DATE DUE

NOVEL VERDICTS:

A GUIDE TO COURTROOM FICTION

by

Jon L. Breen

The Scarecrow Press, Inc.
Metuchen, N.J., & London
1984

Library of Congress Cataloging in Publication Data

Breen, Jon L., 1943–
    Novel verdicts.

    Bibliography: p.
    Includes index.
    1. English fiction—Bibliography. 2. Courts in
literature—Bibliography. 3. American fiction—
Bibliography. 4. English fiction—Stories, plots, etc.
5. American fiction—Stories, plots, etc. 6. Law in
literature—Bibliography. 7. Lawyers in literature—
Bibliography. 8. Judges in literature—Bibliography.
I. Title.
Z2014.F4B69 1984 [PR830.C68] 016.823'008'0355 84–14110
ISBN 0-8108-1741-1

For Bob Samoian

TABLE OF CONTENTS

INTRODUCTION

There are few human situations as inherently dramatic as a trial, whether criminal or civil. This fact has long been recognized by journalists, novelists, short-story writers, and writers for the stage, screen, radio, and television. Works of legal fiction and drama have sometimes been in vogue and sometimes in relative eclipse, but they never disappear completely or lack for an eager audience. The best are often written either by lawyers or laypeople with extensive legal knowledge, but legal proceedings imagined by people with no idea of what goes on in court (except perhaps that gleaned from other legal fiction) can also be entertaining.

This book is a critical bibliography of courtroom fiction in book form. Obviously it is impossible to encompass in a book this size all the novels and short story collections that have had significant portions devoted to trials and other court proceedings. Though there is no claim that this book is comprehensive in its coverage of fictional trials, as complete coverage as possible has been given to certain specialists in courtroom fiction, such as Erle Stanley Gardner, Henry Cecil, Sara Woods, Roderic Jeffries (a.k.a. Jeffrey Ashford), Michael Underwood, William Harrington, Eleazar Lipsky, Edward Grierson, and Arthur Train. Other volumes covered have been selected for their fame, quality, oddity, and general interest. Additional titles I knew about but was not able to include are listed in the supplementary bibliography. Some of these, along with other volumes not yet discovered or still to be published, may be included in a second volume a few years hence.

The following are some general guidelines for selection:

1) The book must either be entirely devoted to describing a trial or include a courtroom scene or scenes of significant length. Novels with legal backgrounds but no trial action have

been excluded. Novels with very brief courtroom interludes, especially those that summarize without quoting testimony, have generally been excluded. In the case of short story collections, all of the stories need not involve courtroom action, but inclusion has generally been limited to volumes about a continuing lawyer character or with a unifying subject of lawyers and the law. There has been no attempt to include individual short stories whether in periodicals or collections.

2) Though it is natural in a work on this subject that a majority of the titles included will be in the mystery/detective genre, mainstream novels with courtroom settings have also been included.

3) Inclusions have been limited to books describing action in British or American courts or courts of other English-speaking countries or colonies. Thus, classics of world literature like Kafka's The Trial, as well as English language novels describing trials in non-English jurisdictions like Margaret Doody's Aristotle Detective, have been excluded. A particularly notable exclusion from the world of detective fiction is Robert van Gulik's Judge Dee series, novels with a background of ancient China written in English by a Dutch diplomat.

4) Especially in the days before 1930, the inquest has been a standard feature of detective novels. Inquests have not been considered courtroom scenes for purposes of the present work, nor have courts of inquiry without clearly drawn adversarial lines.

5) Preliminary hearings, arraignments, and Grand Jury proceedings are considered to be in the work's purview.

6) Scenes taking place in the jury room during actual deliberations are considered to be part of the trial action, though other interchanges involving jurors are not.

7) Quasi-legal proceedings, such as the Court of Seniors in C. P. Snow's The Affair, have not been considered trials for purposes of this work.

The following information has been supplied for each entry:

1) Author, title, place, publisher, and date of first American and British editions. The form of the author's name is generally as it appears on the book. In cases of initials in place

of first names or two initials in place of first and middle names, the complete names are given in parentheses. Author's dates are included if known, as are British or American alternate titles of the first editions. Cross references are used in the following instances: a) joint authors; b) pseudonymous works listed under the author's real or better-known name (e.g. A. A. Fair to Erle Stanley Gardner, Jeffrey Ashford to Roderic Jeffries); c) cases where the author is as well-known or better-known under a name not used on a title covered in the present book (e.g. Cornell Woolrich to William Irish, Cecil Day Lewis to Nicholas Blake). Where a pseudonymous author's real name is not used for writing and/or is less well-known than the pseudonym (e.g. Henry Cecil Leon, A. B. Cox), no cross reference has been made, but the real name has been included in the General Index.

2) A symbol indicating the proportion of trial action included in the book.

A (all or more than three quarters of the book devoted to courtroom action)

½ (one half or more of the book devoted to courtroom action)

¼ (a quarter or more devoted to courtroom action)

B (relatively brief courtroom action, less than a quarter)

C (a collection of short stories or novelettes, proportion of courtroom action not noted)

The B designation is by far the most common, occurring 255 times in 421 entries. Other designations with their frequency of occurrence: ¼ (116), C (29), ½ (12), and A (9).

3) An annotation, usually of one paragraph, including a brief statement of the plot; the type of courtroom action involved; and an evaluation of the book's effectiveness as courtroom fiction. An assessment of the book as a work of fiction generally will usually be included, except in the case of acknowledged classics where such an assessment would be redundant. In some cases, the number of pages of the book concerned with trial action will be indicated as a further aid to the reader. The number of pages is generally given as an estimate, primarily because pagination may differ in various editions of the book.

What factors can be used to judge the quality and effectiveness of courtroom scenes in a book? There are many, but the following are a few of the main ones:

1) Procedural accuracy. Trials in novels are usually not as utterly divorced from real legal procedure as are trials in motion pictures and television, but there are often some incredible gaffes. Though the compiler is not a lawyer, he has had enough experience with legal procedure in real and fictional life to spot the real howlers and has consulted with legal experts in some questionable cases. It is likely that almost any fictional trial can be faulted on procedural grounds by a lawyer. For the most part, the inaccuracies noted here are ones that could be expected to be spotted by a fairly knowledgeable layperson. (For some particularly horrible examples of inaccurate trial procedure, see Barbara Frost's Innocent Bystander, William Ard's Hell is a City, and Harold R. Daniels' The Accused, the last two of which are otherwise estimable novels.)

2) Fairness to both sides. Most courtroom stories have a point of view. The author has a clear intention of which side the reader is supposed to sympathize with and root for, and the story is inevitably slanted in that direction. But the slanting should not be glaringly obvious. The side of the non-angels should be allowed to present its case cogently enough for the reader to understand why the participants are even bothering to have a trial. Just as the master detective deserves to have a suitable opponent in a clever murderer, so the master lawyer should have an opponent worthy of his mettle, not a straw man. Incompetence of counsel in a legal story is permissible, but not just for purposes of stacking the cards for the hero or heroine.

3) Ingenious points of law and procedure and creative trial tactics. This is not essential. The courtroom situation in and of itself is often dramatic enough to carry a story. But many courtroom novels, especially detective stories of the Perry Mason school, are enlivened by rabbit-out-of-a-hat pyrotechnics by the lawyers. (In fact, the lessening opportunity to use surprise in the courtroom has, some believe, taken much of the wind from the sails of the courtroom story, at least if set in the present.)

4) Good Q-and-A. The questioning techniques of the advocates make it almost impossible for a trial to be boring to many courtroom buffs. For a novelist to write a dull cross-examination is almost unforgiveable. It is, of course, possible to

convey the tedium of some parts of a trial without going overboard and writing a tedious novel.

5) General importance of the trial to the book. Is it there just for a couple of dramatic scenes or is it allowed to run its course? Is the problem resolved in a satisfactory way or by some kind of deus ex machina? Does the author make his point, good or ill, about the judicial process believably? Of course, it is possible for a novel to be very good indeed but still not satisfy the special demands of the courtroom buff. Just as a book can be a good novel and a bad detective story, so it can be a good novel and a bad trial novel.

There are at least three ways of using trial action in a novel or a short story: as a dramatic means of presenting the facts in the case; as a means of instructing the reader in points of law and legal procedure; and as a way of commenting on the efficiency, effectiveness, and fairness of the judicial system. Virtually every trial story partakes of the first way. The use of the second is usually limited to those with a specialist's understanding of the law. But the best trial stories partake, in whatever measure, of all three.

In a majority of trial novels, the parties to the case are the central figures and the jury and officers of the court are strictly supporting players with the exception of the lawyer on the side of the angels. In some, however, the attitudes and reactions of the judge and opposing counsel have central importance, and in a few, the jury is at the center of things. (See, for example, titles in this work by Underwood, Wainwright, Bullett, Phillpotts, Jacobs, Postgate, and the team of Goodchild and Roberts.)

Usually a trial appears as the climax of the novel, but there are exceptions. In some cases, the whole novel is a trial (see, for example, Frances Noyes Hart's The Bellamy Trial or Will Oursler's The Trial of Vincent Doon), though this is rarer than might be supposed. Sometimes the trial is the first event in the novel, with the rest of the book reporting the aftermath. (See, for example, Hillary Waugh's A Madman at My Door or John Stephen Strange's Reasonable Doubt.) And sometimes the whole story is aftermath, with occasional flashbacks to testimony in the trial. (See, for example, John Wainwright's Acquittal or Richard Lockridge's Something Up a Sleeve.)

Which are the best courtroom novels included here? To make such a list is a temptation that probably should be avoided,

but I won't.   The following are my personal "Golden Dozen"
courtroom novels (which could easily change from year to year
or week to week):

Henry Cecil, Settled Out of Court
Al Dewlen, Twilight of Honor
Theodore Dreiser, An American Tragedy
Robert L. Fish with Henry Rothblatt, A Handy Death
Erle Stanley Gardner, The Case of the Careless Kitten
Edgar Lustgarten, A Case to Answer (One More Unfortunate)
Cyril Hare, Tragedy at Law
William Harrington, Which the Justice, Which the Thief
Evan Hunter, The Paper Dragon
Meyer Levin, Compulsion
Ellery Queen, The Glass Village
Robert Traver, Anatomy of a Murder

The Cecil and Gardner titles are chosen to represent numerous
excellent books of nearly equal quality. For runners-up, see the
works of Stephen Becker, Anthony Berkeley, Gerald Bullett, John
R. Feegel, C. W. Grafton, Frances Noyes Hart, Roderic Jeffries,
and Raymond Postgate in the pages that follow.

ACKNOWLEDGEMENTS

Many people have offered suggestions and help in the preparation of this work. A few of them deserve special credit.

Francis M. Nevins, Jr., Professor of Law at St. Louis University and one of the most learned detective fiction experts alive, read most of the book in manuscript, making countless worthwhile suggestions and saving me from numerous legal and literary errors. Robert C. S. Adey, a British detective fiction dealer and fan whose knowledge of the field is massive, suggested and provided many volumes that were never published in the United States. My mother, Margaret Breen, proofread the entire manuscript. My wife, Rita Breen, added the accent marks my Xerox 850 word processor couldn't provide, compiled the index, helped locate and identify volumes, and offered suggestions and much-needed encouragement throughout the project.

Others deserving of thanks include Michael Avallone, K. Arne Blom, Michael Bowen, Bill Breen, Robert E. Briney, Tim Brown, Robert Coulson, John Davenport, Gene DeWeese, Ray Esquivel, Joe L. Hensley, Edward D. Hoch, Allen J. Hubin, Angela Irvine, Robert Irvine, Gary Kuris, Marvin Lachman, Chris Lowder, John Mortimer, Warren Murphy, Robert Samoian, Charles Shibuk, and whomever I should have included but forgot. Thanks for the use of their facilities are due the staffs of the Anaheim, Fountain Valley, Fullerton, Garden Grove, Huntington Beach, Los Angeles, Santa Ana, and Whittier, California, Public Libraries and the libraries of the University of California, Irvine and Los Angeles; California State University, Fullerton; Whittier College; and Rio Hondo College.

Printed sources that proved helpful in identifying appropriate titles for this work include two standard library tools, Book Review Digest and Fiction Catalog (both published by Wilson); plus James Sandoe's "Criminal Clef" from his anthology, Murder: Plain and Fanciful (Sheridan House, 1948), and Mary Groff's All Too True (from issues of The Poisoned Pen, book publication pending). Bibliographic works most often used to verify publishers and dates were Contemporary Authors (Gale); the printed catalogs of the Library of Congress and the British Library; Allen J. Hubin's The Bibliography of Crime Fiction, 1749-1975 (Publisher's Inc., 1975) and its updated version, Crime Fiction, 1749-1980: A Comprehensive Bibliography (Garland, 1984); and John M. Reilly's Twentieth-Century Crime and Mystery Writers (St. Martin's, 1980).

AARONS, Edward S. (1916-1975)

1. The Defenders. New York: Gold Medal, 1961. London: Jenkins, 1962. (B)

   The prolific author of the Sam Durell Assignment books here novelizes Reginald Rose's TV series about lawyers Lawrence and Ken Preston, father and son. Two unrelated cases are involved, the Prestons moving from one corny situation to another, but courtroom action is relatively sparse and never notable. At one point, Aarons spurns the courtroom for one of those woman-on-the-ledge situations so popular in the fifties. Though based on a fine program, this novel is no better (and no worse) than what is usually expected of a novelization.

ADAMS, A. K., ed.

2. Favorite Trial Stories: Fact and Fiction. New York: Dodd, Mead, 1966. (C)

   Twelve of the eighteen selections here are fictional, and they are a mostly familiar lot: Irvin S. Cobb's "Words and Music," Erle Stanley Gardner's "The Case of the Irate Witness," Arthur Train's "The Meanest Man," Melville Davisson Post's "Naboth's Vineyard," O. Henry's "The Whirligig of Life," Stephen Vincent Benet's "The Devil and Daniel Webster," Vincent Starrett's "The Eleventh Juror," Agatha Christie's "The Witness for the Prosecution," Charles Dickens' "The Memorable Trial of Bardell Against Pickwick," Rafael Sabatini's "The Night of Charity," Jack London's "The Benefit of the Doubt," and Bret Harte's "Colonel Starbottle for the Plaintiff." Only the Gardner and Benet entries recur from an earlier collection, Albert Blaustein's

Fiction Goes to Court (q.v.). The lack of an overall
introduction or individual notes on the stories and their
authors is regrettable. Quotations about the law follow
each selection.

ALDRIDGE, James (1918-   )

3. A Sporting Proposition. London: Joseph; Boston: Little,
Brown, 1973. (B)

The inhabitants of an Australian bush town choose up sides
in a legal contest over the ownership of a Welsh pony. The
combatants are a 13-year-old boy of poor family and a
prosperous local rancher.   Is Bo, the cart-pulling pony
procured for young polio victim Josie Eyre, really the
mysteriously vanished Taff, inseparable mount of the hell-
raising Scotty Pirie?   This is a fine novel of growing up
that both children and adults can enjoy, and it is also a
considerable courtroom novel with some excellent Q-and-
A, first in a juvenile hearing in Magistrate's Court and
subsequently in a civil case before a visiting judge. The
narrator is the young son of the principled lawyer who
takes the Pirie boy's case. The viewpoint is thus somewhat
reminiscent of Melville Davisson Post's Uncle Abner stories
or some of William Faulkner's tales about Gavin Stevens.
Aldridge's The Untouchable Juli (Joseph, 1975; Little,
Brown, 1976) also logs some court time.

ARD, William (1922-1960)

4. Hell is a City. New York: Rinehart, 1955. (B)

In defense of his sister, a Hispanic youth kills a crooked
vice squad cop in a cheap Brooklyn hotel. Working for a
reform-minded newspaper editor, Manhattan private eye
Timothy Dane becomes involved in the resultant morass of
corrupt officialdom and dirty politics. Unfortunately, the
dozen pages of trial action, concerning a charge of narcotics possession, form the weakest part of a good tough
novel.   The trial, which the judge allows unexpected
television cameras to cover and in which the New York and
Brooklyn District Attorneys, running for office on the same
ticket, are uncomfortable adversaries, seems to be intentionally comic, but its absurdities are too far out of step

with the rest of the book. Francis M. Nevins, Jr., says of Ard's trial, "He couldn't get his characters out of the situation in any sensible way, so he picked a senseless way of tying up the loose ends in jig time in about three minutes of trial."

ARKWRIGHT, Richard

5.   The Queen Anne's Gate Mystery. London: F. V. White, 1889. 2 volumes. New York: Arno, 1976. (B)

This novel has its charms-- some pleasant outdoors writing, occasional humor, and glimpses of upper-class English life of a century ago-- but most of it is hard going for the present-day reader.   The large type indicates it was stretched to fill the then-popular two-volume format, and its thinnish plot has been padded as well. Harry Collingwood is accused of the strychnine poisoning of his wife. Narrator George Pen Owen, Harry's old school chum determined to clear him, forms with his wife Lady Geraldine an early specimen of the husband-and-wife amateur detective team. There are three courtroom sequences. The first and best concerns Harry's arraignment in Westminster police court, where he is ineptly defended by self-important solicitor Joseph Barclay. His Old Bailey trial is merely summarized, and a second Old Bailey trial (with another defendant) consists mainly of speechifying without quotation of testimony. The novel loses coherence at times, and the ultimate solution is a disappointment.

ASHFORD, Jeffrey

See JEFFRIES, Roderic

BAILEY, F(rancis) Lee (1933-   )

6.   <u>Secrets</u>. New York: Stein and Day, 1978. London: Melbourne House, 1979. (¼)

Famed defender Michael Kilrayne is himself charged with murder in a Boston courtroom. Is he responsible for the death of vanished socialite Sarah Hansen? California's L. Ewing Scott case is evoked, as the prosecution tries to prove murder in the absence of a corpse. Evidence presented by the prosecution includes scandalous videotapes of the alleged victim's sex life, in which the legs and torso of one of her partners are said to be "consistent with the legs and torso of Mr. Kilrayne." Lawyer Bailey's first work of fiction is knowledgeable and instructive as well as calculatedly sensational. Interest flags only when he drags in the Mafia and some extraneous aviation action.

BALLINGER, Bill S. (1912-1980)

7.   <u>The Tooth and the Nail</u>. New York: Harper; London: Reinhardt and Evans, 1955. (¼)

The author's specialty was presenting in alternate chapters two seemingly unrelated tales and tying them together at the end. Here the New York trial of an unnamed defendant for the murder of his chauffeur-valet trades off with the first-person account of a professional magician and his wife. The defendant is supposed to have burned his servant's body in a furnace after killing him with a hatchet, and a tooth allegedly from the victim's mouth is a key bit of evidence. The courtroom combat is crisp and effective, and the stunt construction is skillful, though some readers will anticipate the main surprise.

8.   Not I, Said the Vixen. New York: Fawcett, 1965. (¼)

Drunken Los Angeles lawyer Cyrus March is engaged to
defend beautiful Ivy Lorents, who reminds the smitten
counsellor of his lost Beatrice.   The shooting in Ivy's
apartment of Arthea Simpson is not denied, but Ivy claims
to have mistaken Arthea, a close friend whom she did not
recognize outlined against the window, for a burglar. The
prosecution believes she murdered Arthea to conceal from
her wealthy fiancee a Lesbian relationship.   The author,
who often liked to mix his delivery, again alternates first
and third person narration.   Trial action is brisk and
competent, though some of the adversarial byplay seems a
little strained.   This is a good courtroom novel which
Ballinger claimed was heavily edited by the publisher.

9.   The Law. New York: Warner, 1975. (B)

Ballinger is such a consummate pro, he manages (at least
at times) to give the illusion of a real novel rather than a
TV adaptation in this novelization of the teleplay by Joel
Oliansky, from a story by William Sackheim and Oliansky.
Central character is Los Angeles public defender Murray
Stone, who is defending one of four men accused of the
torture-murder of a pro football player. Representing the
other three is Jules Benson, a Great Defender in the
media-conscious, venal mode of Hillary Waugh's Parrish for
the Defense (q.v.).   Another character, Judge Rebeccah
Fornier, is one of the worst and most biassed jurists in
fictional annals. Courtroom action, covering five different
proceedings, totals only about twenty pages, with the main
case dealt with very briefly. A viewing of the film would
no doubt be much more satisfactory.

BARDIN, John Franklin

    see TREE, Gregory

BARLOW, James (1921-   )

10.   Term of Trial. London: Hamilton, 1961. New York: Simon
       and Schuster, 1962. (B)

Graham Weir, an English teacher at Railway Street Secondary Modern School in an unnamed Midland industrial city, is tormented by a wartime act of cowardice, but the reader knows almost from the beginning he is a more worthy and courageous person than he believes himself to be. He is also a bit naive and fails to realize for a long time that student Shirley Taylor, a physically precocious 15-year-old beauty, is in love with him. After he spurns her advances at the end of a school trip to the Continent, her lies land him in Magistrate's Court on a charge of indecent assault. Barlow is a brilliant writer with a gift for characterization and background, and his novel must rank among the best about secondary education. The 55-page courtroom sequence is mostly excellent, though to an American reader that Weir's solicitor is allowed to lead him through his testimony without any objection from the prosecution seems strange indeed. A feature here, not present in many novels with trial climaxes, is the account of the real-life verdict that follows the verdict in court.

11.   The Burden of Proof. London: Hamilton; New York: Simon and Schuster, 1968. (B)

Here Barlow presents a jaundiced and somewhat reactionary view of the swinging London of the the sixties, with an emphasis on the underworld. Main characters include Vic Dakin, a psychopathic professional crook who's good to his aged mother; Gerald Draycott, a perniciously trendy M.P.; and Bob Matthews, a sympathetic police detective. The central event is the bloody robbery of a factory payroll vehicle. (Memorable line of dialogue by one of the fleeing robbers: "We can't drive on two flat tires, six men in a Jaguar, one bleeding. It'd be noticeable.") The 18-page trial of Dakin and three others for the crime illustrates how effective and impressive a good defense lawyer can be even if he hasn't a leg to stand on. As in Term of Trial, Barlow brings his background and characters vividly to life.

BECKER, Stephen (1927-   )

12.   A Covenant with Death.   New York: Atheneum, 1964. London: Hamilton, 1965. (¾)

Judge Ben Lewis, longtime jurist in the southwestern county seat of Soledad City, state unspecified, looks back on a 1923 murder case that provides one of the best legal conundrums in fiction. Bryan Talbot is tried for the strangling murder of his wife Louise, convicted, and sentenced to death. On the day of his execution, his effort to escape from the scaffold results in the death of the state hangman. When the actual murderer of his wife confesses, Talbot is exonerated of that crime but immediately charged with the hangman's murder. Is he guilty or was it self-defense? Both trials are covered, with the young Judge Lewis acting as spectator at the first and longer one and uncomfortably presiding at the second. Becker's best seller is beautifully written, its small-town setting and its law-steeped milieu depicted with equal skill. An earlier Becker novel, Juice (Simon and Schuster, 1958; Muller, 1959), involves very brief courtroom action.

BEEDING, Francis, pseudonym of John Leslie Palmer (1885-1944) and Hilary Adam St. George Saunders (1898-1951)

13.   Death Walks in Eastrepps. London: Hodder and Stoughton; New York: Mystery League, 1931. (B)

A serial killer, dubbed the Evil by the press, wields his knife in the English seaside town of Eastrepps. Chief Inspector Wilkins, called in by Scotland Yard, charges an upper-class mental patient with the crime, but another killing during his incarceration effects his release. A local cop finds evidence against Robert Eldridge, a man with many secrets, and he is tried in the Old Bailey, facing a seemingly air-tight case. The novel has been championed by Vincent Starrett and others as one of the greatest detective novels ever written. There is really more pure suspense than detection, though, and one can easily imagine it as a thirties Hitchcock film. It is also a considerable trial novel, from the prisoner's chillingly described first view of the Old Bailey courtroom to his counsel's very able and dramatic (if apparently hopeless) closing speech to the jury. The shifting points of view during the trial (including the court stenographer, jury foreman, and a playwright-spectator among others) have rarely been done better.

The first American publisher of this classic sold its handsome hard-cover volumes in cigar and drug stores for 50¢, a quarter of the standard price at that time.

BENSON, E(dward) F(rederic) (1867-1940)

14. The Blotting Book. London: Heinemann; New York: Doubleday, Page, 1908. (B)

In a readable but unremarkable novel set in the British
seaside town of Brighton, Benson introduces two characters
with good reason to kill crooked solicitor Godfrey Mills: his
nearly-as-crooked partner Taynton and their slandered (and
unknowingly swindled) client Morris Assheton. When Mills'
body is found, head smashed in by a blunt instrument,
Morris is tried in Lewes Assize Court. The trial wraps up
the rather simple plot neatly enough but is not especially
notable in itself.

BERKELEY, Anthony, pseudonym of Anthony Berkeley Cox
(1893-1971)

15. Trial and Error. London: Hodder and Stoughton; Garden
City, NY: Doubleday, 1937. (B)

This is a classic trial novel with an irresistible basic
situation. Terminally ill Mr. Todhunter decides to commit
a murder for the good of humanity. But when an innocent
man is convicted of killing pernicious actress Jean Nor-
wood, Todhunter must prove himself guilty-- and it isn't
easy. Chief Inspector Moresby thinks he is one of those
cranks who automatically confess to well-publicized
crimes. His Old Bailey trial, covering over eighty pages,
may be a unique one in literature: a civil murder case, a
prosecution brought by a private citizen in a crime for
which another defendant has already been condemned to
die. The novel is rich in humor and irony, and Berkeley's
recurring sleuth Ambrose Chitterwick produces a nice
surprise in the final chapter.

(as Francis Iles)

16. Malice Aforethought. London: Gollancz; New York: Harper, 1931. (B)

Quiet, retiring Dr. Edmund Alfred Bickleigh, physician in
Wyvern's Cross, Devonshire, poisons his domineering wife
Julia in what he thinks is an undetectable way, watches the
net of police investigation close around him, and finally

winds up on trial, still fairly confident he has committed the perfect crime.   As in Trial and Error under the Berkeley name, the author writes expert courtroom scenes. One of the earliest and best novels of this particular type, it struck this reader as even better than his later and more celebrated (non-courtroom) classic, Before the Fact (1932). In an epilogue, Iles shows that the all-cards-on-the-table approach does not preclude a beautifully ironic surprise ending.

BLAKE, Nicholas, pseudonym of Cecil Day Lewis (1904-1972)

17.   A Tangled Web. London: Collins; New York: Harper, 1956. (B)

Eighteen-year-old Daisy Bland becomes the mistress of handsome Hugo Chesterman, who she soon learns is a Raffles-type cat burglar.   When he is accused of killing police inspector Herbert Stone in the seaside town of Southbourne, she is determined to stick by him.   They get little help from their dear-and-trusted-friend Dr. John Jaques (called Jacko), an abortionist who is the most twisted (and thus most interesting) character in the novel. The trial scenes, in Magistrate's Court and Oakhurst Assize Court, are mostly summarized apart from Daisy's testimony and are not especially notable.   The novel, though, is highly recommended for its suspense and the elegant prose style of the future poet laureate. Blake drew the plot from an early-twentieth-century case described in the memoirs of Sir Patrick Hastings, K.C.

BLAUSTEIN, Albert P., ed.

18.   Fiction Goes to Court. New York: Holt, 1954. (C)

In this unique anthology of courtroom short stories, each of the eighteen entries has been chosen by a well-known lawyer, all American save for Great Britain's Lord High Chancellor, Gavin Turnbull Simonds.   Selectors include such political figures as then-Vice President Richard M. Nixon, who picks Arthur Train's Mr. Tutt story "The Dog Andrew," and Presidential candidate Adlai E. Stevenson, who selects A. P. Herbert's "Board of Inland Revenue vs. Haddock: The Negotiable Cow."   Other inclusions and their selectors: Melville Davisson Post's "The Corpus Delicti" (John W. Davis), John Galsworthy's "The Juryman" (Fred M. Vinson), O (Theo Mathew)'s "The Blushing Beginner and the Bearded Juryman" (Simonds), Octavus Roy Cohen's "The Law and the Profits" (Samuel Williston), Irvin S. Cobb's "Boys Will Be Boys" (Roscoe Pound), Ruel McDaniel's "Coroner de Luxe" (Tom C. Clark), A. A. Milne's "The Barrister" (John J. McCloy), William Faulkner's "Tomorrow" (Eric Johnston), Irwin Shaw's "Triumph of Justice" (Estes Kefauver), Richard Harding Davis' "A Wasted Day" (Sam Rayburn), Marc Connelly's "Coroner's Inquest" (Oscar Hammerstein, 2d), Stephen Vincent Benet's "The Devil and Daniel Webster" (Elmer Rice), James Reid Parker's "All the Little Jokers" (William J. Donovan), Cornelia Otis Skinner's "Parcel of Land" (Lloyd Paul Stryker). Only person who is both a selector and a selectee is Erle Stanley Gardner, who champions Harry Klingsberg's "Doowinkle, Attorney" and whose Perry Mason short story, "The Case of the Irate Witness," is chosen by Jerry Giesler. The squibs on the individual stories by their selectors are always brief and seldom very edifying. But Blaustein, himself a distinguished legal scholar, editor, and librarian, certainly managed to recruit an all-star cast, and their choices make for an excellent anthology.

Readers looking for other courtroom anthologies will find the pickings slim beyond A. K. Adams' Favorite Trial Stories and Ephraim London's The World of Law (q.q.v.). Joan Kahn's Trial and Terror (Houghton Mifflin, 1973) sounds promising, but the courtroom items included tend to be non-fictional. The Detection Club's Verdict of 13 (Faber and Faber, 1978; Harper and Row, 1979) collects stories ostensibly concerning juries, but unusually not literal ones, and there is very little courtroom action. For a science fiction anthology with some courtroom stories, there is Joseph D. Olander and Martin Harry Greenberg's Criminal Justice Through Science Fiction (q.v.).

BOK, Curtis

19.   Star Wormwood. New York: Knopf, 1959. (¼)

In an unspecified part of 1931 America, young Depression victim Roger Haike is tried for rape, murder, and mutilation of a dead body (i.e., cannibalism) in the death of

thirteen-year-old Angela Hake, sister of his friend Joe.
The crime, his trial, and his execution are vividly and
harrowingly described. Bok's avowedly polemical novel
uses the case to illustrate his lecture on the failure of the
criminal justice system's emphasis on punishment. Over a
third of the book consists of purely non-fictional commen-
taries on the case. Bok writes, "Someday we will look back
upon our criminal and penal process with the same horrified wonder as we now look back upon the Spanish Inquisi-
tion."

Bok's earlier mixtures of legal fiction and essay, both
published by Knopf, were Backbone of the Herring (1941)
and I, Too, Nicodemus (1946).

BORDEN, Mary (1886-1968)

20.   You, the Jury. New York and London: Longmans, 1952. (¾)

In 1946, faith healer Martin Merriedew is tried on three
counts of treason in Greymouth Assize Court: helping
German prisoners escape from an Army field hospital
where he was employed as an orderly; giving information to
the enemy; and (most damagingly) suborning the troops to
mutiny one Christmas Eve. Told in the first-person by the
sister of one of the charismatic Merriedew's early dis-
ciples, the novel addresses an old question: what if Christ
came to Earth today? Both the background memories in
the first half and the trial in the second are well enough
managed, but the novel doesn't achieve quite the degree of
reader involvement it should. An earlier Borden trial novel
is Action for Slander (London: Heinemann, 1936; New
York: Harper, 1937).

BRAMBLE, Forbes (1939-   )

21.   The Strange Case of Deacon Brodie. London: Hamilton,
      1975. New York: Coward, McCann, and Geoghegan, 1976.
      (B)

William Brodie, cabinetmaker and Deacon of the Wrights,
was a respectable citizen of Edinburgh by day and a burglar
by night. In a fine historical crime saga, something like
the works of John Cashman (q.v.), Bramble briefly but

vividly describes the highly-publicized and somewhat un-
ruly 1788 trial of Brodie and grocer George Smith. The
courtroom action is mostly summarized from the viewpoint
of defendant Brodie, who wonders "how lawyers could
manage to say the same things so often in so many
different ways and end up where they began." Bramble's
subsequent books, Regent Square (1977) and King's Bench
(1979) are legal saga novels with some trial action.

BRAND, Christianna, pseudonym of Mary Christianna Milne
Lewis (1907-   )

22.   London Particular.   London: Joseph, 1952.   As Fog of
      Doubt, New York: Scribners, 1953. (B)

      Though far less prolific, Brand can construct as good a
      classical puzzle as Carr, Christie, or Queen. This tricky
      novel from the Inspector Cockrill series begins with the
      murder of Raoul Vernet during a London pea-souper (called
      a "London particular" in a quote from Dickens' Bleak
      House). The crime occurs in the Maida Vale home of Dr.
      Thomas Evans, with several inhabitants and visitors as
      possible suspects. The Old Bailey trial of Dr. Edwards for
      the crime is efficiently done and unusually rich in detail
      and atmosphere, concluding with a good stunt solution.

BRESLIN, Catherine (1936-   )

23.   Unholy Child.   New York: Dial, 1979.   London: Sphere,
      1981. (B)

      Here are combined some sure-fire best-seller elements--
      law, medicine, religion, and sex-- into something other
      than the exploitative schlock a plot summary might sug-
      gest. Two strong female characters are at the center of
      the story: Sister Angela Flynn, a nun who became pregnant
      and may have killed her own infant, and Meg Gavin, a
      reporter who becomes fascinated with the case. The 50+
      pages of trial action concentrate more on the mental
      processes of the defendant than on courtroom procedure.
      The setting is Minnesota's Twin Cities.

BUGLIOSI, Vincent (1934-   ), and HURWITZ, Ken (1948-   )

24.   Shadow of Cain. New York: Norton, 1981. (B)

In courtroom fiction, reader sympathy is enlisted more often than not on the side of the defense. Bugliosi, who prosecuted the Manson family as an assistant district attorney in Los Angeles and wrote of the case in the nonfiction best seller Helter-Skelter, could naturally be expected to change that in his first fictional effort. The book represents a shift in the emphasis of eighties courtroom fiction also reflected in Henry Denker's Outrage (q.v.).

Convicted multiple murderer Raymond Lomak, allegedly born-again and rehabilitated, is released from prison twenty years after his crimes. Seemingly a new man, he undertakes the direction of a group of charities for an aging cowboy star who owns a football team. Only psychiatrist Richard Pomerantz, who regularly sees Lomak as part of the conditions of his parole, knows how shaky is Lomak's rehabilitation. Two murders occur, and four fifths of the way through the book, Lomak is back on trial, with the reader rooting for the prosecution to put him away for good. The trial scenes are expertly done, highlighted by a brilliant summation by the defense lawyer, for once not on the side of the angels. Though some saw this book as a brief against the parole of Charles Manson, which in part it well may be, it is also a good novel. Raymond Lomak, at times almost an Elmer Gantry for the eighties, is the best character, complex and frightening.

BULLETT, Gerald (1894-1958)

25.   The Jury. London: Dent; New York: Knopf, 1935. (¼)

Bullett's novel is rightly championed by Jacques Barzun and Wendell Hertig Taylor as the greatest of those trial books that focus on members of the jury. The first section ("The Twelve Converging") introduces us to the crime and to the individual jurors. The second ("The Twelve Listening") presents a transcript of the trial of Roderic Strood for the poisoning of his wife Daphne. The final part ("The Twelve Debating") concerns the deliberations, with numerous flashbacks to events in the jurors' lives, and the final

revelation of what really happened. Total trial action in
the longish and very rewarding novel totals over 150 pages.

BUTTERWORTH, W(illiam) E(dmund III) (1929-   )

26.   The Court-Martial. New York: Signet, 1962. (¾)

Civilian Gregory Fitts, of a prestigious Philadelphia law
firm, goes to Wetzlar, West Germany, to defend his old
friend Chief Warrant Officer Joseph Watson, accused of
choking to death his mistress, Hannelore Kummer. Com-
plicating matters is an affair between Fitts and the accused officer's wife. The court-martial is very skillfully
presented, with a feel of procedural authenticity. Butterworth provides an unusual amount of detail in the prelimi-
naries, including the qualifying and swearing in of counsel,
court, law officer, court reporter, and interpreters. (This
novel must also been one of the earliest mass market books
to make free use of the most popular taboo four-letter
expletive.)

CABLE, Mary

27. Avery's Knot. New York: Putnam, 1981. (¼)

Cable effectively fictionalizes a real-life New England murder case of 1832. The Reverend Ephraim K. Avery, a Methodist minister of Bristol, Rhode Island, is accused of the strangulation murder of pregnant mill girl Sarah Maria Cornell of Fall River, Massachusetts. Both a magistrate's hearing in Bristol and Avery's trial in Newport, with Daniel Webster's law partner, Jeremiah Mason, appearing for the defense, are described in considerable detail. The rather mean spirit and hypocrisy of the times are well captured in some of its euphemisms, e.g. the question to one witness, "Did you mistrust her situation?" (Translation: "Did you think she was pregnant?")

CAIN, James M. (1892-1977)

28. The Butterfly. New York: Knopf, 1947. (B)

Somewhat comparable in both brevity and power to the author's celebrated The Postman Always Rings Twice and Double Indemnity, this tale of tangled relationships in the Appalachian coal-mining country concerns Jess Tyler, who receives a surprise visit to his log cabin by his grown daughter Kady. Attracted to her in a non-fatherly way, the upright and religious Jess twice lands in court because of Kady, first on a disorderly conduct charge stemming from an incident in a bar, later and less briefly on a charge of incest. There is also a murder, though no one is tried for it. The title refers to an inherited birthmark that powers the plot. The two hearings, totalling about a dozen pages, are rather loose and informal but not as blatantly unconvincing as later Cain trials.

29.   Galatea. New York: Knopf, 1953. London: Hale, 1954. (B)

Though a loyal Cain fan can find some good lines and scenes scattered through this short novel, it would probably discourage forever a newcomer to his work. Often confusing and occasionally boring, it's vastly inferior to novels like The Postman Always Rings Twice and even a good deal poorer than the less pretentious paperback originals collected in Hard Cain (Gregg Press, 1980). The plot concerns Duke Webster, a former boxer working for a restaurateur named Valenty who had saved him from jail on a robbery charge. Mrs. Valenty is an obese compulsive eater who complacently blames her problem on glands, and both she and her husband seem determined she eat herself to death. Duke prescribes a diet to help her lose weight and falls in love with the trimmed-down version. When Mr. Val drops to his death from a water tower, Duke is charged with murder, and his trial rings as falsely as the Hollywood ending that follows. Locale is Upper Marlboro, Maryland.

30.   The Magician's Wife. New York: Dial, 1962. London: Hale, 1963. (B)

In Channel City, Maryland, meat company executive Clay Lockwood and Sally Alexis, wife of a stage conjurer who is heir to the Gorsuch millions, plot his death by orchestrated traffic accident. The magician's assistant, Edith Conlon (called Buster), is accused of committing the murder by extremely unlikely means. It seems the presence of an extended trial scene in a Cain novel is a bad sign. This fairly late example of his work is truly dreadful, tin-eared and flat. The sloppy 25-page trial, with much argument taking place in front of the jury that surely would never be allowed in a real courtroom, carries no conviction at all.

CARR, John Dickson (1906-1977)

31.   Below Suspicion.   New York: Harper, 1949.   London: Hamilton, 1950. (B)

Patrick Butler, flamboyant Irish barrister who claims to prefer guilty clients, defends nurse-companion Joyce Ellis

on a charge of poisoning her elderly employer, Mildred Taylor. Though Butler gets her off by brilliant cross-examination in the 25 pages of Old Bailey action, the story is only beginning. Dr. Gideon Fell also makes an appearance in a typically ingenious and intricate Carr bamboozlement, albeit lacking a real locked-room problem. The subsequent solo outing of the barrister, Patrick Butler for the Defense (1956), never gets to court. Francis M. Nevins, Jr., points out that Carr's Death Turns the Tables (1941; British title The Seat of the Scornful), "although lacking trial action as such, begins with a powerful sentencing scene."

(as Carter Dickson)

32.   The Judas Window. New York: Morrow; London, Heinemann, 1938. (½)

It appeared only one person could have killed Avory Hume, stabbed with an arrow in an insistently locked room: James Answell, found unconscious in the same room. Sir Henry Merrivale, K.C., accepting his first brief in fifteen years, defends in the Old Bailey trial, rising for his initial cross-examination with a touch of physical humor typical of his cases. The "Old Man"'s one recorded courtroom venture highlights one of the greatest formal detective novels.

CASHMAN, John, pseudonym of Timothy Francis Tothill Davis (1941-   )

33.   The Cook-General. New York: Harper and Row, 1974. London: Hamilton, 1975. (B)

This is an excellent fictionalized account of an 1879 murder case. Irish servant Kate Webster, a terrifying character, is accused of murdering and carving up her elderly employer, Julia Thomas. Cashman spends only about twenty pages on her Old Bailey trial, presumably non-fictional except where he enters the defendant's mind. Cashman's earlier novel on the Neill Cream case, The Gentleman from Chicago (1973) spends even less time in court.

34.   Kid Glove Charlie. New York: Harper and Row, 1978. (B)

Here Cashman fictionalizes legendary Victorian criminal Charlie Peace (1832-1879), a marginally competent and strangely likeable villain who specialized in burglary and had a special affinity for the law courts, often attending other people's trials. Thus, the novel spends slightly more time in court than the author's earlier books, about thirty pages in all. Included are the Manchester trial of the two Habron brothers for shooting a constable, with the actual killer (Charlie) rooting for their acquittal; Charlie's Old Bailey trial on charges of attempting to kill another constable; a Magistrate's hearing in Sheffield, where Charlie is charged with the murder of the husband of his former mistress, Kate Dyson; and his trial on the same charge in Leeds Assizes. The tale is always colorful and frequently very funny. Cashman credits The Trials of Charles Peace (1926) from the Notable British Trials series as one of his sources. In a novel based on a real criminal case, the trial is generally the part that can be expected to offer least opportunity for invention, and that may explain why the trial gets short shrift in some such novels.

CECIL, Henry, pseudonym of Henry Cecil Leon (1902-1976)

35.   Full Circle. London: Chapman and Hall, 1948. (C)

Cecil was one of the most entertaining and instructive of all writers on the British legal system. His first volume of fiction collects sixteen stories, linked by the account of a law professor who, after getting a bump on the head on the way to a lecture at Cambridge, begins to tell his students stories instead of teaching the law more conventionally. Nine tales have courtroom action. Two of these involve dream sequences, one of which, "Portrait in Silk," a particularly weak entry, is a sort of non-seasonal barrister's "Christmas Carol." Other stories, like "The Confession" and "Liberty of the Subject," foreshadow Cecil's later (and better) use of comic legal problems and trick endings, odd judges and quirky witnesses. "On Appeal" marks an earlier use of the central device (kidnapping of a judge's daughter) of No Fear or Favour (q.v.). Others that spend time in court: "Tell Tale," "The Name," "The Case of Mr. Tinker," "The Dream," and "Advertisement."

36.   The Painswick Line. London: Chapman and Hall, 1951. New York: British Book Centre, 1974. (B)

Cecil's first novel opens with a typically incongruous situation: a Church of England vicar tipping horses from the Old Bailey witness box. The case involves Lucy Meeson-Smith, daughter of the Reverend Wellsby Meeson-Smith, accused of defrauding her bookmaker employers by placing bets after the race has already been run. The title refers to Mr. Justice Painswick's son, a rogue involved in the novel's other main case, a libel suit against a Member of Parliament. As usual, Cecil brings in other court scenes and anecdotes to illustrate his little tangential treatises on the law, not the most advisable fiction-writing practice but one a humorist as gifted as he can get away with. The novel marks the debut of the drunken solicitor Mr. Tewkesbury, who will recur even more memorably, and has the requisite surprise twist.

37.   No Bail for the Judge. London: Chapman and Hall; New York: Harper, 1952. (¾)

Sir Edwin Prout, an elderly and upright high-court judge, becomes accused through an improbable combination of circumstances of the stabbing murder of a prostitute named Flossie (surnames various). Prout's daughter Elizabeth enlists the aid of ingenious burglary contractor Ambrose Low to help her father, and Low in turn recruits Cecil's greatest comic witness, the hearty and slightly dense Colonel Brain, to do research among the tarts. Courtroom sequences include a breach of contract suit (very brief) at the beginning, Low's hearing in Magistrate's Court on a pimping charge resulting from his detective work, and finally the Old Bailey murder trial of the judge. The description of the attendees at a cause celebre murder trial is sardonic and amusing, and Cecil provides little essays on various aspects of legal procedure, including how the prisoner/accused should be addressed and the judge's own ruminations over the legal validity of decisions made while he may have been mentally unfit. If not quite as good as some of the Cecils to come, this novel is admirable and inimitable.

38.   Natural Causes. London: Chapman and Hall, 1953. (B)

Central figures here are Alexander Bean, a litigious newspaper publisher who generally avoids testifying in person; Mr. Justice Beverley, who embarrasses Bean in court and becomes a target of his paper; and Sidney York, a World-

War-I comrade of the judge who tries to blackmail him
about his perjured testimony in a court-martial. Major
court proceeding is an inquest on the blackmailer, who dies
in a fall down the stairs of the Bull Inn, with the judge's son
and daughter in suspiciously close proximity. Other court
scenes, totaling about 25 pages, include a libel case involving a Test Match selection (part of it presented in the
style of a newspaper cricket account); an action for
wrongful dismissal against Bean by his former "tame solicitor"; and a Magistrate's Court action on a traffic violation
by the publisher. Despite some serious elements, this is
ultimately Cecil at frothiest, much like an anyone-for-
tennis stage farce. Drunken solicitor Tewkesbury makes an
appearance, and there is a larger dose than usual of the
garrulous Colonel Brain, though not on the witness stand
this time.

39. According to the Evidence. London: Chapman and Hall;
     New York: Harper, 1954. (¼)

This one opens (in uncharacteristically somber fashion for
humorist Cecil) in Cunningham Assize Court with the trial
of Gilbert Essex for the rape and murder of Ellen Wimslow.
A few months after his acquittal by the jury, generally
considered to have been in error, Essex is himself murdered. Ambrose Low, now a stockbroker and married to
the daughter of the man he saved in No Bail for the Judge,
is consulted by Jill Whitby, who fears her fiance, Alec
Morland, will be accused of the crime. Low enlists Colonel
Brain in an elaborate scheme to get Morland charged and
acquitted, thus saving the young lovers further worry. The
course, though, does not run smooth. Other courtroom
scenes in the novel involve Morland's hearing in Magistrate's Court, another case in the Court of Criminal
Appeal, and finally Morland's trial. As ingeniously plotted
and lightly told as ever, this one also explores some serious
philosophical questions about vigilante justice.

40. Brothers in Law. London: Joseph; New York: Harper,
     1955. (¼)

The first of the trilogy about barrister Roger Thursby
(appropriately played on the screen by Ian Carmichael),
this represents Cecil at his lightest and funniest but also
most informative about the British legal system. Beginning
with Roger mulling over the last question of his Bar Final

Examination, we follow the 21-year-old novice through his observational apprenticeship and his earliest briefs, including a divorce case that looks simple but has disastrous pitfalls and a successful Old Bailey debut defending Mr. Green, a typically comic Cecil defendant who by requesting a dock brief may pick his own counsel from barristers seated in the court, on a charge of writing himself a fraudulent reference. The day of the Green case begins badly with an embarrassing coincidence: Roger finds his mother seated on the jury. Besides the cases covered first hand, there are a wealth of legal anecdotes from Henry Blagrove, a comparative veteran of the chambers, played just as appropriately in the film version by Richard Attenborough.

41. Friends at Court.   London: Joseph, 1956.   New York: Harper, 1957. (¼)

As the second Thursby novel opens, Roger has been twelve years at the Bar and is contemplating taking silk, i.e. becoming a Queen's Counsel, an advancement Henry Blagrove has already made. The novel's principal case involves a charge of police bribery against Mr. and Mrs. Glacier, operators of the Glorious Hotel. Roger and Henry appear on opposite sides as the case is followed from Magistrate's Court all the way to the Court of Criminal Appeals, where there is lengthy disquisition on the meaning of the word "sure" in the judge's charge. Mr. Green reappears from the earlier novel, and Roger nearly takes his dock brief for old times' sake. Cecil introduces a memorable comic advocate in Crabtree, who seems incapable of finishing a question. Highly entertaining though not quite as good as its predecessor.

42. Much in Evidence.   London: Joseph, 1957.   (As The Long Arm, New York: Harper, 1957.) (¼)

Professional horseplayer William Richmond is burgled of a hundred thousand pounds in cash that he had insured only the day before. Insurance claims assessor Miss Clinch is suspicious, as is the reader. When the company delays payment, he brings suit before a comically garrulous judge. In subsequent proceedings, his solicitor Mr. Tewkesbury is arraigned on a drunk charge and offers a brilliant oddball defense; Richmond is tried on criminal charges in the Old Bailey; and still another defendant tries to use the verdict in Richmond's case to his own benefit. Playing variations on a theme of coincidence, Cecil offers some of his funniest court scenes and a convoluted plot with a double-twist ending, only part of which many readers will see coming.

43.   Sober as a Judge. London: Joseph; New York: Harper, 1958. (¼)

In the final novel of the Thursby trilogy, another thirteen years have passed and 46-year-old Roger is appointed as a High Court Judge. Even more episodic than the first two entries in the series, the novel has much good anecdotage on the peculiarities of judges.   Cases include a unique instance of "libel-by-ice" and a blackmail-con game played on a horseplaying society woman.   Roger has various run-ins with a practical joking school friend known as Plummer. At the end of the novel, he encounters from the bench some barristers as inexperienced and ill-prepared as he was at the beginning of Brothers in Law.

44.   Settled Out of Court. London: Joseph; New York: Harper, 1959. (¼)

Wealthy Lonsdale Walsh is a man so averse to telling lies, he has an allergic reaction to them.   Outraged at being convicted of murder on perjured evidence, he arranges to escape from jail and stage a mock retrial, with a hand-picked judge and defense barrister and all the witnesses held prisoner while the rehearing progresses.   Best part of the book is a dozen-page tour of the law courts by Walsh's daughter, Angela, who is shopping for the judge and barrister.   In one of the most delightful patches of unadulterated Cecilism, we sees Mr. Tewkesbury defending a prostitute in Magistrate's Court, his cross-examination of a policeman a masterpiece of delay and obfuscation; a receiving-stolen-goods case including a hilarious lost-cause address to the jury by the defense; a High Court judge making the advocates' arguments for them; and a Court of Appeals hearing compared to center court at Wimbledon.   The surprise twist represents one of the author's deftest reader bamboozlements.   All in all, this is one of a handful of candidates for best Cecil novel. (The mock trial has been considered courtroom action for purposes of arriving at the quantity symbol.   Readers who object can change the ¼ to a B.)

45. Alibi for a Judge. London: Joseph, 1960. (B)

William Burford, on trial for bank robbery before Mr.
Justice Carstairs, is convicted and sentenced to ten years
when he fails to provide a convincing alibi or to pin the
crime on a mysterious lookalike acquaintance known as
Thompson. The judge, troubled by an accusation of unfair-
ness by a juror, comes to doubt the verdict and tries
unsuccessfully to help Burford win his appeal. He even
takes up the search for Thompson himself, in tandem with
Burford's wife, Lesley. Trial action, in the original court
and the Court of Criminal Appeal, runs about 45 pages. In
his most informal-essayist vein, Cecil conveys a lot of
interesting information about the appeal process.

46. Daughters in Law. London: Joseph; New York: Harper,
1961. (¼)

Major Claude Buttonstep, who has a strong aversion to
lawyers due to an unfortunate family history of litigation,
objects to the plans of his two sons to marry the twin
Coombe sisters, solicitor Jane and barrister Prunella. Not
surprisingly, they wind up representing him in the case of
Buttonstep vs. Trotter, a teapot tempest arising from the
loan of a lawnmower. The final twist is straight out of
musical comedy. Here more than ever Cecil is the P. G.
Wodehouse of legal fiction, and judging from numerous
dust-jacket quotes, Wodehouse was one of his most enthusiastic fans.

47. Unlawful Occasions. London: Joseph, 1962. New York:
British Book Centre, 1974. (¼)

The jacket illustration showing a loudly-dressed man strew-
ing red herrings in the path of police, press, barristers, and
solicitors is most appropriate, for this is one of Cecil's
most wonderfully complicated plots, a reader-as-detective
story in which all the enigmas are resolved at the end.
Brian Culsworth, Q.C., is asked by an attractive neighbor,
Margaret Verney, for advice in dealing with a possible
blackmailer, Mr. Sampson, and soon is dealing with him
himself. He also briefly represents a Mr. Baker in a
dispute over the dividing up of a football pools win. The
story begins in court and darts in and out throughout,
following Baker's case through various courts, and finishing
with Sampson's libel trial.

48. Independent Witness. London: Joseph, 1963.   New York: British Book Centre, 1974. (½)

Michael Barnes, Member of Parliament, goes on trial for dangerous driving in a book that exemplifies Cecil's ability to create ample suspense out of a less than life-or-death situation. For a time it appears Barnes will have to face the dreaded Mr. Justice Grampton, who "collected motorists." Including some of the author's best and most extensive wigged combat, the novel provides more of the excitement of the law than most "big" courtroom books. Though it is less purely comic than some Cecil products, there are plenty of laughs when Colonel Brain, almost a professional witness, testifies for the prosecution. The ending is both surprising and credible.

49. Portrait of a Judge and Other Stories.   London: Joseph, 1964. New York: Harper, 1965. (C)

Cecil's second collection gathers 22 tales, most short-short stories with twist endings, a form the author could handle as masterfully as the comic novel. Most concern legal matters but only eight actually get in court: "I Killed Gordon McNaghten," "The Lesson," "The Application," "The Patient," "Striking the Balance," "The Limit," "Mock Trial," and "The Wife in the Train." One of the non-courtroom stories, "The Wanted Man," was later expanded into a novel of the same title (q.v.).

50. Fathers in Law.   London: Joseph, 1965.   (As A Child Divided, New York: Harper, 1966.) (¾)

This grimmer-than-usual entry begins with adoptive parents Bill and Mary Woodthorpe menaced by blackmailer Eric Smith, who may be part of the biological father's attempt to take away little Hugh. After Smith's trial in the Old Bailey, we have a custody battle between the natural and adoptive parents, with something to be said on both sides. There's interesting material on British adoption laws and fun with psychiatric testimony, but on the whole this is lesser Cecil, mainly because the kind of wild plotting that works fine in a farce is less effective in a basically serious story.

51. A Woman Named Anne.   London: Joseph; New York: Harper, 1967. (½)

The titular Anne is named as a corespondent in the divorce case of Amberley vs. Amberley. The main question of the tale, which begins and ends with her on the witness stand, is simple: did she or didn't she? The reader is kept guessing until the highly satisfying surprise ending. This novel also exists as a play, and judging from the stage-like entrances and exits designed to keep the setting unified, it may have been a play first.

52. No Fear or Favour. London: Joseph, 1968. (As The Blackmailers, New York: Simon and Schuster, 1968.) (¾)

Clifford Ledbury is tried in the Old Bailey for conspiracy to commit blackmail under the guise of an organization called the Association for the Suppression of Slander. Presiding is Mr. Justice Hereford, who expresses the doubt that he has ever done anything for which he could be blackmailed. But there is a way of putting pressure on him in an attempt to influence his conduct of the case: kidnapping his young daughter. The situation makes the novel less light-hearted and humorous than most Cecil products. The 80+ pages of courtroom action are up to the usual standard, and justice is finally done by a cute trick.

53. Brief Tales from the Bench. London: BBC, 1968; New York: Simon and Schuster, 1972. (C)

The eight first-person stories in this volume, all including courtroom action, were originally BBC radio plays with Andrew Cruickshank in the role of the judge-narrator. In his introduction, Cecil states that four of the cases are entirely fictitious and four are based at least in part on his actual experiences as a county court judge. In an appendix, he reveals which are which. The implied challenge-to-the-reader adds to the volume's enjoyment. (I guessed right on six out of eight.) Cecil was equally entertaining and informative at whatever length he chose.

54. Tell You What I'll Do. London: Joseph; New York: Simon and Schuster, 1969. (B)

The novel opens with silence in the Old Bailey court. The reason: everyone is eating toffee during the fraud trial of likeable con man Harry Woodstock. Harry abruptly changes his plea to guilty and is convicted, and the rest of the novel recounts his determined efforts to get (and then stay) in prison. There is much theological discussion with the prison-visiting Canon Abdale. Main trial scene concerns a group of shoplifting offenses prosecuted in Magistrate's Court by the offensive Randall Blower, Q.C. Though entertaining, the book falls short of Cecil's best work.

55. The Wanted Man. London: Joseph, 1972. New York: British Book Centre, 1974. (B)

Is Norman Partridge, well-liked newcomer to the village of Little Bacon, really escaped bankrobber John Gladstone, as some of his neighbors suspect? As usual, Cecil discusses very serious ethical and moral dilemmas in a light-hearted, unsolemn way. He feels a duty to educate that could be fatal in a novelist less skilled at his craft. In chapter three of this book, his didactic impulses for once clash with the best interests of fiction, as his characters spend improbable amounts of time lecturing to each other about the need for more police and better justice. Though Judge Herbert Ward is the focal character, court action is much slighter than usual, totaling only about a dozen pages. Cecil provides the usual well-orchestrated surprise ending, though it is somewhat telegraphed this time.

56. Hunt the Slipper. London: Joseph, 1977. (B)

This final, posthumously published Cecil novel is a disappointment. The only trial action comes in a dozen early pages, describing a combined divorce and probate proceeding brought by Harriet Hunt, whose husband Graham vanished seven years before. Just as she is about to make the big step of taking another man into her bed, Graham reappears as if nothing had happened. While Graham's seven-year hiatus remains a mystery, Cecil has fun with the situation and the tale grips the reader. But when it is explained, by a strained and far-fetched combination of circumstances, interest drops sharply. Cecil includes an au courant hostage situation in his finale, but action and suspense really were not his milieu.

The following late Cecil titles, published only in Britain, all by Joseph, were not examined for the present work: Juror in Waiting (1970), The Buttercup Spell (1971), Truth with her Boots On (1974), and Cross Purposes (1976). An earlier unexamined work is Ways and Means (Chapman and Hall; British Book Service, 1952). The Asking Price (1966) is a possibly unique Cecil in its failure to get into court at all.

CHRISTIE, Agatha (1890-1976)

57.   The Mysterious Affair at Styles. London: John Lane, 1920.
       New York: Dodd, Mead, 1927. (B)

       Although her short story "The Witness for the Prosecution"
       became one of the most famous of courtroom dramas both
       as a play and as a film, Christie rarely wrote trial scenes.
       Her first novel, however, sees John Cavendish charged in
       the Old Bailey with the poison murder of his stepmother,
       Emily Inglethorp. The defendant's barrister in a sequence
       of about fifteen pages bears the Dickensian name, Sir
       Ernest Heavywether.   Hercule Poirot springs his initial
       least-suspected-person solution (and a fine one) outside of
       court.

58.   Sad Cypress.   London: Collins; New York: Dodd, Mead,
       1940. (B)

       Here Christie starts in the courtroom in her prologue, with
       Elinor Carlisle in the dock for the murder by poison of the
       wealthy and elderly Mary Gerrard. After a lengthy flash-
       back to how Elinor got in this particular spot, Christie
       returns near the end for some thirty pages of adequate
       trial action. Though we do not learn the content of his
       testimony until the case is over, the most important
       witness for the defense is Hercule Poirot.

CLARK, Douglas (1920?-   )

59.   Roast Eggs.   London: Gollancz; New York: Dodd, Mead,
       1981. (B)

       This is one of those rare novels (see also Bugliosi and
       Cozzens) where the reader's sympathies are enlisted on the
       side of the prosecution. The gimmick is that Scotland Yard
       detectives Masters and Green must do some high speed
       detection on the weekend between direct and cross exami-
       nation of defendant James Connal, on trial for the murder
       (by fire) of his wife, in order to beef up the tottering case
       against him. It's a pure intellectual puzzle for readers
       nostalgic for R. Austin Freeman, Freeman Wills Crofts,

J. J. Connington, and their Golden Age colleagues. The forty-or-so pages of courtroom scenes are nicely done. As in other Clark novels, his pharmaceutical expertise comes into play.

COBB, Irvin S. (1876-1944)

60. Back Home. New York: Doran, 1912. (C)

Cobb was a good writer and is worth rediscovery, but the stories about Judge William Pitman Priest, Kentucky arbiter and Civil War veteran, are much stronger on local color than trial action. Three of the ten tales in this first collection get into court, but they offer little of interest to the buff. In "Words and Music," Judge Priest appears as a witness for the defense in the Forked Deer County, Tennessee, trial of Breck Tandy for killing the county clerk. Southern patriotism is used to sway the jury with very little revealed on the merits of the case. Presiding in "Five Hundred Dollars Reward," the judge also manipulates the result to get off the defendant, who shot a bully in an incident arising from a family feud. "When the Fighting was Good" begins in court with the judge regretfully sentencing a fellow veteran to two years' hard labor in an assault case. A Cobb novel with some courtroom action is Alias Ben Alibi (Doran, 1925). One of the novelettes in Judge Priest Turns Detective (Indianapolis: Bobbs-Merrill, 1937) logs at least some court time.

CONROY, A. L.

61. Storefront Lawyers. New York: Bantam, 1970. (B)

This novelization of a TV series created by David Karp frequently betrays its small-screen origins. Three brilliant young law graduates join a stuffy corporate firm on the condition it bankroll them in a storefront office giving free legal service to the poor. One of their first clients is retiree Karl Holder, who has shot to death socialite Howard Weston Woodward, a man he has never seen before, saying the victim "stole" his house. In the climactic trial, advocates are allowed to mix interrogation and argument to the jury unchallenged, and the result lacks credibility.

COOPER, James Fenimore (1789-1851)

62.   The Ways of the Hour.   New York: Putnam; London:
      Bentley, 1850. (B)

      In the town of Biberry, Duke's County, New York, young
      Mary Monson (not, everyone believes, her real name) is
      charged with arson and murder.   Are Peter and Dorothy
      Goodwin the charred skeletons found in the ashes of their
      burned house, or (as one expert medical witness believes)
      are the remains those of two women?   Lawyer Tom
      Dunscomb appears for the defense.   The novel is Cooper's
      brief against the jury system.   In the numerous eloquent
      and intelligent conversations (or lectures in dialogue),
      which bring the plot but not the reader's interest to a
      grinding halt, other issues of the day are touched on as
      well: capital punishment, trial by press, slavery (jarringly
      to the modern reader, Cooper's hero comes out for it), and
      (most prominently) the rights and roles of women.   To put
      it mildly, the author of the Leatherstocking tales was no
      feminist.

      This is anything but a great novel, partly because most of
      the characters are barely solid enough to hang opinions on.
      It is, however, a fascinating document of its times, both in
      and out of the courtroom.   About a hundred pages are spent
      on the mystery woman's trial, covering jury selection
      through verdict and sentencing, followed by last-minute
      revelation and retrial.   Under all the excess verbiage is a
      tale not so different in structure from many twentieth-
      century courtroom and detective novels.

COZZENS, James Gould (1903-1978)

63.   The Just and the Unjust.   New York: Harcourt, Brace,
      1942. London: Cape, 1943. (¼)

      Assistant District Attorney Abner Coates, grappling with a
      decision to overcome his distaste for politics and run for
      the soon-to-be-vacant top spot, is the focal character in
      the story of a small-town murder trial of big-city crimi-
      nals.   Setting is an unspecified Eastern Commonwealth,
      probably Pennsylvania.   The case itself, a gang kidnap-
      killing, is among the most boring ever to have a whole
      novel devoted to it.   Neither the victim nor the defendants

are very interesting to the reader, nor are they intended to be. This circumstance lends added authenticity to a trial that has a definite feel of reality about it but challenges the author to retain the reader's interest. He does, however, in a novel pleasantly old-fashioned in its leisurely pace, accumulation of detail, and avoidance of wrought-up histrionics. Almost uniquely (at least to this buff), the out-of-court scenes carry the most interest, though there is some effective exposition of trial tactics and argument. A secondary case, briefly in court, involves a high school teacher accused of sexual improprieties (short of rape) with students. At times, the conservative Cozzens seems almost as contemptuous of juries as James Fenimore Cooper in The Ways of the Hour (see above), but ultimately he does not suggest their abolition.

CREASEY, John (1908-1973)

(as Michael Halliday in Britain, Kyle Hunt in U.S.A.)

64. Sly as a Serpent. London: Hodder and Stoughton; New York: Macmillan, 1967. (B)

Brian Callard, a very severely dominated son, strangles his mother. Dr. Emmanuel Cellini, psychiatrist and sometime detective, believes he can get Callard off with a unique self-defense plea. Not a whodunit and very slightly plotted, this shares with many Creaseys a failure to fulfill its early promise. The Old Bailey trial is very abbreviated, giving it a rather TV-ish feel. Human interest and readability are strong, however.

65. Too Good to be True. London: Hodder and Stoughton; New York: Macmillan, 1969. (B)

Justin Gray, a man of rigid ethical standards others can't seem to understand, refuses to agree when his three partners in a realty firm want to acquire valuable land cheap from Mrs. Pantanelli, a wealthy and somewhat senile elderly lady. When she is poisoned, Justin is accused by eyewitnesses, and the beautiful client who could provide his alibi has disappeared. Dr. Cellini takes a hand and sorts everything out. The very brief (11-page) Magistrate's Court hearing is undistinguished, and if anyone fails to guess the ending, it will be because the solution gimmick was considered hopelessly old hat in 1910, let alone 1969.

CURTIS, Richard

See TOUSTER, Irwin

DANE, Clemence (1887-1965), and SIMPSON, Helen (1897-1940)

66. Enter Sir John. London: Hodder and Stoughton; New York: Cosmopolitan, 1928. (B)

Matinee idol Sir John Saumarez, who ranks (in a very tough field) as one of the most egotistical detectives in fiction, attends the trial of actress Martella Baring, who is accused of the fireplace-poker murder of Edna Warwick, the wife of actor-manager Gordon Druce. After her conviction, in a setting she finds "not nearly as impressive as a court on the stage," the balance of the book is a racing-the-hangman plot, though one lacking in much real tension. The scene in the jury room, like most such in fiction, does not make one sanguine about the system. Following the final secret's revelation is a dreadfully elongated aftermath. Re-Enter Sir John (1932), reputed to be much the better of the two Saumarez novels, gets in court only very briefly.

DANIELS, Harold R. (1919-   )

67. The Accused. New York: Dell, 1958. London: Deutsch, 1961. (B)

Though not prolific, Daniels was one of the most highly-regarded paperback original writers of the fifties. Here excerpts from the transcript of college teacher Alvin Morlock's Massachusetts trial for the murder of his wife Louise alternate with flashbacks to the events leading up to her death. The novel is an efficient piece of story-telling, but the courtroom sequences are a procedural disaster, reading more like a TV trial than a real one: the judge inexplicably offers the prosecutor an exception on a very minor point; the prosecutor repeatedly cross-examines his own witnesses; the lawyers offer gratuitous snide comments without challenge and routinely use "loaded" language; prosecution and defense witnesses at times appear to be testifying in arbitrary order. The following exchange illustrates scrambled terminology. Gurney (prosecutor): "Mrs. Carofano, would you say that they were happy while they were living in your house?" Leibman (defender): "Objection, Your Honor. The answer would be argumentative."

DANIELS, Norman

68. Arrest and Trial. New York: Lancer, 1963. (¼)

This is an original (in one sense of the word) novel based on characters from the TV series. The challenge to the show's script writers (and to Daniels) was to put both the investigating officer (played by Ben Gazzara) and the defense attorney (played by Chuck Connors) on the side of the angels. Though this is probably above average as TV novelizations go, it is a fairly tepid novel, written by an efficient but unscintillating old pro with no particular flair for courtroom action. The plot concerns an executive tried for the attempted murder of another executive who beat him out for a corporate presidency. Much of the story is concerned with tiresome affairs of the heart.

69. The Missing Witness. New York: Lancer, 1964. (¼)

The second Arrest and Trial novelization has an intriguing plot but quicky execution. A surgeon is thanked by the father of a mentally retarded baby who died in surgery for an act of euthanasia the surgeon claims he didn't commit. (Typically of TV "problem" shows of the time, the novel does not confront head-on an instance of actual euthanasia.) There are two trials here: the surgeon's slander suit against the police and the trial of both father and doctor for murder. There are numerous unlikely happenings, unbearably corny dialogue in the man-woman scenes, and a general soap-opera aura to the whole enterprise.

(as Harrison Judd)

70. Shadow of a Doubt. New York: Gold Medal, 1961. London:

Muller, 1962. (B)

High school science teacher Hal Griffith sees a contorted-faced man leaving the vacant house next door to his Westwood, California, home. When a ten-year-old girl is found there raped and murdered, Griffith becomes key witness in the case against bank president Neil Morrison. But he's just not sure, despite the strong circumstantial case built up by Sgt. Casey Cole, and the novel becomes less the traditional threatened-witness story than an uncertain-witness story. A rare pro-capital punishment tract, the book starts very strong in the best paperback-original tradition of crisp story-telling, but goes downhill in the second half. The author promises a big trial but doesn't really deliver, getting in court for only a dozen pages or so. It's just as well, for the grasp of courtroom procedure is very loose. The author inserts the vague statement, "there were legal arguments," but makes no attempt to explain what they were. The defense counsel inserts questions willy-nilly during the prosecutor's direct examination, and no one seems to find it odd. There is so much in-court conversation among the central characters it's a wonder the judge doesn't shut them up.

DAVIES, Valentine

71. Miracle on 34th Street. New York: Harcourt, Brace, 1947. (B)

This novelization puts between covers a movie trial that many will know by heart from repeated Christmas viewings: the sanity hearing of Kris Kringle, Macy's Department Store Santa Claus, threatened with being committed because he believes himself the real St. Nick. The novel follows the film trial word-for-word and is more enjoyable when one can picture Edmund Gwenn, Jerome Cowan, John Payne, William Frawley, and (as the judge, worried about the next election) Gene Lockhart in the main roles.

DAY LEWIS, Cecil

See BLAKE, Nicholas

DE FELITTA, Frank (1921-   )

72.   Audrey Rose. New York: Putnam, 1975. London: Collins,
       1976. (B)

       The allegedly ideal existence of Janet and Bill Templeton,
       an exasperating young couple, is disturbed when a man
       named Elliot Hoover claims their daughter Ivy is the
       reincarnation of his daughter Audrey Rose, burned to death
       in a car accident only moments before Ivy's birth. When
       Hoover is charged with kidnapping, his defense by ambi-
       tious lawyer Brice Mack depends on establishing the truth
       of reincarnation. Overwrought trial action is plentiful
       (over eighty pages) but unrewarding. Though this is a
       second-rate horror novel, the basic idea is not bad. It
       would be interesting to know what Stephen King could have
       done with it.

DENKER, Henry (1912-   )

73.   A Place for the Mighty. New York: McKay, 1973. (¼)

       U.S. Supreme Court Justice Harvey Miller is assassinated
       during a session of the Court by a black gunman in the
       public gallery. The accused is Midgely Grove, a badly
       confused and uncommunicative man who insists on having
       as his defender civil rights lawyer Lincoln Winkler, a
       caricature of an activist attorney who puts radical politics
       and his own self-aggrandizement ahead of his client's best
       interests. (Winkler is clearly a non-humorous lampoon of
       William Kunstler, and the novel crawls with other roman à
       clef liberals.) Lawyer Denker, writing in the by-the-
       numbers prose of Irving Wallace and other blockbusterites,
       knows how to tell an involving story and writes good
       courtroom Q-and-A, but the book fails to convince. Its
       card-stacking and strawman-building are too blatant, and
       Winkler seems too transparently phony to fool so many
       people. Even his sharp young co-counsel Scott Ingram III is
       very slow to get onto him. And could he possibly get away
       with what he does in a Federal courtroom even in the
       climate of the early 1970's? The defense revolves around a
       trendy concept called the Doctrine of Social Inevitability,
       but Winkler has another curve to throw at the Supreme
       Court when the verdict is appealed. The climactic address
       of liberal Justice Ben Robertson to his colleagues will

delight some and invite groans and catcalls from others, depending on whether they agree with Denker's views.

Coincidentally, this was one of two 1973 novels dealing with the assassination of a Supreme Court Justice, the other being Edward Linn's The Adversaries.

74. Outrage. New York: Morrow, 1982. (½)

Dennis Riordan's daughter was raped and murdered, but the perpetrator was released on a technicality. Riordan seeks out and personally executes the rapist-killer, then demands a trial. Idealistic young defender Ben Gordon takes the case, but his client refuses to cooperate in an insanity plea, wanting the reasons for his act to have a full airing in court. The course of the trial is followed from jury selection to deliberation.

Denker's novel is undeniably readable and skillfully constructed but just as undeniably a polemic against the supposed overemphasis on the rights of the accused in today's courts. With a keen feel for the breezes of popular opinion, the novel reverses the liberal spirit that characterized most courtroom fiction of the previous few decades. As Denker stacks the cards, of course, the reader can only sympathize with Riordan, and indeed the particular technicality on which his victim escaped the law (the inadmissibility of certain evidence applied to a parolee that would be admissible applied to an ordinary citizen) does seem wrongheaded. The characters are not deep but they are well-differentiated (medium-grade cardboard, you might say), and ultimately this is better than some "message" fiction.

DERLETH, August (1909-1971)

75. Sign of Fear. New York: Loring and Munsey, 1935. London: Newnes, 1936. (B)

Judge Ephraim Peck stars in a series of ten detective novels, forming one odd corner of the Wisconsin author's massive Sac Prairie Saga. In this one, archaeologist Christopher Jannichon is drawn back to his hometown of Prairie du Chien by a series of subtly threatening postcards. Murder follows by one of those ingenious means beloved of detective novelists of the thirties. Derleth has a clever least-suspected-person gimmick as well, but his fair play is questionable and the use of a trial structure for exposition after the solution has been revealed is ineffective. Judge Peck, old-fashioned enough to address a jury with three women on it as "gentlemen," appears for the defense. The two advocates allow each other to get away with too much testifying of their own. There is a rather archaic feel to both narrative and dialogue.

76. Sentence Deferred. New York: Scribner's; London: Heinemann, 1939. (B)

Though Judge Peck's cases only occasionally find him in court, in this one there are two trials, with a pair of defendants accused in turn of the apparent murder of banker Henry Hornly. In Hornly's burned house, a skeleton is found, identified as Hornly's by dental evidence and with two dissimilar bullets rattling around in its skull. Peck is an observer rather than a participant in the trials, until the time comes to spell out the solution.

Courtroom action totals about fifty pages, not counting Peck's final summing up to the court after the second jury verdict is in. In the tradition of its time, the solution is at its most ingenious when at its farthest-fetched, i.e. in the matter of where the two bullets came from. Other aspects of the plot are readily guessable by experienced mystery readers, and Derleth must suffer by the obvious comparison to R. Austin Freeman (q.v.). The novel is ultimately more notable as a regional period piece, giving a strong feeling of the problems of the Depression era, than either a detective or trial novel, though Derleth does have some fun with technicalities of the law. The court procedure has its oddities, however. Most strikingly, the prosecuting attorney is repeatedly allowed to stop between questioning witnesses to argue his case to the jury.

DEWLEN, Al (1921-   )

77. Twilight of Honor. New York: McGraw-Hill, 1961. London: Longmans, 1962. (½)

Lawyer Owen Paulk, disenchanted with the criminal law since an acquitted client committed murder and his young wife died in an accident on the same night, is appointed by the court to defend Ray Priest, a drifter accused of killing the Texas Panhandle town's leading citizen, Big Jess Hutcherson. Owen finds the cards (including an impressive-looking but sleepy and marginally competent judge and a jury panel studded with powerful local citizens) stacked against him but an elderly and ailing legal mentor (with beautiful daughter) in his corner. Dewlen's book belongs in the top echelon of Big Trial novels. The case is one of the most thoroughly presented, from jury selection through eloquent closing arguments through verdict, in all of fiction. Adding to the interest are the contrasts of Texas trial procedure with that of most other states. For example, all the witnesses are sworn in at once; the jury actually sleeps in the jury room (necessitating separate quarters for the recently enfranchised female jurors); and the judge's charge precedes the closing arguments of the prosecution and defense.

DICKENS, Charles (1812-1870)

78.   The Posthumous Papers of the Pickwick Club. London: Chapman and Hall, 1837. American publishers various. (B)

One chapter recounts the breach of promise suit against Mr. Pickwick by his former landlady Mrs. Bardell, one of the most famous trials in literature. Dickens' exploitation of the comedic possibilities of the courtroom may have inspired later humorists like Henry Cecil (q.v.). The author's Bleak House, though much involved with matters of law, spends hardly any time in court.

DICKSON, Carter

See CARR, John Dickson

DONAHUE, Jack (1917-   )

79.   Pray to the Hustlers' God.   New York: Reader's Digest/Crowell, 1977. (B)

In the first of a projected series about flamboyant attorney Harlan Cole, it soon becomes clear that Donahue is trying to create a new Perry Mason, and we could use one. He offers saltier language than Erle Stanley Gardner, slightly more graceful prose, a fresh background of Houston, and a cast that includes a Della Street-type secretary, Paul Drake-type private eye, and Hamilton Burger-type D. A. The case involves the beating murder of a Houston basketball coach arising from an attempt to fix the NBA playoffs. Cole's client is a wealthy underworld figure, John (the Paymaster) Heywood. The climax comes in an "examining trial" before a Justice of the Peace. Unfortunately, this is not nearly as involving or exciting as a Gardner novel, and even the courtroom action doesn't liven things up much, especially since the solution is prematurely revealed.

80.   The Lady Loved Too Well. New York: McGraw-Hill, 1978. (B)

The impression of a Mason imitation is even stronger in the second Harlan Cole novel despite surface differences: Cole has a sex life and is given to saying "you-all." Donahue even copies Gardner's early habit of plugging the next book in the series in the closing pages. (As of mid-1984, the next book had not appeared.) Again what is missing is Gardner's incomparable sense of pace. The case involves the trial of feminist author Cornelia Sherry, accused of the steak-knife murder of her lover. Courtroom action covers some forty pages late in the book-- again, like a Perry Mason.

DREISER, Theodore (1871-1945)

81.   An American Tragedy. New York: Boni and Liveright, 1925. London: Constable, 1926. (B)

Dreiser was a writer of immense power, and the hundred pages of trial in this massive novel constitute a classic of courtroom fiction. Twenty-one-year-old Clyde Griffiths is accused of the rowboat drowning of poor and pregnant Roberta Alden, carried out in order to marry wealthy and socially prominent Sondra Finchley, known during the trial as Miss X. Dreiser based the novel on the 1906 case of Chester Gillette, convicted and executed for the murder of Grace Brown. Every florid word of the lawyers' speeches to the jury rings true. Most testimony is summarized, until the very detailed (in 60+ pages) account of the defendant's time on the stand, one of the most elongated and harrowing examinations in all trial fiction.

DYER, George (1903-1978)

82. <u>The People Ask Death</u>.   New York: Scribner's; London: Heinemann, 1940. (¾)

There is much fun to be had in this specimen of the American-style Golden Age detective novel, complete with photos, floorplans and footnotes, though by the evidence of this plot, Dyer was no Ellery Queen. F. Austin Scarborough, a member of the San Francisco Board of Police Commissioners, has been shot at the Thermopylae Club pool, in circumstances that seem to allow for no other killer than <u>Times</u> reporter Persen "Buzz" Drake. Drake's fellow members of the Catalyst Club, a group of six amateur criminologists featured in other Dyer novels, leap into action to prove his innocence. A rival paper tries to drum up public sentiment against Drake, as shown by the inflammatory clippings that begin each chapter. Prosecuting Drake is flamboyant and politically ambitious D.A. Haywards Nonni. Defending is socially conscious young attorney Richard Victor, who confronts a classic situation of legal fiction: trying to stretch out his case while awaiting the arrival of the missing key witness from halfway around the world. In a less standard occurrence, most of his defense materials are stolen at tommy-gun point on the eve of the trial. The courtroom action is designed more for drama than for realism, and all pretense of accurate procedure is thrown to the winds for the windup. Dyer offers much humor throughout, suggesting that the florid closing statements of the advocates are at least semi-satirical.

E

EHRLICH, J. W.

See WILLIAMS, Brad

F

FAIR, A. A.

See GARDNER, Erle Stanley

FALL, Thomas, pseudonym of Donald Clifford Snow (1917-   )

83.   The Justicer. New York: Rinehart, 1959. London: World
      Distributors, 1962. (B)

      A rare courtroom western, set on the plains of 1889. In the
      town of Ridgefield, just north of the Kansas border,
      dedicated young lawyer Angus DeWolfe gets a new trial for
      Indian Marcus Maywood, accused of murdering a family of
      four.   The principled anti-gallows defender must go up
      against Federal District Court hangin'-judge Willard Ring,
      with some support from the judge's daughter, who taught
      the defendant in an Indian school. It's a readable story that
      makes good use of its historical background but is not
      otherwise notable.

FEEGEL, John R. (1932-   )

84.   Autopsy. New York: Avon, 1975. (¾)

      The author of this Edgar-winning paperback original is both
      a lawyer and an M.D. specializing in pathology, giving him
      qualifications similar to R. Austin Freeman's Dr. Thorn-
      dyke. Here he uses his expertise to present a procedural
      masterpiece, with fascinating detail about the work of
      morticians, autopsy surgeons, and attorneys. Flordia toma-
      to grower Myrl Caton, an appropriately unpleasant charac-
      ter, is found shot to death in his Connecticut motel room.

He is presumed to have committed suicide and is shipped home following a perfunctory and slipshod investigation. Citing a Flordia law that allows a two-year waiting period before an insured can commit suicide to enrich his beneficiaries, the insurance company declines to pay off on a recently signed policy. The widow brings suit in Florida's Federal District Court, where her lawyers try to show the death was not suicide but murder. The friendly rivalry of the opposing lawyers is beautifully done, and the reader gets a good sense of the differences in procedure between Federal and state courts in such matters as jury selection and adversarial demeanor. The irascible judge's disgust at a squeamish juror is a nice touch.

FISH, Robert L. (1912-1981)

85. Trials of O'Brien. New York: Signet, 1965. (B)

An original story based on the short-lived Peter Falk TV series, this is one of the few such products to stand on its own as a good novel. Daniel J. O'Brien, a Runyonesque character with a wide acquaintence of small-time criminals, is better realized on the printed page than most TV characters, and his murder defense of safecracker Benny Kalen does not have the over-simplified feel of a TV trial. Fish demonstrates his flair for courtroom action in twenty pages of well-staged cat-and-mouse.

86. The Murder League. New York: Simon and Schuster, 1968. London: New English Library, 1970. (B)

Carruthers, Simpson, and Briggs, a trio of elderly British writers considered over the hill by younger members of the Mystery Authors' Club they founded, form a murder-for-hire organization. Sir Percival Pugh, phenomenally successful barrister, defends Simpson in the elevator-shaft death of a charity executive. In a good comic trial, Pugh tricks his opponent into behaving quite foolishly. The American Fish writes of a British milieu with remarkable sure-footedness, except when Carruthers and Briggs go directly to Pugh without a solicitor as middleman. The two subsequent Murder League novels, Rub-a-Dub-Dub (1971) and A Gross Carriage of Justice (1979) also feature Pugh and some comic legal finagling but no extended trial scenes, though the former does include a shipboard inquest.

87. (with Henry Rothblatt) A Handy Death. New York: Simon
     and Schuster, 1973. London: Hale, 1975. (B)

     Attorney Hank Ross, apparently based on co-author Roth-
     blatt as Sam Benedict was based on Jake Ehrlich, defends
     former Met pitcher Billy Dupaul on an eight-year-delayed-
     action murder charge. He was originally convicted of
     assault, but when his victim dies years later as a direct
     result of the bullet wound, another trial is necessitated.
     The story also involves an Attica prison riot that begins
     during a convict baseball game.

     First Ross performs some fancy footwork in the prelimi-
     nary hearing, almost seeming to lead the judge around by
     the nose. He gets the original conviction set aside, then a
     second-offender sentence on another charge reconsidered.
     Finally, with wonderful chutzpah, he asks bail for his
     convict-client. In the jury trial that follows, he confronts
     the real killer on the witness stand in true Perry Mason
     style. Indeed, this is among the best novels in the Mason
     vein by someone other than Erle Stanley Gardner. Roth-
     blatt's involvement guarantees the book is about the law,
     not just the facts of a mystery plot, and Fish did courtroom
     sequences so effectively, it's regrettable he didn't do them
     more often.

FITZMAURICE, Eugene

88. Circumstantial Evidence. New York: Jove, 1978. (¼)

     This novel offers a prime example of the Inflated Block-
     buster Syndrome. At half the length, it would have been a
     pretty good legal detective story, even though the murder-
     er comes out of a hat.   Scenes from the Pennsylvania
     murder trial of surgeon Paul Oslo cover most of the second
     half of the book and are competently done. But the pre-
     trial discussion of the opposing lawyers (pages 190-192) is
     as incredible as it is pretentious.

FLANNAGAN, Roy

89. County Court. Garden City, NY: Doubleday, Doran, 1937.
     London: Heinemann, 1938. (B)

In the small town of Juliaville, Virginia, farmwife Anna Fry is on trial for the shooting murder of her husband. Central enigma of the novel is a healer-prophet-troubador and alleged halfwit known as Captain Jinks, and the reader is led to wonder if he is detective, murderer, or just some kind of authorial metaphor. Among the witnesses is the defendant's son, a rare fictional instance of a "court witness," called by judge and open to cross-examination by both sides. This is an interesting and readable novel with a good sense of setting and adequate courtroom action.

FOOTE, Shelby (1916-   )

90.   Follow Me Down. New York: Dial, 1950. London: Hamilton, 1951. (B)

An early novel of a well-known Civil War historian concerns Bible-reading Mississippi farmer Luther Eustis, who astonishes his acquaintences by spending three weeks on a deserted island with young Beulah Ross and then killing her. He is represented with an insanity defense by burned-out lawyer Parker Nowell. Foote uses a multi-narrator format, summarizing Eustis' trial through the eyes of the court clerk in the first chapter, then describing it in more detail from Nowell's perspective late in the book. The time-shifting mosaic of viewpoints eventually gives a picture of what happened and why. A fine novel with good court scenes and observations of the judicial process.

FOOTNER, Hulbert (1879-1944)

91.   The Whip-poor-will Mystery. New York: Harper, 1935. As The New Made Grave, London: Collins, 1935. (B)

Weir Lambert, Yankee editor of the Kent County Witness, a small-town weekly in an unnamed Southern state, tries to find the girl who put an anonymous personal ad addressed to "Whip-poor-will" in his pages. He finds Leila Cowdin, helps her bury the body of her father, and winds up her codefendant on a charge of shooting him to death. The circuit-court trial before a three-judge panel and a jury is a singularly boring one, and the young couple's soppy romance is nearly as hard to take as the book's egregious racism. A dismal piece of work to be avoided by detection and trial buffs equally.

FOX, Gardner F. (1911-   )

92.   Witness This Woman. New York: Gold Medal, 1959. London: Muller, 1961. (B)

At a time when Robert Traver's Anatomy of a Murder (q.v.)
was a runaway bestseller and courtroom fiction was very
much in vogue, a number of old pros whose hearts weren't
really in it turned to the field.   Like Norman Daniels
(writing as Harrison Judd) in Shadow of a Doubt (q.v.), Fox
pretends to write a trial book but manages to avoid getting
in court for all but about 17 pages.   We open with the
windup of a Westchester County, New York, rape case,
prosecuted by politically ambitious Assistant D.A.   David
Kirwan and defended by his beautiful fiancee, Myra Star-
ling.   The subsequent prosecution of labor organizer Bill
Matson for the shooting murder of building foreman Joe
Farella (who in a prime example of careless character
naming works for a powerful contractor named Big Jim
Farragut) could make David's career, but is he really sure?
Fox can be a good storyteller, but this shallow study of
ambition piles on the clichés relentlessly.

FOX-DAVIES, A(rthur) C(harles) (1871-1928)

93.   The Testament of John Hastings. London: John Long, 1911.
(¼)

In the opening chapter, an Old Bailey jury finds artist John
Hastings guilty of the shooting murder of barmaid Phyllis
Dalison.   Proclaiming his innocence to the last, Hastings is
hanged, but in his will he provides for an investigation to
clear his name, with the ultimate goal of a prosecution of
the real murderer by barrister Ashley Tempest.   For a time
midway, the novel turns from straightforward detection to
political/spy thriller, with a German plot for a British
revolution centering on a Welsh parliamentary election.
Two more defendants are charged in turn with the Dalison
murder, with most of the somewhat repetitious but pro-
cedurally sound in-court action concerning the trial of the
German Schiller for the crime.   When the opposing barristers discuss the case after the verdict, the prosecutor

thinks the defendant innocent while the defender opines his
guilt. The plot takes some interesting twists, though the
detection/future-war combination is a somewhat uneasy
one. The author wrote several other novels about Tempest,
at least some of which presumably also have trial action.

FREEMAN, R(ichard) Austin (1862-1943)

94.   The Red Thumb Mark. London: Collingwood, 1907. New
      York: Newton, 1911. (¼)

      The first novel about Dr. John Evelyn Thorndyke, specialist
      in medical jurisprudence, has as one of its announced
      purposes "drawing attention to certain popular misappre-
      hensions on the subject of finger-prints and their evidential
      value" (Freeman's preface). The fifteenth and sixteenth
      chapters (about 80 pages) are devoted to the trial of
      Reuben Hornby for stealing diamonds from his uncle.
      After the vaunted fingerprint experts have their say,
      Thorndyke bursts their bubble by demonstrating how fin-
      gerprints can be forged. The book is told by Dr. Jervis, a
      medico even denser than Watson but with a charming
      Victorian prose style. The trial runs its full course from
      swearing in of the jury to verdict, and the procedure seems
      correct and realistic, centering more on points of fact than
      points of law. Though the novel remains highly readable
      and involving, contemporary readers may be looking for an
      extra twist that does not materialize-- at the time, de-
      bunking fingerprint evidence was enough novelty.

95.   The Eye of Osiris. London: Hodder and Stoughton, 1911.
      As The Vanishing Man, New York: Dodd, Mead, 1912. (B)

      Egyptian scholar John Bellingham has vanished and is
      presumed dead. Under the terms of his bizarre will, he
      must be buried in a certain parish churchyard (or reason-
      able facsimile) for his deserving brother to inherit. A
      collection of bones found in various locations may or may
      not be his. The neatly-presented probate court proceeding,
      on an application to establish Bellingham's death two years
      after his disappearance and to decide the nutty will in
      favor of his cousin George Hurst, is not the climax of the
      book. In fact, Dr. Thorndyke doesn't even attend. The
      denouement is elongated by present-day standards, but this
      is a fine detective novel with an especially interesting

murderer.

Freeman, an undervalued writer, has an almost Dickensian
touch with secondary characters, and the proper Edwardian
romances that have irritated some critics charmed no less
demanding a reader than Raymond Chandler.

96.   For the Defence: Dr. Thorndyke. London: Hodder and
      Stoughton; New York: Dodd, Mead, 1934. (¼)

      This time Thorndyke appears as a barrister, rather than in
      his usual role as expert witness. His client, painter Andrew
      Barton, finds himself through an odd combination of cir-
      cumstances on trial for his own murder. The body found at
      the base of a cliff, its face battered to unrecognizability
      by a block of chalk, is identified as Andrew but is actually
      his cousin Ronald Barton, whose place Andrew has taken.
      Though there is some effective Q-and-A, Freeman empha-
      sizes speechifying: the opening for the prosecution, for
      example, takes about twenty of the ninety-odd pages of
      trial. The author manages to work in some sniping at a
      favorite target: non-representational modern art.

97.   The Jacob Street Mystery. London: Hodder and Stoughton,
      1942.   As The Unconscious Witness, New York: Dodd,
      Mead, 1942. (B)

      The final Dr. Thorndyke novel finds Freeman's ability as
      well as his general approach unaffected by the passing
      years. He did not choose to follow the changing fashions of
      detective fiction. Again, trial action is in the probate
      court, where the questions of whether the vanished Lotta
      Schiller is dead or alive, and whether the will in question is
      actually hers, are addressed.   About 35 pages of trial
      action are handled with Freeman's usual meticulousness.
      (Note that many Freeman novels involve inquests, some-
      times described at considerable length, that are outside the
      scope of the present work.)

FROST, Barbara

98.   Innocent Bystander.   New York: Coward-McCann, 1955.
      (B)

Though she has to go through some of the traditional
damsel-in-distress had-I-but-knowning, New York attorney
Marka de Lancey is ahead of her fictional times as an
independent female professional.   There's also a woman
jurist in this novel, Judge Louise Breen (no relation to the
present writer).   However, Marka calls in a male criminal
law specialist to defend her client, Italian violinist-com-
poser Gregory Trefani, accused of the morphine poisoning
of nightclub singer Trixie Maxon.   Unfortunately, the 17-
page trial is sadly inept, unconvincing, and TV-ish, including florid addresses by the attorneys that sound more like
1890 than 1955, objections that have no perceptible rhyme
or reason to them, and the opinion of Marka and her
creator that closing summations are the same as opening
statements "only more so"!   That Trefani is tried before an
all-male jury is not remarked upon as anything unusual.
The two earlier novels in the series, The Corpse Said No
(1949) and The Corpse Died Twice (1951), were not examined, but internal references suggest they probably did
not involve courtroom action.   Which is just as well.

G

GALSWORTHY, John (1867-1933)

99. <u>The Silver Spoon</u>. London: Heinemann; New York: Scribners, 1926. (B)

The middle volume of the nine-book Forsyte Chronicles offers a vivid view of twenties culture shock in London high society. The exasperating Fleur Mont, daughter of Soames Forsyte, is the defendant in a mountain-out-of-a-molehill upper-crust libel suit which culminates in a trial no one really wants. The defense strategy is an attack on "modern morality." There is some entertaining testimony about a scandalous "dirty book" of the time, and the cross-examination of the plaintiff is a masterpiece. Galsworthy gives forgotten issues and discredited attitudes a rare sense of immediacy.

100. <u>Over the River</u>. London: Heinemann, 1933. As <u>One More River</u>, New York: Scribners, 1933. (B)

Central event of the final Forsyte Chronicles volume is the divorce case of Corven vs. Corven. Sadistic Sir Gerald, left by wife Clare in Ceylon, is bringing the action on grounds of her adultery with young Tony Croom, whom she had met on the return voyage to England. The reader knows the adultery never took place, but the circumstantial evidence is strong: on shipboard, he was seen leaving her stateroom, and back on land they spent an incredibly innocent night together in a disabled car. One of the few Forsytes in evidence is a solicitor known irritatingly as "very young Roger." This posthumously-published novel is generally less enthralling than <u>The Silver Spoon</u>, but the courtroom give-and-take (of about fifty pages) is admirably done, especially (as before) the cross-examinations.

GARDNER, Erle Stanley (1889-1970)

101. The Case of the Sulky Girl.   New York: Morrow, 1933.
     London: Harrap, 1934. (B)

Since Perry Mason's debut, The Case of the Velvet Claws
(1933), lacks a trial scene, his second case represents a
milestone: the first Gardner courtroom novel.   Though
many of the series regulars are not yet in place, secretary
Della Street and private detective Paul Drake are in their
accustomed roles helping the brilliant defender. Of the
rest of the Perry Mason saga, only The Case of the Lucky
Legs (1934), The Case of the Dangerous Dowager (1937),
The Case of the Baited Hook (1940), The Case of the
Empty Tin (1941), The Case of the Drowsy Mosquito (1943),
and the novelette "The Case of the Crying Swallow"
(collected in 1971) spend no time in court. The Case of the
Lame Canary (1937) and The Case of the Perjured Parrot
(1939) involve inquests, disqualifying them from coverage
here.

Under the terms of her late father's will, Frances Celane's
inheritance is held in trust by her uncle, Edward Norton,
who has the option of giving most of the fortune to charity
if Fran marries before the age of 25.   Now 23, she asks
Perry Mason to work out a way she can marry Rob Gleason
and get the money. It soon develops the couple are already
married, and when Norton is clubbed to death, both are
charged with his murder. The engrossing trial is presented
in somewhat more detail than those in later books. At one
point Gardner even switches to an essay format for a
couple of pages to underscore the bleakness of Mason's
position and his client's chances.   But the pattern is set for
the spirited and free-wheeling courtroom combat to come
in subsequent cases. The opponent is assistant-D.A. Claude
Drumm, a forerunner of the better-known Hamilton Burger.   Mason's young assistant Frank Everly, who never
really established a firm niche in the series, appears with
him in court. Judge Markham is determined not to allow
any chance for Mason's courtroom theatrics. In the trial's
first day, Mason maneuvers Drumm into leaving an un-
wanted juror on the panel and capitalizes on his adversary's
tactical error by getting in the session's last question and
thus receiving the lion's share of the next day's press
coverage. Both lawyers try to use objections as a vehicle
for arguing their cases, to the annoyance of the judge.

Perry often appears to be leaving damaging testimony
unchallenged and eschewing objection to material detri-
mental to his clients, behavior that baffles judge, D.A., and
witnesses but of course proves fully justified in the end.
Mason uses a deft application of witness psychology on a
court-wise judge who is a witness for the prosecution.
Finally he confronts the real killer on the witness stand,
though he doesn't get an automatic confession.

A word is in order about the notorious "incompetent,
irrelevant, and immaterial" objection, which turns up in
nearly every volume of the Mason saga and can become
quite irritating, especially when several Gardner novels are
read in a row. Indeed the three-I objection is almost the
only blight on Gardner's wonderful courtroom scenes.
Gardner didn't invent it-- it turns up, albeit with the three
I's in different order, in Theodore Dreiser's An American
Tragedy (q.v.), which antedates the first Perry Mason by
eight years. Gardner probably did most to popularize it,
though, and other writers picked it up in subsequent novels.
Though its stubborn recurrence suggests it probably was a
standard courtroom recitation early in the century, I'm told
by lawyers that this smorgasbord objection is a refuge of
the desperate advocate who doesn't really know what he
wants to object to but knows he wants to stop his opponent
in any way he can and hopes for a fortuitous ruling.
Indeed, this is how it is often used in the Mason novels.
But it is not always the befuddled D.A. who resorts to the
three I's. The first three triple-I objections in this novel
come from Mason himself. Drumm soon joins in, and even
the judge invokes the three I's on his own at one point.

At the end of Sulky Girl is a scene previewing the third
novel in the series, The Case of the Lucky Legs, a practice
followed in most of the early Mason novels. These teasers
were usually cut in paperback reprints of the novels but are
retained in Aeonian's more recent hardcover reprints.

102. The Case of the Howling Dog. New York: Morrow, 1934.
London: Cassell, 1934. (B)

Arthur Cartwright consults Mason about two matters: he
wants to make a will leaving his money to a neighbor, Mrs.
Clinton Foley, and he wants to complain about Mr. Foley's
howling dog, which Cartwright insists was taught the
behavior just to annoy him. When Cartwright subsequently

sends him ten $1000 bills through the mail as a retainer, Mason is convinced he has an insane client. Arriving for an appointment with Foley, Mason finds man and dog shot to death and is soon being grilled under glaring lights by the disagreeable Sgt. Holcomb, Mason's principal police neme- sis until the advent of the more sympathetic Lt. Tragg later in the series.

Bessie Forbes, whose real identity is in some doubt, is the defendant in the trial sequence, with Judge Markham, Claude Drumm, and Frank Everly all recurring from the earlier novel. Though many later Masons would involve preliminary hearings, this is another full-scale jury trial, beginning with a description of jury selection. The Q-and- A is sharp and Mason's solution comes in his closing speech to the jury. The ending has an uncharacteristic ambiguity. (Question: Does it seem likely that Mason would have to explain the double jeopardy rule to savvy legal secretary Street?)

103. The Case of the Curious Bride. New York: Morrow, 1934. London: Cassell, 1935. (B)

Rhoda Montaine is charged with the iron-poker murder of confidence man Gregory Moxley, who may have been her first husband. Thinking Gregory dead, Rhoda had recently married Philip Montaine, a weak-willed former drug addict with a wealthy father. This was the first Mason to involve two courtroom proceedings. In domestic relations court, the D.A.'s office tries to get Philip an annulment, which would allow him to testify against Rhoda. Her trial, with Judge Markham again presiding, follows the pattern of early Masons in beginning with jury selection. John Lucas is an especially sneering and unpleasant prosecutor. In- stead of playing shell-and-pea with guns, this time Perry does it with doorbells. There's plenty of exciting razzle- dazzle in and out of court, including more out-and-out deception by Mason than he would practice later in his career.

104. The Case of the Counterfeit Eye. New York: Morrow; London: Cassell, 1935. (B)

Peter Brunold, who has a collection of artificial eyes for various times of day and degrees of sobriety, tells Mason one of his eyes has been stolen and replaced with a fake.

He fears the stolen eye will be used to frame him for murder, and indeed millionaire Hartley Basset is found shot to death with a bloodshot glass eye clutched in his hand. Brunold and the widow, Sylvia Basset, are charged with the crime in a preliminary hearing, the first such in the Mason series. The somewhat looser format could accommodate more of Mason's flamboyant stunts than could a full-scale jury trial. The novel, one of the most intricate and exciting of the pulp-flavored early Masons, also has a Nick Carter-ish touch when Perry and Paul Drake impersonate window-cleaners. There is a wealth of technical information about the art and craft of glass eye manufacture.

This novel marks the debut of Hamilton Burger, personally handling the first major murder case in his term of office as District Attorney. In their first conversation, he tells Perry, "I have a horror of prosecuting an innocent person." What a horror-filled existence he was to lead, prosecuting the wrong person in most of the Mason novels to follow.

105. The Case of the Caretaker's Cat. New York: Morrow, 1935. London: Cassell, 1936. (B)

The will of miserly Peter Laxter, who died in a fire, guarantees a perpetual job as caretaker of his estate and a home for life to 65-year-old Charles Ashton-- but principal legatee Sam Laxter claims he is not similarly obligated to Ashton's Persian cat, Clinker. Two more murders follow, unusually high carnage for a Mason novel, caretaker Ashton by strangulation and woman-who-knew-too-much Ethel De-Voe, clubbed with a blunt instrument that may have been Ashton's crutch. Mason defends young Douglas Keene on the latter murder. Though there is generally plenty of artistic license in a Gardner courtroom sequence, this one seems looser than most, again taking advantage of the more informal atmosphere of a preliminary hearing. There is plenty of adversarial byplay, enlivened by a lawyer for one of the legatees who constantly insinuates his oar though his client is technically not a party to the case. Perry and Della are both called as witnesses for the prosecution, with Mason doing some of his summing up in that role. The hearing ends with a series of dei ex machina bursting into court with new evidence. The plot machinery, powered by a MacGuffin of hidden money and diamonds, is elaborate enough for any Golden Age detective story practitioner, and the key clue is a good one.

106. The Case of the Sleepwalker's Niece. New York: Morrow;
     London: Cassell, 1936. (B)

     Mason is retained by Edna Hammer, who is worried about
     her uncle Peter Kent's potentially murderous sleepwalking
     episodes. Kent winds up on trial for the nocturnal murder
     of his half-brother P. L. Rease, supposedly having mistaken
     him for business partner Frank B. Maddox, who had traded
     bedrooms with Rease. The jury trial is an excellent one,
     including a fine cross-examination by Mason of a fellow
     lawyer giving eyewitness testimony and one of D.A. Bur-
     ger's best smorgasbord objections: "...argumentative, im-
     proper, no proper foundation laid, insulting, not proper
     cross-examination, incompetent, irrelevant, and im-
     material." This is a strong early Mason that crackles in
     and out of court.

107. The Case of the Stuttering Bishop. New York: Morrow,
     1936. London: Cassell, 1937. (B)

     Anglican Bishop William Mallory of Sydney, Australia,
     consults Mason about the statute of limitations in a man-
     slaughter case, a drunk driving death that occurred 22
     years ago (i.e., 1914). The man's stutter makes Mason
     suspect he's an impostor. Treacherous millionaire Renwold
     C. Brownley, whose daughter-in-law Julia drove the car
     involved in the 1914 accident, is found dead in his sub-
     merged car. Did a gunshot kill him or did he drown? Julia
     is charged and her preliminary hearing is a briefer one than
     usual, some seventeen pages. Despite a complex plot of
     shifting identities, this is only about an average Mason for
     the period. Burger, thinking of charging Mason, puts in a
     brief appearance but leaves the trial work to a deputy.

108. The Case of the Substitute Face. New York: Morrow;
     London: Cassell, 1938. (B)

     This one opens in an unusual setting for Gardner: an ocean
     liner returning from Hawaii with Perry and Della among
     the passengers. The voyage climaxes in a "man-overboard"
     situation. Among the elements: embezzlement from the
     dead man's firm, his daughter's strong resemblance to a
     movie star, and a nurse-attended passenger with a broken
     neck. In a well-handled San Francisco preliminary hearing,
     Perry defends Anna Moar, accused of the murder of her
     husband. For once it's secretary Della Street who conceals

information from Perry-- she vanishes without word at one
point and commits some other idiotic and very un-Della-
like behavior.   In a novel marked by strong narrative
movement and snappy dialogue, Perry admittedly is slow to
catch on to an amply-clued if rather far-fetched plot.

109. The Case of the Shoplifter's Shoe. New York: Morrow,
      1938. London: Cassell, 1939. (B)

      Mason's rescue of an elderly woman accused of shoplifting
      in a department store tea-room leads to a case involving
      missing diamonds, a traffic accident, two deaths by shoot-
      ing, and Gardner's old reliable sleight of hand with guns and
      bullets.   In puzzle and courtroom action, this is no better
      than an average Mason.   It illustrates the increasing
      influence of the slick magazines (and decreasing influence
      of the pulps) on Gardner's style.   Assistant D.A. Larry
      Sampson's coaching of a prosecution witness (to convince
      him he saw more than he really did) forms an interesting
      chapter.   In the trial itself, another full-dress jury pro-
      ceeding, Sampson may set a series record for "incom-
      petent, irrelevant, and immaterial" objections.

110. The Case of the Rolling Bones. New York: Morrow, 1939.
      London: Cassell, 1940. (B)

      In one of the most intricate and fairly-clued Masons, the
      lawyer is first consulted by the niece and the fiancée of
      millionaire Alden Leeds about moves by family members to
      have him declared incompetent.   Much of the plot hinges
      on Leeds' days in the Klondike in the early days of the
      century, and questions of identity become tangled indeed.
      There are two court actions involved, a habeas corpus
      hearing early in the tale, wherein Mason gets his way by
      reading the judge cleverly, and the customary preliminary
      hearing where he defends the millionaire on a murder
      charge.   Among the well-laid clues to the truth is the
      double-meaning title. The final stages concern themselves
      almost as much with the ethics of Mason's courtroom
      trickery (here involving switchboard operator Gertie in
      possibly her first appearance) as with the unraveling of the
      crime. The wild comedy of Chapter V (concerning Mason's
      later-corrected reckless driving and a fire in his office)
      belies the alleged predictability of this series.

111. The D. A. Draws a Circle. New York: Morrow, 1939.

London: Cassell, 1940. (B)

This is the third book about District Attorney Doug Selby of Madison County, California, but it is the first to have courtroom action and the first to introduce the series' most memorable character, slick big-city criminal lawyer A. B. Carr. In several of the Selby books, Gardner reversed the Mason formula, as the heroic D.A. foiled the tricky defender again and again. One factor does not change, however: the defender is still more interesting to read about than the prosecutor. Most of the D.A. books do not get in court, given the difficulty of having both a court-room drama and a whodunit when the prosecutor is the hero.

A nude corpse, victim of an apparent gang killing, is found near the house where unwelcome stranger Carr has recent-ly bought a palatial home. The body shows two almost coincidental bullet holes, each made by a bullet from a different gun. It is impossible to tell which one killed him. Meanwhile, Carr's unhappy neighbor Rita Artrim is thought to be either, depending on whom Selby believes, the murderer of her husband, supposedly killed in an auto-mobile accident, or a potential victim of her crippled, amnesiac father-in-law. The thirty pages of court action (not the climax of the book in this case) involve the preliminary hearing of Peter Ribber, accused of the shoot-ing of fellow-crook Morton Taleman, the nude man. The reader is fairly certain that the object of Selby's prosecu-tion is guilty of something, if not of the murder he is charged with. Carr's questioning of Madison City police chief Otto Larkin, a political foe of Selby and Sheriff Rex Brandon and surely one of the stupidest cops in detective fiction, ranks among Gardner's funniest cross-examina-tions. Though the plot is not one the author's best, this smooth novel avoids some of the romantic excesses of later Selby books.

112. The D. A. Goes to Trial.   New York: Morrow, 1940. London: Cassell, 1941. (B)

The Doug Selby books generally fall short of the Perry Masons, but not because the intricate plotting or the exposition of legal ins-and-outs is any less impressive. Mason had roots in the pulps, while Selby is strictly a slick-paper hero, and the romantic angle (involving the triangle of Selby, reporter Sylvia Martin, and lawyer Inez Stapleton) gets pretty unbearable at times. Here Gardner manages to get Selby into court by having a hostile Grand Jury return a too-hasty indictment and forcing a trial, with Selby going up against old girl friend Inez. The trial runs only eight pages, though, with the rather informal Grand Jury sequence covering another eleven.

The background of a small city in the California desert, with constant political pressure on the elected officials, gives the D.A. series its uniqueness in the Gardner canon. The desert background offered an opportunity for some colorful outdoor descriptions. This one begins with a corpse on a railway trestle a mile outside town, apparently a hobo struck by a train. But the dead man may have some connection with a lumber company bookkeeper who seems to have been living a double life. Subsequently a banker is found shot to death in the vault. There is much shell-and-pea with fingerprints (which, as in most mystery fiction, can be taken from any surface, anywhere, any time). The painfully transparent least-suspected-person killer and some incredibly corny and sententious dialogue mark the novel as distinctly below average for this period of Gardner's career. One awful purple sentence cries out to be quoted: "Then he quietly replaced the receiver, and returned to the window to stare out over the sleeping city, to look up at the lopsided moon, at the brighter stars which gazed steadily down in the unblinking splendor of a universe rolling majestically on its course through eternity in response to the unchanging majesty of divine law, a law which functioned smoothly and impersonally." (p. 282)

113. The Case of the Silent Partner. New York: Morrow, 1940. London: Cassell, 1941. (B)

This nicely complicated case is one of Gardner's best from a standpoint of Golden Age puzzle-spinning, complete with alibi-breaking and least-suspected-person killer. Comprising the MacGuffin are some certificates of stock in a chain of flower shops, jointly owned by two sisters, Mildreth Faulkner and Carlotta Faulkner Lawley, the latter convalescing from a heart ailment. Competitor Henry Peavis, who unknown to the sisters has acquired the small holding of the firm's third director, wants Carlotta's stock, unfortunately in the hands of her weak, gambling husband Bob. Mason must keep his client (Carlotta) safe not just

from prison but from strain on her heart that would kill
her, and he is determined to save her the stress of a trial.
For once, the only courtroom action involved is a civil
proceeding, Peavis vs. Faulkner Flower Shops, as the
villainous competitor demands possession of the stock
certificates. Though the 15-page trial is one of Gardner's
shortest, Mason manages to prevail on a nice legal point.
This is one of Lt. Tragg's earliest and most extensive
appearances in the saga. As the tale ends, there is even
romance on the horizon for the lieutenant.

114. The Case of the Haunted Husband. New York: Morrow,
     1941. London: Cassell, 1942. (B)

Here is an untypical Mason, including more variations in
pace and mood than usual, somewhat more running-in-
place, a rare involvement with Hollywood movie people, an
uncharacteristic philosophical digression by Mason on the
subject of death, and a touch of Philo Vance in the
denouement. Again the relationship of Mason and Tragg is
prominent, and the byplay of the continuing characters
offers more humor than some Mason novels.   Waitress
Stephane Olger, hitchhiking from San Francisco to Los
Angeles, is involved in an accident with a cad and masher
who disappears, leaving her at the wheel to face accusations of car theft and drunk driving. Her preliminary
hearing begins before the halfway point, with a long gap
between sessions. The ultimate clue is an interesting one.

115. The Case of the Drowning Duck. New York: Morrow, 1942.
     London: Cassell, 1944. (B)

Rancher John L. Witherspoon, who fears his daughter is
about to marry the son of a murderer, asks Mason to study
the transcript of an 18-year-old murder trial and assess the
defendant's guilt. Perry decides to do more than armchair
detection, and soon there are fresh murders, of a blackmailing private eye and of a disabled houseguest of Witherspoon's. The weapon in both cases is cyanide gas. Witherspoon is charged with the second murder and begins his
preliminary hearing in the desert community of El Templo
with another lawyer, temporarily putting Perry in the
unaccustomed role of spectator. This one is a trifle over-
complicated and over-populated, but it has its moments of
ingenuity. (Note for animal lovers: no ducks actually
drown in this book, but they have some narrow escapes.)

116. The Case of the Careless Kitten.   New York: Morrow,
     1942. London: Cassell, 1944. (B)

Helen Kendal's kitten Amber Eyes almost dies from a dose
of strychnine. Is the poisoning of the cat connected with
the sudden reappearance (by telephone) of Helen's wealthy
uncle Franklin Shore, who had vanished several years
before? Henry Leech, the go-between who was supposed to
take Helen to her uncle, is found shot to death in his car.
The trial, not for Leech's murder, is unique in the Mason
saga. When frustrated D.A. Burger can't get anything on
Perry himself, he charges Della Street with spiriting away
Shore, allegedly a material witness in the assault with
intent to commit murder on Helen's friend Jerry Templar.
Mason demands a jury trial but declines to question or
challenge any jurors, leaving all the grilling to Burger. The
trial runs its full course, Burger jumping through hoops
throughout. There are even closing speeches to the jury by
both sides.   Fair play to the reader was not always
manifest in Gardner's novels, but this time he showcases
and explains his clues as carefully as Ellery Queen or Helen
McCloy.   The result is one of the best pure detective
novels he ever wrote.

117. The Case of the Buried Clock. New York: Morrow, 1943.
     London: Cassell, 1945. (B)

Notable features this time include one of Gardner's better
puzzle plots (and an exceedingly clever faked alibi); an
explicit World War II period, as a returned Purple-Heart
veteran finds Jack Hardisty shot to death in a mountain
cabin; an opening away from Mason's office, with Perry and
Della among the last characters introduced; a reflection of
Gardner's outdoor interests in some eloquent descriptive
prose few readers would expect from him; and a full-scale
jury trial, with one of the two accused acting in his own
defense.

118. The Case of the Crooked Candle. New York: Morrow,
     1944. London: Cassell, 1947. (¾)

A traffic accident in which a client rear-ends an abruptly
stopping sheep truck gets Perry involved in the affairs of
the shadowy Skinner Hills Karakul Company. Shortly after
the midway point, he is representing Roger and Carol
Burbank (father and daughter) on charges of murdering

Fred Milfield by a blow to the head on the Burbank yacht. Their preliminary hearing is Gardner's longest sustained trial scene to date and a good one. Jacques Barzun and Wendell Hertig Taylor recommend this Mason above all others to enthusiasts of formal detection: there is much fascinating technical testimony and analysis of physical evidence, principally the leaning candle of the title, and at one point there are even a diagram and timetable to delight fans of Freeman Wills Crofts and J. J. Connington. This is one of the best Masons, if not the one-of-a-kind Barzun and Taylor imply.

119. The Case of the Black-Eyed Blonde. New York: Morrow, 1944. London: Cassell, 1948. (B)

Diana Regis, a radio actress employed as a paid reader by wealthy Jason Bartsler, gets a shiner and an accusation of theft from the boss's good-for-nothing stepson Carl Fretch. This event proves the iceberg-tip of a complex plot involving adoption and kidnapping, and Diana is soon charged in a preliminary hearing with the shooting murder of her look-alike roommate Mildred Danville. Assistant D.A. Drumm and the despicable Sgt. Holcomb return after multi-book absences from the series. This is a strong Mason but less notable than most for its twenty-or-so pages in the court-room. Gardner offers a rare fast-action climax (with Perry still showing a tendency to drive too fast) in lieu of legal theatrics.

120. The Case of the Golddigger's Purse. New York: Morrow, 1945. London: Cassell, 1948. (B)

Sally Madison, a very sympathetic golddigger, is trying to get money from wealthy Harrington Faulkner for TB-stricken pet shop employee Tom Gridley, who has developed a cure for the gill disease afflicting goldfish collector Faulkner's rare Veiltail Moon Telescope (a.k.a. the Fish of Death). When Faulkner is found shot to death, a broken fish bowl and several dead goldfish in the vicinity of the body, Sally is charged and Perry represents her in a preliminary hearing. This is another good entry from Gardner's peak period.

121. The Case of the Half-Wakened Wife. New York: Morrow, 1945. London: Cassell, 1949. (¾)

Though Mason seldom has it easy, this case brings him to a lower ebb than most: a failed hunch backfires, causing uncharacteristic self-doubt and depression; the same incident results in a defamation-of-character suit against him and Paul Drake; Hamilton Burger's case seems more airtight than ever; and as a final indiginity, Perry is fired by his client in the midst of a jury trial. As a byproduct of these problems, his relations with Della Street are more openly amorous (almost embarrassingly so to long-time fans!) than anywhere else in the series. The plot involves the oil-lease rights to an island that Jane Keller is selling to millionaire Parker Benton. In an effort to reach an agreement, Benton invites all the principals for a cruise on his yacht, with Perry and Della included to represent the Keller interests. Scott Shelby, who owns the oil lease and is endangering the sale, disappears overboard, and his wife Marion, smoking gun in hand and telling an unlikely story, is accused of his murder. Mason's doubts that Shelby is really dead precipitate the failed stunt. The trial sequence, among the longest in a Mason novel, includes interesting technical testimony regarding seagoing telephone systems and ballistics. The climax finds Mason taking a deposition from his opponent in the defamation suit. Though technically out of court, this cross-examination ranks with his best. The complicated solution, satisfactory if far-fetched, reveals some ingenious clueing. Jackson, Mason's rarely-seen assistant, a scrupulous researcher who can't make a move without a precedent, makes one of his most extended appearances early in the book.

122. The D. A. Breaks a Seal.   New York: Morrow, 1946. London: Cassell, 1950. (B)

Army Major Doug Selby returns to Madison City on furlough, his D.A. job having been taken by an ass of Hamilton-Burger proportions. Meeting Sylvia Martin at the station, he wonders at the number of people wearing white gardenias, including lawyer A. B. Carr. Later he goes with Sheriff Rex Brandon to the scene of hotel guest Fred Roff's mysterious death and detects the odor of bitter almonds. Then he helps out Inez Stapleton, who is representing a relative contesting the will of wealthy Eleanor Preston on grounds of undue influence by the woman's companion, Martha Otley. Both were killed in the same automobile accident, and Martha's heir, a Hollywood type made over in demure fashion by lawyer Carr, stands to inherit. Carr's cross-examination of one plaintiff's witness is a dandy-- soon, however, he is befuddled enough to resort to the three I's. The solution is fair (if not unforeseeable) and on the whole this is top-notch Gardner.

123. The Case of the Borrowed Brunette. New York: Morrow, 1946. London: Cassell, 1951. (B)

When he sees a succession of brunettes, all of comparable size and all wearing furs, standing on street corners, Perry's curiosity leads him into a tangled case involving impersonation. Why is Eva Martell recruited to take the place of Helen Reedley and why is go-between Robert Hines shot to death? In a preliminary hearing, Perry defends Eva and her middle-aged chaperone Adelle Winters, one of many formidable liberated women in Gardner's work. Prosecuting is Harry Gulling, Hamilton Burger's right-hand man, whom Perry calls "the shrewd legal mind that guides the policy of the district attorney's office," a dubious compliment if there ever was one. The climax comes before the Grand Jury. Sound, average Mason for the period.

124. The Case of the Fan Dancer's Horse. New York: Morrow, 1947. London: Heinemann, 1952. (¼)

Perry and Della find a fan-dancer's costume in an old car involved in an Imperial Valley traffic accident. Perry advertises to find the owner, but the ad's vague reference to her "property" is taken by several claimants to refer to a horse. When rancher John Callender is found run through with a Japanese sword (an unusually exotic weapon for Gardner), a piece of ostrich feather in the wound connects the crime to Mason's client, fan-dancer Lois Fenton. The jury trial is satisfactorily strong and lengthy, but surely most of the Mason-Burger byplay, mutual accusation, and argument would not be allowed in the presence of a jury.

125. The Case of the Lazy Lover. New York: Morrow, 1947. London: Heinemann, 1954. (B)

Amnesia was a staple of mystery fiction in the forties (and after), and Gardner has some fun with it here. There's an especially amusing scene where switchboard operator Gertie claims to be the alleged amnesiac's wife. Mason's

client is Lola Faxon Allred, who first comes to his attention via a $2500 check in his morning mail, soon to be
followed by another. Lola, charged with the murder of her
husband Bernard, found dead in a wrecked car, proves to be
one of Mason's least reliable clients, changing her story
again and again. The puzzle of the footprints around the
car is about as close as Gardner ever got to a "miracle
problem," admittedly not very close. For once the trial
scene has a good-natured prosecutor, D. T. Danvers. This
one is highly enjoyable but very far-fetched, even for a
Mason.

126. The Case of the Lonely Heiress. New York: Morrow, 1948.
     London: Heinemann, 1952. (B)

One of the funniest Perry Masons, with some scenes more
suggestive of Gardner's alter ego, A. A. Fair. Initial client
is the publisher of a lonely hearts magazine, trying to
locate an heiress who has (for some reason) advertised in
his pages. Other elements include a will contest, a
thumbprint on a check, and a wonderful new invention: the
"ballpoint fountain pen." Trial action is only about average
for a Mason, and the final explanation has a touch of self-
parody.

127. The Case of the Vagabond Virgin. New York: Morrow,
     1948. London: Heinemann, 1952. (¾)

Department store executive John Racer Addison engages
Perry to get Veronica Dale, a young woman charged with
vagrancy, out of jail. But when Addison is charged in a
preliminary hearing with the shooting murder of his partner, Edgar Ferrell, hitchhiker Veronica is a key witness
against him. D.A. Burger's extreme solicitousness of his
fragile young witness is overdone and, predictably, backfires on him. Detailed testimony on tire tracks and
ballistics highlight another solid addition to the saga.

128. The Case of the Dubious Bridegroom. New York: Morrow,
     1949. London: Heinemann, 1954. (B)

Mining executive Ed Garvin, worried about the validity of
his Mexican divorce from first-wife Ethel, is charged with
murder when she is found shot to death in her car near
Oceanside, California. The change in jurisdiction puts
Perry up against San Diego County District Attorney

Hamlin Covington. The overwrought Covington, surely too excitable and unstable a man to attain such high office, gets tied in knots even faster than Hamilton Burger, and Mason's conduct of the jury trial is in a more playful mood than usual. (His opening statement must be one of the briefest on record: "He can't prove it.") Courtroom highlights include some fun with the interpretation of tire tracks and a dandy cross-examination of an eye witness. Again, though, the extensive sniping by counsel, marginally credible in a preliminary hearing, seems totally unbelievable in front of a jury. But Gardner is too entertaining to be denied his poetic license. The finale involves some clever alibi-breaking.

129. The Case of the Cautious Coquette. New York: Morrow, 1949. London: Heinemann, 1955. (B)

Perry begins in the unusual role of personal-injury lawyer, seeking witnesses to a hit-run accident that left his college-student client with a broken hip. After a newspaper ad produces two suspect vehicles, Perry becomes concerned with the murder of chauffeur Hartwell L. Pitkin, found shot to death in a parking structure. The victim is the ex-husband of Mason's mendacious and reluctantly acquired client, Lucille Barton. Among the most entertaining novels in the series, this one involves some of Perry's most dazzling pre-court wire-walking and in-court fireworks. One highlight of the preliminary hearing is a classic exchange between Sgt. Holcomb and the judge on the subject of hearsay.

130. The Case of the Negligent Nymph. New York: Morrow, 1950. London: Heinemann, 1956. (¼)

Surveying George Alder's private-island mansion from a canoe, Perry comes to the aid of a fleeing young woman. Dorothy Fenner has taken from the house a bottle containing a message about the death of Minerva Danby, drowned from Alder's yacht a few months before. Mason defends Dorothy first in a bail hearing on a charge of jewel theft, later in a jury trial for the shotgun murder of Alder. Perry ties the local sheriff (of an unspecified rural county) in knots on the witness stand over the identification of a wet purse. Though less enthralling than some Masons, the novel has a neat resolution.

131. The Case of the Musical Cow. New York: Morrow, 1950.
     London: Heinemann, 1957. (B)

     This is atypical Gardner on a number of scores. Designed
     to celebrate the work of the State Police, it represents in
     part his closest approach to a police procedural novel; it is
     the last of his novels not to feature a series character; its
     preliminary hearing occurs not in California but in an
     unnamed Eastern state; and it begins (of all places) in
     Europe, where dog trainer Rob Trenton is on vacation. As
     a result of meetings with some strangers on his trip and on
     the voyage home, Rob inadvertently becomes involved with
     heroin smuggling and winds up accused of the houseboat
     murder of narcotics agent Harvey Richmond. The fine
     courtroom chapter, with Rob represented by a marginally
     competent defense attorney recommended by a friend of
     doubtful status, features some interesting expert testimony
     by pathologist Dr. Herbert Dixon on the cause of death. As
     a whole, though, the book lacks the snap of a Perry Mason
     or Lam/Cool adventure.

132. The Case of the One-Eyed Witness. New York: Morrow,
     1950. London: Heinemann, 1956. (B)

     Myrtle Fargo is accused of the stabbing murder of her
     husband, real estate man Arthman (whose odd first name is
     solidly in the Gardner tradition). Star witness for the
     prosecution is Mrs. Newton Maynard, a prickly busybody
     who appears on the stand with one eye bandaged, ostensibly
     because of an infection. For once D.A. Burger seems to
     have Mason, whose effort to produce an alibi for his client
     has apparently failed, dead to rights, and he is irritated
     that the open-and-shut nature of the case has discouraged
     the usual mobs of spectators at a Mason-Burger prelimi-
     nary hearing. Gardner provides much interesting technical
     information about eyeglass making. It's hard to be objec-
     tive about this novel, the first Mason I ever read and thus a
     memorably dazzling experience. A quarter century later,
     I would still rank Mason's duel with Mrs. Maynard among
     his most entertaining courtroom exploits.

133. The Case of the Fiery Fingers. New York: Morrow, 1951.
     London: Heinemann, 1957. (¾)

     This very strong entry features two jury trials, each with a
     different defendant. Practical nurse Nellie Conway, who

had consulted Mason about how to prevent her patient, Elizabeth Bain, from being murdered by husband Nathan, is accused of petty larceny of some costume jewelry. The book's title refers to the main evidence against her: flourescent paint on the jewel box and her fingers. The second trial accuses Victoria Braxton, the victim's sister, of the arsenic poisoning of Elizabeth. Testimony on wills and dying declarations is particularly intriguing. Once again, Mason and Burger get away with murder in their remarks in front of the jury.

134. The Case of the Angry Mourner. New York: Morrow, 1951. London: Heinemann, 1958. (¼)

Arthur B. Cushing, in a wheelchair following a skiing accident, is shot to death in his lakeside cabin in the mountain community of Bear Valley. Neighbor Belle Adrian, after trying to destroy all evidence of her 21-year-old daughter Carlotta's possible connection to the crime, consults vacationing Perry Mason, who soon defends Belle in a preliminary hearing. The victim's wealthy father brings in a high-priced corporation lawyer to advise the small-town D.A. In a proceeding with an unusually large lawyer population, Perry's tactics seem even more bizarre than usual: he asks one witness to scream and another to throw a heavy mirror at the judge's bench. The courtroom action and a well-clued solution mark this as an above average specimen.

135. The Case of the Moth-Eaten Mink. New York: Morrow, 1952. London: Heinemann, 1958. (B)

Restaurateur Morris Alburg asks Mason's advice when a waitress vanishes without explanation, leaving the titular mink coat behind. Soon Alburg and waitress Dixie Dayton are accused in a preliminary hearing of the shooting murder of blackmailer George Fayette. D.A. Burger unsuccessfully tries to have Mason disqualified from the case because he is to be called as a witness for the prosecution. (Unlike lawyer Ephraim Tutt in Arthur Train's "Mr. Tutt Takes the Stand" (q.v.), Perry does not cross-examine himself.) The novel has an unusually dramatic ending, with the least-suspected-person killer not named until half a page from the end.

136. The Case of the Grinning Gorilla. New York: Morrow,

1952. London: Heinemann, 1958. (B)

At a public administrator's auction, Perry spends five bucks on the personal effects of Helen Cadmus, a secretary who supposedly died a suicide, jumping off the yacht of millionaire Benjamin Addicks. The fat promptly entering the fire, Mason is soon defending Josephine Kempton, accused of the carving-knife murder of Addicks. The dead man had been involved in psychological experiments on simians. The preliminary hearing, one of the few in which Mason works with a co-counsel, is less notable than usual in a below-average book most remembered for a couple of scenes where the gorilla menaces Mason.

137. The Case of the Hesitant Hostess. New York: Morrow, 1953. London: Heinemann, 1959. (¼)

The structure here is most unusual for a Mason novel. It begins in court, with retired salesman Albert Brogan on trial before a jury for robbing Rodney Archer, who was sitting in his car with a female companion, stopped for a traffic light at the time of the crime. Nightclub owner Martha Lavina is the supposed companion, and it is her testimony Perry spends the whole novel trying to discredit. Though some of the out-of-court action is less diverting than usual, the plot is an extremely clever one and the witness-stand pursuit of Archer and Lavina brings forth some of Gardner's very best Q-and-A. There is a murder involved, though the trial involves robbery only. The climactic damsel-in-distress rescue of Della Street, like something out of a Mr. and Mrs. North novel, is another uncharacteristic touch.

138. The Case of the Green-Eyed Sister. New York: Morrow, 1953. London: Heinemann, 1959. (¼)

Private detective George Brogan is acting as blackmail intermediary for J. J. Fritch, who has a tape recording purporting to connect ailing Ned Bain with a bank robbery. Sylvia Bain Atwood, one of Bain's daughters, initially consults Mason, but it is her sister Harriet who is accused of the icepick murder of Fritch, found dead in Brogan's apartment. The preliminary hearing is one of Gardner's longest non-stop courtroom scenes and an excellent one. There is extended technical testimony on post-mortem lividity and determination of the time of death.

139. The Case of the Fugitive Nurse. New York: Morrow, 1954.
     London: Heinemann, 1959. (¾)

     Dr. Summerfield Malden, a surgeon who has been under
     Bureau of Internal Revenue investigation and may have
     been overly friendly with his vanished nurse and office
     manager Gladys Foss, has reportedly died in a private-
     plane crash. Young widow Steffanie is accused of causing
     the crash by drugging Malden's whisky. Another major
     question: who cleaned out the wall safe in the deceased
     medic's love-nest? The plot provides a complicated iden-
     tity puzzle, and the Mason-Burger duel in Mrs. Malden's
     preliminary hearing is brisk and bitter-- at one point,
     Perry is actually sentenced to jail for contempt of court.

140. The Case of the Runaway Corpse. New York: Morrow,
     1954. London: Heinemann, 1960. (¾)

     Myrna Davenport, encouraged by relative Sara Ansel to
     consult Perry, says her husband Ed, now ill and possibly
     dying in a motel room, has left a sealed note in his
     Paradise, California, office accusing her of poisoning him
     and another relative, Hortense Paxson. When Ed is re-
     ported dead, Perry goes to the office to represent his
     client's interests, opens the envelope (which proves to
     contain only blank paper) and reseals it, then learns the
     supposedly deceased Ed has vanished. Myrna's preliminary
     hearing for the murder of her husband is longer but less
     exciting than average-- by the climax, Fresno D.A. Talbert
     Vandling (no Hamilton Burger) is more Mason's collaborator
     than his adversary. The puzzle is clever, intricate, and
     fair, even though Gardner severely bends one of the basic
     rules of murderer selection. Best scene depicts Mason's
     hilarious verbal duel with the D.A. of Butte County, who is
     trying to question him about his activities in Davenport's
     office. In this masterpiece of fast footwork and lawyerly
     obfuscation, Mason is so slippery, he reminds the reader of
     A. B. Carr from the Doug Selby series.

141. The Case of the Restless Redhead. New York: Morrow,
     1954. London: Heinemann, 1960. (¾)

     This is one of only two Mason novels to begin in court, as
     Perry observes the Riverside trial of waitress Evelyn
     Bagby, accused of jewel theft and represented by a nervous
     young lawyer, Frank Neely. Thanks to Mason's lunch-break

advice to Neely, she is acquitted, but later in Los Angeles she is accused of shooting actor Steve Merrill, scheming second husband of film star Helene Chaney. The two lawyers work as a team on her preliminary hearing. Recurring expert witness Alexander Redfield makes one of his most prominent appearances in a novel especially recommended to ballistics buffs and fans of thin-ice skating.

142. The Case of the Glamorous Ghost. New York: Morrow, 1955. London: Heinemann, 1960. (¼)

A near-nude woman's late-night dancing in the park distracts a necking couple and precipitates a leering newspaper article, written in Gardner's odd version of journalistic prose. Olga Corbin Jordan, identifying the supposedly amnesiac "ghost" as her much-hated half-sister Eleanor, hires Mason to get her out of whatever jam she is in and save the family embarrassment. In a jury trial, Eleanor is accused of killing Douglas Hepner, a government informant on jewel smuggling whom she claimed to have married. Hepner was found shot to death in the same park, same night. The plot is not one of Gardner's best, but the courtroom windup is among his most dramatic.

143. The Case of the Sun Bather's Diary. New York: Morrow, 1955. London: Heinemann, 1961. (B)

Arlene Duvall, who calls for help from the fourteenth hole of a golf course with a claim her clothes have been stolen, proves to be one of Mason's sneakier clients, and the lawyer comes close to a murder charge himself. Featuring both a scene before the Grand Jury and a preliminary hearing, this is a solid Mason, with Hamilton Burger at his loudest, most overwrought, and at times stupidest. A sequence where Burger calls Mason as a witness is especially entertaining.

144. The Case of the Nervous Accomplice. New York: Morrow, 1955. London: Heinemann, 1961. (¼)

This is one of the purest trial books in the Mason saga, with about 40% of the action taking place in court, including both a preliminary hearing and a jury trial. It begins with Perry uncharacteristically taking on a domestic relations case with situation-comedy overtones: Sybil Harlan, determined to hold onto her straying husband Enright, hires Mason to buy stock in a real estate investment company and make a nuisance of himself at a director's meeting, thereby introducing an irritant into the relationship of Enny and his client-lover Roxy Claffin and possibly making his loving wife look better to him. Sybil is subsequently accused of the shooting murder of George Lutts, from whom Perry bought his stock. The clever plot turns (as so often) on ballistic trickery, and the trial action is as enthralling as it is plentiful. In the preliminary hearing, Judge Hoyt, a stern hardliner, admonishes Perry at the outset against fireworks, but after the defense attorney passes opportunities to cross-examine nearly all D.A. Burger's witnesses, His Honor assures Mason he wasn't trying to intimidate him!

145. The Case of the Terrified Typist. New York: Morrow, 1956. London: Heinemann, 1961. (¼)

The Morrow jacket copy makes no secret of the unique event that occurs late in this novel: this is the one where Gardner answered all the readers who wanted Hamilton Burger to win just once. Though we all know Perry Mason never defends a guilty client, the jury delivers a guilty verdict, and the only question is how (not whether) Perry will show it didn't really happen and rob Burger of his victory.

Is Mae Wallis, the frightened but fast extra typist who comes to work in Mason's office one morning, the same young woman who searched the office of a gem importing company in the same building? Before disappearing from the office, she left two diamonds stuck to the underside of her desk with chewing gum. Mason is retained to defend Duane Jefferson, a partner in the gem firm, on a charge of killing for gain diamond smuggler Munroe Baxter. Though no body was found, Jefferson allegedly knifed Baxter in a rowboat after assisting him in a faked suicide from a cruise ship. Courtroom action is fine, and the way Perry extricates himself from a loser's ignominy is very cute indeed.

146. The Case of the Demure Defendant. New York: Morrow, 1956. London: Heinemann, 1962. (B)

Under sodium pentothal, Nadine Farr confesses to the poison murder of her uncle, Mosher Higley. Her doctor,

who used the truth serum in treating her for emotional
disturbances, consults Perry Mason. Perry plays shell-and-
pea with poison bottles, and there is an interesting legal
argument over confidential communications and the admissibility of the doctor's tape recordings. Much ballyhooed as
the fiftieth Perry Mason novel, this is not one of Gardner's
best but a worthy enough milestone.

147. The Case of the Gilded Lily. New York: Morrow, 1956.
London: Heinemann, 1962. (B)

This one starts in the office with a boss/secretary combo
other than Perry and Della. Businessman Stewart G.
Bedford becomes the target of blackmail over the criminal
record of his new (and twenty-years-younger) wife Ann,
who had been charged with insurance fraud. Secretary Elsa
Griffin is a true-crime buff who once took a correspon-
dence course in detective work. When blackmailer Binney
Denham is found shot in a motel room, Bedford is accused.
Mason enters the story unusually late, on page 57 of the
244-page Morrow edition. Burger, hostile and snapping
from the outset, opposes Mason in a jury trial, with much
fingerprint sleight-of-hand involved. This is a cut below
average for the series, with the solution a trifle loose
compared to the author's best.

148. The Case of the Lucky Loser. New York: Morrow, 1957.
London: Heinemann, 1962. (¼)

An anonymous female caller wants to pay Perry merely to
be a spectator at the trial of Ted Balfour, accused of hit-
and-run manslaughter of an unidentified victim. Balfour is
convicted but subsequently is accused of murdering the
same man (now known to be Jackson Eagan) by shooting. In
a habeas corpus hearing, Perry makes an intriguing use of
the double jeopardy rule in opposing the prosecution's
application. He subsequently defends Balfour in a jury trial
for murder, bringing the number of courtroom actions in
the novel to three. (A series record?) In both plot and
legal interest, this ranks with Gardner's best.

149. The Case of the Screaming Woman. New York: Morrow,
1957. London: Heinemann, 1963. (¼)

Client John Kirby, at his wife's insistence that he needs a
lawyer, tells Mason that he picked up a girl carrying a gas

can on a deserted road and took her on a fruitless search to find her car. But he winds up accused of the murder of physician-surgeon Dr. Phineas Lockridge Babb, who supposedly named Kirby as his assailant before he died. The preliminary hearing is one of Gardner's longer trial scenes and produces some strong Mason-Burger fireworks, leaving the D.A. at his most flummoxed and frustrated, especially when he calls Della Street as a witness. There are some nice clues to the solution, but many will find it overly transparent.

150. The Case of the Daring Decoy. New York: Morrow, 1957. London: Heinemann, 1963. (B)

Oil executive Jerry Conway, involved in a bitter proxy fight, calls on Mason when he thinks he has been framed (but isn't sure for what) by a mysterious phone caller named Rosalind. Soon he is on trial before a jury for the hotel-room shooting of Rose Calvert. The trial is marked by interesting technical evidence, and the identity of the killer is both surprising and fairly clued.

151. The Case of the Long-Legged Models. New York: Morrow, 1958. London: Heinemann, 1963. (B)

Model Stephanie Faulkner has inherited majority interest in a Las Vegas casino from her murdered father, Glenn. A mysterious Mr. X wants to buy her stock, and she fears someone is trying to profit by her father's death. Soon she is accused of the shooting murder of George Casselman, and Perry defends in a jury trial. This is a fairly routine Mason, involving some heavy gun shuffling. The killer confesses on the witness stand, a rarer occurrence in the Mason novels than on TV.

152. The Case of the Foot-Loose Doll. New York: Morrow, 1958. London: Heinemann, 1964. (¾)

Fleeing the scene of a collapsed romance, Mildred Crest takes over the identity of hitchhiker Fern Driscoll, killed in an accident, and becomes a possible suspect in her own murder. But it is for the delayed-action icepick murder of blackmailer Carl Harrod that she goes on trial. In a long and satisfying preliminary hearing, Mason does some of his most inspired weapons juggling, and the rather obvious murderer is fairly clued. It is rather careless of Gardner, though, to have a Harriman Baylor and a Hamilton Burger in the same book, even in the same scene.

153. The Case of the Calendar Girl. New York: Morrow, 1958. London: Heinemann, 1964. (¾)

Here Perry spends over 40% of the book in court, defending two different clients on the same murder charge. Building contractor George Ansley consults Mason about a traffic accident he is involved in with model Dawn Manning. Ansley is soon accused of the shooting murder of photographer Meridith Borden. The preliminary hearing, with its rebuttals and surrebuttals, takes on the aspect of a multiple-overtime basketball game. At one point, when both sides seem to be using a slowdown offense, the judge is asking most of the questions. When Ansley gets off, Perry defends Dawn in another preliminary hearing. As in many late Masons, the courtroom combat is much stronger than the plot.

154. The Case of the Deadly Toy. New York: Morrow, 1959. London: Heinemann, 1964. (¾)

Seven-year-old Robert Selkirk, center of a custody battle between divorced parents Mervin and the remarried Lorraine, is one of the rare child characters in Gardner's fiction. Mervin is found shot to death in his car at a golf course, and Norda Allison, who broke off with the dead man over his insensitive treatment of his son, is accused in a preliminary hearing. Did Robert actually do the shooting, as his grandfather claims? This is an average Mason, competent but not notable. (Gardner specialized in ornate character names, but invention fails when he introduces a dog named Rover.)

155. The Case of the Mythical Monkeys. New York: Morrow, 1959. London: Heinemann, 1965. (¾)

Gladys Doyle, secretary-companion to best-selling novelist Mauvis Niles Meade, is accused of shooting an at-first-unidentified man in a mountain cabin, one of Gardner's favorite murder locations. There's not much literary background here, but the author has a chance to grouse about the sort of sexy, steamy novels that make best-seller lists. The lengthy preliminary hearing lumbers to a TV-ish climax, and despite the presence of gangsters and G-men, this is less diverting than average. The titular monkeys appear only on a scarf.

156. The Case of the Singing Skirt. New York: Morrow, 1959. London: Heinemann, 1965. (¾)

Ellen Robb, night-club singer in the corrupt and wide-open small town of Rowena, is framed for robbing the till after she refuses to cooperate with her employers in a card-cheating scam. Later, she is charged in a preliminary hearing with the shooting murder of Nadine Ellis, wife of a local gambler who lost money at the club. Familiar elements include gun-switching and a body on a yacht. An unusual number of intriguing appellate decisions are cited by Mason, and the solution is satisfactory though very complicated. The ending brings a nice irony in the strained Mason/Burger relationship.

157. The Case of the Waylaid Wolf. New York: Morrow, 1960. London: Heinemann, 1965. (¾)

Stenographer Arlene Ferris, an employee of the Lamont Rolling, Casting, and Engineering Company, is the victim of unwelcome sexual advances by her boss, Loring Lamont. She tells Perry Mason she wants to teach him a lesson by bringing civil or criminal charges, but it develops that Lamont is beyond lessons, having been murdered with a butcher knife at the rural lodge in Chatsworth where he had taken Arlene. Perry defends in a lengthy preliminary hearing in this medium-grade entry.

158. The Case of the Duplicate Daughter. New York: Morrow, 1960. London: Heinemann, 1965. (B)

This time the client is a juror in one of Mason's previous cases. Muriell Gilman consults Perry about the sudden mid-breakfast disappearance of her father, Carter Gilman, who had told her to seek the lawyer in case of any unusual occurrence. Gilman reappears but is accused of strangling private detective Vera Martel in his woodworking shop and pushing her car over a cliff. Court action involves a preliminary hearing. The whole enterprise is only so-so among the later Mason novels.

159. The Case of the Shapely Shadow. New York: Morrow, 1960. London: Heinemann, 1966. (¾)

Here is another of the quantitative leaders among Gardner novels, with more than 40% of the action in court. Janice Wainwright, secretary of Morley Theilman who downplays her beauty in order not to make Mrs. Theilman jealous, fears there is blackmail money in the heavy suitcase she is to deliver to one A. B. Vidal via a key to a Union Depot locker. When Janice is accused of shooting Theilman to death at an abandoned mountain realty subdivision, Mason defends in a jury trial. His slashing cross-examination of a medical witness is especially impressive. Both puzzle and witness-stand thrust-and-parry rank high among Masons of the sixties.

160. The Case of the Spurious Spinster. New York: Morrow, 1961. London: Heinemann, 1966. (B)

Susan Fisher, secretary to the manager of the Corning Mining, Smelting, and Investment Company, is Mason's client in a case involving a shoe box full of money carried by the boss's 7-year-old son; two elderly ladies in wheelchairs claiming to be Amelia Corning, absentee owner of the company; and finally the stiletto murder of the operator of the Mojave Monarch mine, which should have been operating and wasn't. This is a very good specimen of late Mason with a fairly logical if not too surprising solution. The fast pace and breathtaking plot twists of the early part of the novel are more notable than the preliminary hearing, which is only about average. This, of course, is the latter-day establishmentarian Perry with pleas for safe driving sprinkled throughout.

161. The Case of the Bigamous Spouse. New York: Morrow, 1961. London: Heinemann, 1967. (¾)

Gwynn Elston, a children's encyclopedia saleswoman, discovers her best friend's husband, Felting Grimes, is leading a double life under the name Frankline Gillett. Grimes is shot to death and Gwynn accused. When Perry subpoenas wealthy and powerful George Belding Baxter to testify in the preliminary hearing, he gets a civil lawsuit for his trouble. Though fairly routine overall, this one has some interesting elements.

162. The Case of the Reluctant Model. New York: Morrow, 1962. London: Heinemann, 1967. (B)

Art dealer Lattimer Rankin wants to sue for slander Collin M. Durant, who claimed a painting Rankin sold to collector Otto Olney was not a genuine work of French artist Phellipe Feteet but a poor imitation. The trial, though, involves murder as Maxine Lindsay, the young art student who heard the alleged slander, is accused of the shooting murder of Durant. The preliminary hearing is a good one, with some particularly interesting technical testimony. A fairly strong Mason of the later period.

163. The Case of the Blonde Bonanza.   New York: Morrow, 1962. London: Heinemann, 1967. (B)

Why does Dianne Alder, the beautiful blonde of Bolero Beach, daily gorge herself on fattening foods? Ostensibly to model fashions for the fuller-figured woman, but Perry Mason has some questions about her contract with modeling agent Harrison T. Boring. When Boring is found dead via blunt instrument in a room at the Restawhile Motel, Perry defends Dianne in a Riverside County preliminary hearing. This is one of the Mason novels that is most like the TV series. The witness-stand accusation and confession seem too pat and too easy, as does the reasoning that leads up to them.

164. The Case of the Ice-Cold Hands. New York: Morrow, 1962. London: Heinemann, 1968. (¼)

Perry and Della go to the races with instructions to cash some mutuel tickets if client Nancy Banks' horse is a winner. But soon Nancy is accused of the shooting murder of shady Marvin Fremont, employer of her embezzling, gambling brother Rodney. Fremont was found shot at a motel, his body allegedly packed in dry ice from the adjacent Osgood Trout Farm to confuse the time of death. During the jury trial, Hamilton Burger grants Rodney immunity from prosecution so that he can be forced to testify against his sister. This action precipitates one of the most delightful legal thunderbolts in the Gardner canon.   The courtroom fireworks are some of his best, though the final revelation depends on two incredibilities: Mason's luck and the murderer's stupidity.

It has been claimed that Gardner came up with some of his odd character names by reversing first and last names of phone-book listings.   In support of that theory can be offered the judge in the present book: Novarro Miles.

165. The Case of the Mischievous Doll. New York: Morrow,
     1963. London: Heinemann, 1968. (¾)

     Devious client Dorrie Ambler enters the scene demanding
     to show Mason her appendectomy scar as a proof of her
     identity. She subsequently behaves even more oddly,
     fearing she is being groomed as a double for "madcap
     heiress" Minerva Minden. In a tangle of confused iden-
     tities, Minerva winds up on trial before a jury, charged
     with murdering private detective Marvin Billings and also
     suspected of killing Dorrie, with Mason as her lawyer. The
     trial is notable for Perry's cross-examination of Dunleavy
     Jasper (another of Gardner's best reverse names), an al-
     leged accomplice testifying in exchange for immunity, and
     for his cryptic refusal to hear something his client wants to
     tell him. There is also much fun with fingerprint evidence.
     The solution is really far-fetched, but there's a good clue
     to the main secret.

166. The Case of the Stepdaughter's Secret. New York: Mor-
     row, 1963. London: Heinemann, 1968. (¾)

     Harlow Bissinger Bancroft, self-made millionaire, consults
     Mason when he discovers his stepdaughter Rosena Andrews,
     about to marry socially prominent Jetson Blair, is being
     anonymously blackmailed about Bancroft's criminal past.
     Wife Phyllis Bancroft is accused of murder in a preliminary
     hearing when Willmer Gilly is found shot to death on the
     Bancroft yacht. In an amusing sequence, Orange County
     District Attorney Robley Hastings acquires a newspaper
     job so that he can attend the defendant's press conference
     and ask questions. Otherwise, this is distinctly below
     average.

167. The Case of the Amorous Aunt. New York: Morrow, 1963.
     London: Heinemann, 1969. (¾)

     Client Linda Calhoun fears her wealthy widowed aunt,
     Lorraine Elmore, will be murdered by alleged Bluebeard
     Montrose Dewitt. But when Perry catches up with the pair
     (and seemingly most of the rest of the cast) at a motel in
     Calexico, it is Lorraine who's charged with Dewitt's mur-
     der. Going up against a publicity-conscious Imperial Coun-
     ty D.A. in the preliminary hearing, Mason makes one of his

rare appearances with a co-counsel, young local attorney
Duncan Crowder, Jr., clearly intended as a romantic alternative to Linda's unworthy fiancé. Though fairly routine,
this is better than some from the period.

168. The Case of the Daring Divorcee. New York: Morrow,
1964. London: Heinemann, 1969. (B)

This one begins with a phantom-client situation, similar to
that of The Case of the Lazy Lover (q.v.): a woman
claiming to be Adele Hastings leaves her purse and gun in
Mason's office and disappears. Did the gun kill her husband
Garvin Hastings? A cute trick with a lineup of women
wearing dark glasses foils Lt. Tragg's attempt to get Gertie
to identify Mason's client. The traditional gun-juggling this
time includes the theft of a Smith and Wesson from the
desk drawer in Mason's office. There's an interesting
question of probate law, as Hastings' second wife, Minerva,
claims that since she didn't carry through with a Nevada
divorce, the marriage to third wife Adele was invalid. The
sharp give-and-take in Adele's preliminary hearing helps
make this a better than average late Mason, though the
main clue may be a little too obvious. (At one point, Tragg
confides that the police rarely find usable prints on a gun--
how many earlier detective stories, including some by
Gardner, does that admission render invalid?)

169. The Case of the Phantom Fortune. New York: Morrow,
1964. London: Heinemann, 1970. (B)

Business executive Horace Warren offers Perry $500 to
attend a dinner party. Paul Drake poses as a caterer to
identify a fingerprint that may belong to a servant or
guest. Soon Perry is defending Warren in a preliminary
hearing on a charge of shooting his wife's former employer,
the shady Collister Gideon, found dead in a deserted
storeroom. Burger threatens Mason with criminal prosecution or bar association sanctions over his evidence juggling.
This is very routine late Mason.

170. The Case of the Horrified Heirs. New York: Morrow, 1964.
London: Heinemann, 1971. (B)

Lauretta Trent, with a houseful of potential heirs, seems a
likely victim in a standard which-greedy-relative-or-ser-
vant-is-poisoning-the-rich-lady plot. Perry defends ex-

legal secretary Virginia Baxter, a witness to Mrs. Trent's will, in preliminary hearings on two separate charges: first, drug trafficking; then, with the same opposing prosecutor, ambitious deputy D.A. Jerry Caswell, the murder of Lauretta Trent, though no body has been found. That the prosecutor in the second case has an exceedingly weak case on the face of it marks this as the least interesting of the two-trial Masons. There is a nice closing surprise, however.

171. The Case of the Troubled Trustee. New York: Morrow, 1965. London: Heinemann, 1971. (¾)

Mason's client is smooth Kerry Dutton, trustee of a spendthrift trust who did some well-intended but legally dubious reinvesting. Dutton loves beneficiary Desere Ellis, who is being taken in by bearded beatnik Fred Hedley, whose pseudo-hip dialogue is as unconvincing as his plan to set up a foundation for the support of starving geniuses. Perry defends Dutton in a jury trial for the golf-course shooting of Rodger Palmer. Hamilton Burger gets a rare chance to cross-examine Perry's witnesses and does a masterful job, though his end result is no different. The plot has less twists than usual, and for once Gardner seems to be guilty of a bit of padding. Again, weakish late Mason.

172. The Case of the Beautiful Beggar. New York: Morrow, 1965. London: Heinemann, 1972. (B)

In the absence of his faithful niece Daphne, 75-year-old Horace Shelby has been declared incompetent by action of his half brother Borden Finchley and wife Elinor. The Finchleys claim Daphne is not really his daughter. There are two courtroom sequences: a hearing on the conservatorship of Shelby's estate and a preliminary hearing on Daphne for the asphyxiation murder of Ralph Exeter, a friend of the pernicious Finchleys. The method of murder gives Perry a chance to play musical gaspipes. The book is notable for the portrait of an elderly but quite competent man (about the same age as author Gardner at the time of the book's writing) faced with a charge that he is non compos mentis. Otherwise, however, this is below par, especially in courtroom action.

173. The Case of the Worried Waitress. New York: Morrow, 1966. London: Heinemann, 1972. (B)

This is one of Gardner's weakest efforts, with the brief
trial action too tepid even to bring forth a three-I objection. Waitress Katherine Ellis buys Mason's table from a
colleague and seems on the verge of asking advice-- he
leaves an $11 tip, saying $10 is his usual office consultation
fee. She is concerned about the odd behavior of her aunt,
who studies the newspapers for grocery bargains then takes
a cab to the store. A preliminary hearing finds her accused
of a flashlight assault on the aunt. A blind woman is a key
element in the very far-fetched plot. There are some
fairly interesting sidelights on the restaurant business.

174. The Case of the Queenly Contestant. New York: Morrow,
1967. London: Heinemann, 1973. (B)

Ellen Adair, who won a midwestern beauty pageant twenty
years before, is the object of unwelcome press attention
and quizzes Mason about her right of privacy. Soon she is
charged in a preliminary hearing with the shooting murder
of blackmailer Agnes Burlington. The novel's central
puzzle is what happened to the fatal bullet. Offering
comparatively bland court action and a loosely reasoned
solution, this is a tired effort. The overall impression of a
weary author is exemplified by the brevity and perfunctori-
ness of Gardner's foreword/dedication.

175. The Case of the Careless Cupid. New York: Morrow, 1968.
London: Heinemann, 1972. (B)

Selma Anson is accused of the arsenic murder of her
husband Bill at an Arlington family cookout. Covetous
relatives of Delane Arlington, a potential future husband of
Selma, fan the fires of suspicion. Perry does much press
manipulation in this one, using a neat trick to cover up for
his fleeing client. In defending Selma, he opts for a trial
by judge rather than jury. For the most part, this is a
sharper Mason novel than the weak efforts that preceded
and followed it. The solution, though, is a real groaner.

176. The Case of the Fabulous Fake. New York: Morrow, 1969.
London: Heinemann, 1974. (B)

As the two posthumously published Mason novels (see
below) were written earlier in Gardner's career and set
aside, this subpar exploit is the last he wrote in his lifetime
about the famous lawyer. In an early sequence uncon-

nected with the rest of the plot, Mason defends a young
black accused of a pawnshop robbery and makes a telling
point about eye-witness testimony. In the main case, he
represents Diana Douglas, charged with the shooting murder of blackmailer Moray Cassel, before a judge who is a
"strict constructionist" on the role of the preliminary
hearing.

177. The Case of the Crimson Kiss. New York: Morrow, 1971.
London: Heinemann, 1975. (C)

Gardner wrote enough stories for the pulps and slicks to fill
dozens of volumes, but only after his death did his publishers begin to issue collections of his shorter works. The
entertaining title story is one of two Mason novelettes
Gardner wrote for American magazine in the forties. Fay
Allison is accused of the poisoning murder of Carver C.
Clements, found dead in his apartment with a red lipstick
mark on his forehead. Mason questions a prosecution
expert, who is testifying to the numerous fingerprints of
Fay found in the apartment, on the subject of lip prints and
follows up with some courtroom histrionics flamboyant
even for him. The volume's other four tales stay out of
court and do not involve Mason.

A non-courtroom Mason novelette heads a subsequent collection, The Case of the Crying Swallow (1971). Both
Mason novelettes were earlier included in a book club
edition of The Case of the Cautious Coquette (1949).

178. The Case of the Irate Witness. New York: Morrow, 1972.
London: Heinemann, 1975. (C)

The title piece of this collection is the only Perry Mason
short story (as well as a rare non-murder case) and a very
cleverly plotted tale. More than half the story takes place
in court, as Perry (his fishing trip interrupted) defends
Harvey L. Corbin, accused of robbing the vault of the
Jebson Commercial Company. The three non-Mason novelettes in the collection have no trials.

179. The Case of the Fenced-in Woman. New York: Morrow,
1972. London: Heinemann, 1976. (¾)

This was the first of two posthumously-published Mason
novels, "written a few years earlier and set aside," accor-

ding to the publisher. Bachelor Morley Eden consults Perry Mason when Vivian Carson has a barbed wire fence put up, dividing his house and grounds in half, and moves in, claiming half the house and lot is hers. Gardner has much fun with the unusual situation, but the rest of the plot is sub-standard. Morley and Vivian, once they get to know each other better, become co-defendants in the stabbing murder of her estranged husband Loring, supposedly having conspired to purloin some securities the decedent had hidden on the property. The clients are even more close-mouthed than usual, and Perry goes through the whole trial, including one of his rare closing speeches to the jury, completely in the dark. For once, he gets his clients off with a brilliant defense without figuring out who actually committed the crime. That revelation comes in the trial's aftermath, the killer coming from even farther out in left field than was usual in late Masons.

180. The Case of the Postponed Murder. New York: Morrow, 1973. London: Heinemann, 1977. (B)

Gardner expert Francis M. Nevins, Jr., dates the writing of this last Mason novel in the thirties by virtue of its tough-as-nails Depression ambience, in contrast to the compara-tively staid and Establishmentarian Masons of later years. Supporting this theory is the courtroom scene, a prelimi-nary hearing before Justice of the Peace Emil Scanlon, much shorter and less satisfactory than those of the forties and fifties. Scanlon runs a faster and looser prelim than most judges, asking many of the questions himself. The client is Mae Farr, who begins the novel posing as her sister Sylvia, accused of shooting to death womanizer Penn Wentworth on his yacht. (Yachts, along with cars and mountain cabins and motel rooms, were among Gardner's favorite murder sites.) This is not prime Gardner, though better than most of the novels of the sixties.

(as A. A. Fair)

181. The Bigger They Come. New York: Morrow, 1939. As Lam to the Slaughter, London: Hamilton, 1940. (B)

Suspended attorney Donald Lam, a little man with a large brain, applies for a job with Bertha Cool, a fat, elderly, and tough private detective, beginning a durable series in which Donald would stay about the same and Bertha would get a bit slimmer and younger but no less tough.   The plotting technique and legal shenanigans are similar to those found in the Perry Mason series, but the first-person style is somewhat different, and for many years the Fair-Gardner connection, though widely suspected, was officially a secret.   Many prefer the Lam-Cool novels to the Masons for their more extensive use of humor.   Donald's first assignment is to serve papers on one Morgan Birks for his estranged wife, client Sandra Birks.   When Morgan is shot to death, Donald has the opportunity to prove the claim for which he was suspended from law practice: that he has a sure-fire method to get away with murder.   In a ten-page Arizona habeas corpus hearing, he spells the trick out to an astonished judge.

182. Give 'Em the Ax. New York: Morrow, 1944. As An Axe to Grind, London: Heinemann, 1951. (B)

This was the first Lam-Cool case after Donald's return from World-War-II Navy duty, his work hampered by recurring symptoms of malaria. (Though other fictional detectives, including Rex Stout's Archie Goodwin, were in uniform, is Donald unique as a character who left his series for war service, leaving Bertha to handle at least one case on her own?)   The story is about medium for the series, with a good surprise killer but a solution-by-discovery taking the place of real clues. Though there is no trial as such, the novel's best scene describes the in-office taking of Bertha's deposition concerning a traffic accident she had witnessed. A sharp lawyer's devastating cross-examination provides a prime specimen of Gardner's witness-stand Q-and-A.

183. Beware the Curves. New York: Morrow, 1956. London: Heinemann, 1957. (B)

Claiming to be a writer, client John Dittmar Ansel engages Donald Lam and Bertha Cool to locate a man named Karl, living in an Orange County community, who once told him a great story he'd like to turn into fiction. The tale is as trumped up as it sounds, and the client and the victim's wife wind up on trial for the murder of Karl Carver Endicott. Most Cool-Lam novels after the first have no courtroom sequence, but some of the later ones are more Perry Mason-ish with Donald propping up a shaky defense attorney. The effect is like a Mason novel with Paul Drake calling the shots. This one has much tricky plot movement, business finagling, political machinations, and a nice legal trick in the conclusion. The writing lacks the snap of some earlier Lam-Cool titles, though, and the trial scenes are not really up to Gardner's best standards. (Uncharacteristically, the case runs its full course and goes to the jury.)

184. Try Anything Once. New York: Morrow, 1962. London: Heinemann, 1963. (B)

Client Carleton Allen says he was with a woman-not-his-wife at the Bide-a-wee-bit Motel the night assistant district attorney Ronley Fisher died of a suspicious fall into the empty swimming pool. He wants Donald Lam to take his place the next night, pretending to be the customer sought by police. In the very brief courtroom scene (a mere dozen-or-so pages but still enough to work in three triple-I objections), Lam is for once feeding lines to the prosecutor rather than the defense attorney, helping Fisher's replacement nail Staunton Cliffs and Marilene Curtis for the murder of Cliffs' wife. This is distinctly below-average Fair, with the relationship of Lam and Cool with Sgt. Sellers (who should know them better by now) still amusing but getting a little tired.

185. All Grass Isn't Green. New York: Morrow; London: Heinemann, 1970. (B)

Young tycoon Milton Carling Calhoun, who asks Cool and Lam to look for missing novelist Colburn Hale, winds up accused of a murder related to a drug smuggling operation. During his preliminary hearing, ex-lawyer Lam induces Calhoun to fire his lawyer and act in his own defense with Lam's coaching. The last novel by Gardner to be published in his lifetime is undeniably one of his poorest books, despite a good (and au courant) title. But all Gardner trials are worth the enthusiast's attention. He was spotting killers in the courtroom and spreading around the three "I's" to the very end.

(as Charles J. Kenny)

186. This is Murder. New York: Morrow, 1935. London: Methuen, 1936. (B)

Sam Moraine, an advertising executive and yachtsman who

longs for mystery and adventure, becomes involved as intermediary in the ransom kidnapping of Ann Hartwell. Eventually he is suspected of the murder of political boss Pete Dixon. Making a deal with his pal the D.A., one of the few honest men in a corruption-ridden small city, Sam is allowed to question witnesses at a climactic Grand Jury hearing intended to charge him with murder. The proceeding thus is very much like a Perry Mason trial, though not quite as interesting as most. This pulp-flavored novel is probably closest in style and mood to Dashiell Hammett's work of any of Gardner's books. It offers a fairly good mystery puzzle and swift narrative movement. Moraine may have been intended as a series character, but he never reappeared. Gardner makes no use of his potentially interesting advertising background. (The author's occasional carelessness in character naming is rampant in this novel, including a Morden and a Moraine, a Pete Dixon and a Phil Duncan.)

GILBERT, Michael (1912-   )

187. Death has Deep Roots. London: Hodder and Stoughton, 1951. New York: Harper, 1952. (¼)

Young Frenchwoman Victoria Lamartine is charged with the knife murder of Major Eric Thoseby, a British hero of the resistance. Solicitor Gilbert writes some of the best Q-and-A in the business. Trial scenes alternate with an account of an investigation in France by one of the defendant's solicitors. From the opening scene of a discussion among court-watchers in the queue to the expertly executed conclusion, this is an excellent novel.

188. Blood and Judgement. London: Hodder and Stoughton; New York: Harper, 1959. (B)

The body of Rosa Ritchie, wife of a known criminal recently escaped from prison, is found on the bank of a reservoir by two youths. Boot Howton, successor to her husband's territory, is accused of her shooting murder. Young Scotland Yard detective Patrick Petrella has his doubts about the case, despite the confidence of his superior, Superintendent Chris Kellaway, cast by the press (and his own memoir-writing vanity) in the Great Detective mold. A fine specimen of the police procedural novel with much humor and realistic investigative detail, this novel is also unusual in following the same case from Magistrate's Court, through Old Bailey trial, to the Court of Criminal Appeal, though the action in the latter is basically pro forma.

189. The Dust and the Heat. London: Hodder and Stoughton, 1967. As Overdrive, New York: Harper and Row, 1967. (B)

World War II veteran Oliver Nugent, noted by fellow soldiers for his coolness and daring, applies these same attributes to the post-War revitalization and diversification of a drug and cosmetics firm. The climactic trial (about seventeen pages) is a civil case, Mallinson Pharmaceutical Supplies vs. Quinn and Nicholson, involving Nugent's firm's one-upping the opposition by anticipating a perfume called Lucille with a bathroom product called Loo-Seal. This is a fine novel of industrial espionage with knowing views of boardroom jockeying and advertising strategy.

190. Stay of Execution and Other Stories of Legal Practice. London: Hodder and Stoughton, 1971. (C)

Of the thirteen entries in this collection, there is courtroom action in only three: "The Blackmailing of Mr. Justice Ball" describes a comic trial over a wealthy lady's will, which attempts to tie up her fortune for the lifetime of her Siamese cat Sunny and "her legitimate offspring." "Murder by Jury" is a slight tale involving a man on trial for strangling his wife-- his defense: that he did it in his sleep. The title novelette (of some 56 pages) begins in court with the sentencing to death of Harry Gordon for the murder of actress Janine Mann and ends there with the fruit of some of Gilbert's most devious plotting. The title story and some of the volume's non-trial entries appear in the American collection, Amateur in Violence (Davis, 1973), edited by Ellery Queen.

191. Death of a Favourite Girl. London: Hodder and Stoughton, 1980. (As The Killing of Katie Steelstock. New York: Harper, 1980.) (B)

When a London TV celebrity returns to her small-town home to attend a dance, her murder creates a national cause celebre. Gilbert follows a large cast through the police investigation and subsequent legal proceedings with his usual expertise and feeling of authenticity to a surprising but credible final revelation. The climax comes in Magistrate's Court.

GOLDMAN, Lawrence Louis

192. Judd for the Defense: The Secret Listeners. New York: Paperback Library, 1968. (¾)

Ten-year-old Duane Werner dies in a schoolyard accident when a wire-mesh fence gives way during a daredevil game. His father Hugo at first engages TV lawyer Clinton Judd to bring an action for criminal negligence against his son's "murderers" but ends up on trial for shooting to death cement contractor Frank "Lucky" Chance, whom he admits visiting but claims he did not kill. Judd is the same self-righteous stuffed shirt I remember from the small-screen performance of Carl Betz. The story centers on his reluctance to use tape recordings obtained by "bugging." There's a Craig Kennedy-ish use of "infallible" voice prints. This is nothing great, but it has more law in it (though Judd gets away with murder in court) and less of a quicky feel than most media adaptations. It falls well short of Robert L. Fish's Trials of O'Brien (q.v.) but is a clear winner over the TV spin-offs of Edward S. Aarons, Elsie Lee, Norman Daniels, and A. L. Conroy (q.q.v.).

An earlier Goldman volume, Judd for the Defense (Paperback Library, 1968), was not examined. According to an ad in the present book, it deals with a college professor accused of murdering a student via a sugar cube of LSD.

GOODCHILD, George (1888-1969), and ROBERTS, Bechhofer (1894-1949)

193. The Dear Old Gentleman. London: Jarrolds, 1935. New York: Harper, 1936. (¾)

The narrator of this classic courtroom novel is a newspaper publisher and a juror in the trial of Margaret Sampson, former servant in the Aitken household accused of the axe-murder of a current servant, Bessie McIntosh. Is she guilty or, as her defenders preposterously claim, is the real killer the 87-year-old father of the house, Angus Aitken? Of the title character's tag, only "old" is uncontested. The trial occupies most of the first half of the book, the remainder devoted to the investigations of the narrator and a young reporter for his paper. This is a Scottish case and provides some interesting observations on Scottish vs. English legal procedure, appropriately ending in that famous Scots verdict, Not Proven. Astonishingly (at least to a present-day American reader), the jurors are allowed to read newspaper accounts of the trial during its course. The case is based on the 1862 trial of Jessie M'Lachlan, recounted in William Roughead's "The Sandyford Mystery."

194. The Jury Disagree. London: Jarrolds, 1934. New York: Macmillan, 1955. (A)

Based like numerous other works of fiction on the Julia Wallace murder case, this unusual novel takes place entirely (save the last twenty-or-so pages) in the jury room as they deliberate the fate of John Tanner, accused of the blunt-instrument murder of his wife despite an elaborate alibi. The jurors, identified except for the foreman by their occupations (watchmaker, publican, schoolmistress, actress, etc.), each take up a single aspect of the case in turn. One problem is that, like characters in a radio drama, they spend a lot of time telling each other things they obviously already know. This is an interesting example of the rare structure pioneered by Eden Phillpotts in The Jury (q.v.) and later used most effectively by Reginald Rose in the TV play and film "Twelve Angry Men," but it is not a complete success. There is much repetition, occasional tediousness, and a solution that embodies a preposterous coincidence. As in the Rose drama, one character brings in his own personally-gathered data on the case, not a part of the evidence presented in court. And is it credible that a journalist who investigated the crime for his newspaper would be allowed on the jury?

GORDON, Richard, pseudonym of Gordon Ostlere (1921-   )

195. The Medical Witness. London: Heinemann, 1971. As Witness for the Crown, New York: Simon and Schuster, 1971. (B)

An author renowned for his comic medical novels (Doctor

in the House, etc.) here presents the very serious portrait of pathologist John Rumbelow, a renowned expert witness in most of the major murder cases of his day (a well-realized 1936). Regarded by juries as infallible, Rumbelow is a cold and unbearably stuffy, though not totally unsympathetic, character who collects the neckbones of hanged murderers. His story is told in rich prose with some very explicit descriptions of post-mortem examinations. There are three very good trial sequences, totalling about sixty pages: the Old Bailey case of chauffeur Thomas Vickery, charged with the murder of his bigamous second wife, where Rumbelow comes up against a rival Scottish pathologist who is the expert for the defense; the Old Bailey prosecution of Dr. Elgin, an accused abortionist; and finally the trial in Mortlake Assizes of Mrs. Stella Jeavons for the arsenic poisoning of her husband.

GRAEME, Bruce, pseudonym of Graham Montague Jeffries (1900-1982)

196. Though the Eyes of the Judge. London: Hutchinson; New
      York: Lippincott, 1930. (A)

Patrick Spencer is tried in the Old Bailey for the murder of his cousin and lifelong rival, George Douglas Bourne, whose mutilated body is found in a privately owned woods. Viewpoint character is Mr. Justice Raymond, trying his last case before retirement. Graeme, the father of Roderic Jeffries (q.v.), one of the best of the British courtroom specialists, employs considerable artistic license in this all-trial novel: 1) evidence is introduced in illogical order for dramatic impact, with the actual fact and manner of death not discussed until a third of the book has passed; 2) some witnesses testify to obvious hearsay, clearly not the "best evidence"; 3) there is much blatant leading of witnesses, nearly always unchallenged; and 4) as in many trial books, there are some fireworks that would not have taken place had the advocates been properly prepared. Puzzlingly, the judge indicates in his charge to the jury that the prosecution must prove motive. Embarrassingly, he becomes smitten with the defendant's faithfully-attending fiancée. Graeme was a writer of considerable gusto and versatility, but this is not his best work. The solution reflects a xenophobia common in Golden Age British detective fiction.

GRAFTON, C(ornelius) W(arren) (1909-1982)

197. <u>The Rope Began to Hang the Butcher</u>. New York: Farrar
and Rinehart, 1944. London: Gollancz, 1945. (B)

Gilmore Henry, small-city attorney in Kentucky's Calhoun
County, is hired by an insurance agent in trouble over an
unofficial policy on a real estate entrepreneur who vanished seven years before. The short, chubby, and uncon-
ventionally heroic attorney does some fancy footwork
worthy of Perry Mason in his approach to the case. The
fifty pages of trial action involve his disputed option to buy
a house built by the missing man in a projected but
unrealized housing development, an area now in demand for
an aircraft factory. (The tale is set in 1941 America,
before entry into World War II but with clouds clearly on
the horizon.)

The trial takes place in a backwoodsy court where the
judge (not an admirable figure) wears no robes and sometimes wanders around the courtroom so that visitors from
out of the county often have trouble telling judge from
lawyer from witness. Grafton, who would produce even
better courtroom action later (see below), is such a good
writer, it's a pity he wrote no more than four novels. The
tricky plot structure and legal background seem influenced
by Gardner (alluded to at one point), the breezy style by
Raymond Chandler and Rex Stout. But Henry and Grafton
have attractions all their own. The first novel about
Henry, <u>The Rat Began to Gnaw the Rope</u> (1943), lacks any
trial action.

198. <u>Beyond a Reasonable Doubt</u>. New York: Rinehart, 1950.
London: Heinemann, 1951. (¼)

Championed as a classic by Jacques Barzun and Wendell
Hertig Taylor (among others), this is one of the most
cleverly plotted and suspenseful trial novels of them all.
Narrator-lawyer Jess London kills (with some justification)
his brother-in-law Mitchell Sothern. He immediately confesses, later recants, but winds up on trial, acting in his
own defense in over a hundred pages of expert cat-and-
mouse. Thus, for once, the defendant the reader is invited
to root for is guilty. The first-person narration and
Kentucky setting (though the court here is less backwoodsy) recall Grafton's Gil Henry books.

Lawyer Mike Bowen agrees that the trial scenes are effective but challenges their realism: "The protagonist, who was conducting his own defense and doing the cross-examination of all the key witnesses, took chances that no sane lawyer would ever take, and he always got away with it. He didn't get burned a single time....It was a little bit like a Socratic dialogue where one guy is writing both sides and the guy he favors gets all the zingers. It doesn't happen that way in the real world."

GREEN, Anna Katharine (1846-1935)

199. Hand and Ring. New York: Putnam, 1883. London: Ward, Lock, 1884. (B)

Green is seldom read today, and many no doubt regard her novels strictly as museum pieces. This one, though, has the dignity of a stately old car, and many contemporary readers might find it surprisingly diverting if allowance can be made for the Victorian writing style. The death of a reclusive widow in a small upstate New York city produces two equally likely suspects. The novel, published four years before the debut of Sherlock Holmes, includes such detective fiction staples as the dying message, the nutty will, the closely-timed alibi, and even the mysterious hunchback of earlier mystery fiction. The trial, occupying some fifty of the novel's more than four hundred pages, is expertly done, though the judge seems oddly unobtrusive, allowing the opposing lawyers much cross-talk without intervening. Both the defendant and his lawyer are suitors of the tortured heroine, whose problems give an all-too-vivid picture of the plight of women in Victorian society. Green's series sleuth Ebenezer Gryce appears late in the going to wrap up the mystery. A Green novel can be approached like a silent film drama: if you want it to be ridiculous, it will be ridiculous, but if you are willing to meet it on its own terms, you can be caught up in it.

There is also some trial action in The House of the Whispering Pines (New York: Putnam; London: Eveleigh Nash and Grayson, 1910).

GREENBERG, Martin Harry

See OLANDER, Joseph D.

GREENLEAF, Stephen (1942-   )

200. State's Evidence. New York: Dial, 1982. (B)

A fine private eye novel in the tradition of Ross Macdonald, this is one of the few of its type to include
measurable trial action (about twenty pages' worth). Former lawyer John Marshall Tanner is the sleuth, San Francisco the locale. Strong in all areas-- action, dialogue,
plot, characterization, theme, and a mannered style that
avoides self-parody-- and the author's legal training makes
the courtroom scenes crisp and accurate. Tanner's job is to
track down a model who witnessed a hit-run killing and get
her to testify against a Mob leader.

GRIERSON, Edward (1914-1975)

201. Reputation for a Song. London: Chatto and Windus; New
York: Knopf, 1953. (¼)

In the small cathedral city of Turlminster, eighteen-year-
old Rupert Anderson is charged in Assize Court with the
murder of his father, solicitor Robert. The action opens in
court before flashing back to the events leading up to the
crime. The Anderson family has plenty of conflict, with
husband and wife at loggerheads over their respective
favorites among the three children. Grierson leads up to
the death of the father with mounting suspense, and the
tension does not lessen through the harrowing hundred-page
march to the final courtroom verdict. A fine novel.

202. The Second Man. London: Chatto and Windus; New York:
Knopf, 1956. (¼)

Marion Kerrison, a gifted but inexperienced barrister,
defends Australian John Maudsley, accused of the scarf
strangling of his elderly aunt. Assisting her is narrator
Michael Irvine, her office-mate in the provincial Northern
chambers where she is the first Portia. Though the case
appears open-and-shut, Marion disbelieves the eye-witness

testimony of the dead woman's companion, who she believes is shielding the "second man" of the title. The
account of the trial is superb, one of the best described in
all fiction. The courtroom scenes have a full measure of
atmosphere, particularly in the appeals court sequence.
This is Grierson's masterpiece.

203. The Massingham Affair. London: Chatto and Windus, 1962.
Garden City, NY: Doubleday, 1963. (¼)

In 1891, two poachers, Patrick Milligan and Michael Kelly,
are accused and convicted in Belcastle Assizes of burgling
the home of an elderly rector. Eight years later, young
solicitor Justin Derry has reason to think them innocent
and tries to prove it with the help of a local vicar, Mr.
Lumley. After new confessions permit the release of
Milligan and Kelly, the police who faked the evidence are
tried for criminal conspiracy. Grierson's style and characterization reflect the period admirably, and he provides a
good surprise ending. In a prefatory note, he indicates the
tale was partially based on "the celebrated Edlingham
Burglary that convulsed Northumberland towards the end
of the last century," a case that helped create Britain's
Court of Criminal Appeal.

204. A Crime of One's Own. London: Chatto and Windus; New
York: Putnam, 1967. (B)

In what must be one of the very few novels about the
bookshop-lending library business, Warmouth bookseller
Donald Maitland has reason to suspect spies are passing
messages to each other via his circulating collection. His
amateur detective work lands him in Assize Court, charged
with the murder (by his own office paperknife) of customer
Margaret Weir. There is much gentle satire of the British
book world and the espionage craze of the sixties, a light
narrative touch, and the author's usual sharp courtroom
interplay, totalling about forty pages.

H

HALLIDAY, Michael

See CREASEY, John

HAMILTON, Bruce (1900-   )

205. The Brighton Murder Trial: Rex v. Rhodes. London: Boriswood, 1937. (A)

This is an intriguing and possibly unique experiment in political science fiction, carried out with considerable skill. The entire novel is the transcript of communist James Brandleigh Rhodes' trial for the hammer murder of Bertram Handley Haywood, Commander of the Brighton branch of Great Britain's National Youth Movement. Though written in the thirties, the story is set in the early forties in a nation perilously close to fascism but still enjoying a relatively free and even-handed system of justice. Hamilton's foreword and afterword are ostensibly written from the perspective of 1950, by which time Britain has become a communist state and the case is looked on as "one of the most perfect specimens of the operation of bourgeois justice in the period of decline." The transcript format conveys quite a bit of the tediousness and repetitiveness of a real trial, but these elements underscore the sense of reality and human drama.

206. Let Him Have Judgment. London: Cresset, 1948. As Hanging Judge, New York: Harper, 1948. (B)

Sir Francis Brittain, a hard-line High Court judge, is himself accused of murder when a man named Teal is found dead in a well at the holiday house Sir Francis annually visits under the alias Willoughby. For a time, he seems to be escaping a murder charge on account of his eminence, but public opinion won't allow it. His trial at Norwich Assizes is seen through the eyes of watchmaker Denis Bowman, determined not to let a bad cold keep him off the jury in a celebrated case. The courtroom action is expertly done in a witty, suspenseful entertainment. Hamilton's earlier novel To Be Hanged (1930) involves only very slight courtroom action.

HANSHEW, Mary E. and Thomas W. (1857-1914)

207. The Riddle of the Frozen Flame.   Garden City, NY: Doubleday, Page, 1920. (B)

Though about 25 pages of this book's climax are spent in the Old Bailey, it is not a notable scene for trial buffs. Detective Hamilton Cleek is so renowned for his infallibility that the judge, just as the verdict is about to be announced, completely surrenders control of his courtroom to Cleek, allowing the Man of Forty Faces to line up all the witnesses (i.e., suspects) in a row, exonerate the defendant, nail the real murderer, and explain everything, including the mysterious and deadly lights on the Fens that incite local superstition and give this dreadful novel its title. The Hanshews justify the distortion of procedure by stating "the English law...unlike American practice does not allow counsel to becloud the issue with objection and technical argument." (p. 256)

HARE, Cyril, pseudonym of Alfred Alexander Gordon Clark (1900-1958)

208. Tragedy at Law.   London: Faber, 1942.   New York: Harcourt, Brace, 1943. (B)

In one of the great legal novels, we follow a High Court judge, Sir William Barber, as he travels the Southern Circuit in early wartime England. It is not an untroubled trip, as the judge is threatened by anonymous letters and possible attempts on his life. Among the other major characters are barrister Francis Pettigrew, to reappear in several later Hare novels; Inspector Mallett, Scotland Yard sleuth of the author's earlier volumes; and the judge's wife, a barrister felled by sexism, whose legal brain is far keener than her husband's. Hare offers much quiet humor, insightful characterization, and a vivid and knowledgeable picture of the British legal system, its nuts and bolts as well as its pomp and ceremony. The clever detective plot, with a solution turning on a fascinating point of law, seems almost secondary to the background. The longest of the book's several brief courtroom scenes describes the trial of John Ockenhurst for killing his wife's lover, Pettigrew defending. It illustrates how an unsympathetic or biassed judge can quite destroy an advocate's presentation of his case without doing anything truly exceptional.

209. He Should Have Died Hereafter. London: Faber, 1958. As Untimely Death, New York: Macmillan, 1958. (B)

In the author's final novel, titled with bitter irony in both its British and American editions, barrister Pettigrew returns to the scenes of his youth on Exmoor and finds the dead body of a man at a remote spot on the moor: the same hill where he found a dead man in his boyhood many years before. But the body disappears. Later Pettigrew observes a case in Chancery Court, where the settlement of an estate hinges on which of two Gormans died first. The twenty pages of courtroom action are as sharply observed as ever, and the puzzle is neatly resolved. Inspector Mallett also puts in an appearance.

HARNESS, Charles L.

210. The Catalyst. New York: Pocket Books, 1980. (B)

This near-future (2006) science fiction novel concerns a patent dispute over an application of the wonder drug trialine. In seventeen pages of deposition-taking, a computer acts as "Reporter" (in effect judge, for purpose of ruling on objections). Voice stress tests are available in an advisory capacity to measure witness veracity. Later, arguments are made to a three-person panel of Patent Office examiners. Though this is not a completely successful novel (very hard s.f. rich in science lectures plus a touch of mysticism), there is some delightful humor and satire, and the possibilities of a computer as judge (plus other unusual but highly possible computer applications) are entertainingly explored.

211. The Venetian Court. New York: Ballantine, 1982. (¼)

The main premise here is very tough to swallow: in the
U.S.A. of 2021, patent infringement carries the death
penalty. Harness never makes it quite believable. Principals include intrepid lawyer Quentin Thomas; Ellen Welles,
who must die if it is found her small company infringed the
patent on Fiber K; Judge Rex Speyer, an insane, spider-
collecting jurist who loves to send defendants to their
death; and an inventing computer called Faust, who gives
Universal Patents its firm grip on world invention. Trial
action includes the Welles case and very brief U.S. Supreme Court deliberations on the constitutionality of the
existing patent law. Lawyer Harness writes good court
scenes, and (as in the author's The Catalyst and many
science fiction novels) the ingenious ideas somewhat make
up for the book's other problems.

HARRINGTON, William (1931-   )

212. Which the Justice, Which the Thief. Indianapolis: Bobbs-
Merrill, 1963. London: Joseph, 1965. (A)

Roger Louis and Ruth Gibson are accused of the armed
robbery of a jewelry store in a small Ohio town. Clerk
Paul (Doc) Russell is the one important witness against
them, the prosecution succeeding or failing on his credibility. Narrating the account is 92-year-old ex-judge
William H. H. Applegate, an observer at the trial, whose
successor has let him keep a courtroom office. In conversations with his fellow townspeople, he avoids commenting
on how Judge Kemp does things differently from the
practice in his day, but he withholds no comments from the
reader on the course of criminal justice. He is a knowledgeable, likeable, and very humane guide. The courtroom
and all the principals are described in leisurely fashion.
Jury selection is presented in possibly the greatest detail
to be found in any novel. The action leaves the courtroom
only occasionally for lunch breaks, overnight recesses, and
the wait for the jury to return. The climax offers a verdict
but no neat answer to the defendants' guilt or innocence--
and that is one of the author's main points.

Lawyer Harrington intended his first novel to educate
readers about what criminal justice is really like and "to

see how very different it is from what they see on
television." He has succeeded admirably in that goal, but
he has also brought his people and their town to life with
unusual skill and craftsmanship. I believe this is one of the
finest trial novels ever written.

213. The Power. Indianapolis: Bobbs-Merrill, 1964. As The
Gospel of Death, London: Joseph, 1966. (B)

As a result of assurances from faith healer Rob Jones that
she is healed, a farm woman suffering from diabetes and
heart trouble stops taking her insulin and digitalis and dies
the next day. The family and some others call it murder.
Cutler County, Ohio, prosecutor Nelson (Chunk) Connaway
brings a charge of manslaughter against the evangelist.
Harrington does not stack the cards unduly: both Jones and
Conaway are presented sympathetically, and their views
are given a fair hearing. Both the trial and the novel come
to an ambiguous conclusion. As in his earlier novel, the
author eschews easy answers. Another fine book by a
powerful and undervalued novelist.

214. Trial. New York: McKay; London: Barrie, 1970. (B)

In the course of robbing a neighborhood grocery store,
Johnny Hall shoots to death Mama Rosa Rovigo and wounds
her 80-year-old husband Papa Pete. By a lucky coincidence, Cleveland police detective Clement Yacobucci, a
decent and troubled man who has been celebrated in the
press as a contemporary Sherlock Holmes, finds Hall out.
The outcome of the trial, economically described in little
more than a dozen pages halfway through the book, is
never really in doubt. Harrington includes an event presumably commonplace in real life but rare in fiction: a
post-verdict discussion between the losing lawyer and one
of the jurors. The paradoxical point is made that "it's
easier to send a particular man to his death than to endorse
capital punishment in principle." The condemned Hall's
fate becomes interlocked with the campaign for governor
of Republican Attorney General Bill Sherman, who employs
Hall's lawyer as a campaign manager and takes Yacobucci
on as an investigator when he suddenly resigns from the
police department. More than anything this ambitious,
wide-canvas novel is an essay on the politics of capital
punishment. Once again, Harrington gets a major story out
of a relatively routine crime.

215. Partners. New York: Seaview, 1980. (B)

Houston lawyer Teejay Brookover is in Harris County Jail
accused of hiring Kevin Flint to murder her wealthy and
devious client Benjamin Mudge.   Thinking she is being
prosecuted in part because she is a woman, Teejay chooses
a woman lawyer, Lois Farnham Hughes, to represent her
and also wants a woman judge, Norma Jean Spencer.
Events in the present (1978) alternate with flashbacks to
the previous twenty years, following the rise of the three
women in the Texas legal world.   The trio are all highly
capable, all young and attractive, and none wholly admirable or wholly villainous.   Harrington's feel for courtroom
scenes is as sure as ever in Teejay's climactic trial and half
a dozen other court proceedings briefly visited along the
way.   The ending illustrates once again that the truth and
the proper verdict on the evidence are not necessarily the
same thing.

HARRIS, John Norman (1915-   )

216. The Weird World of Wes Beattie. New York: Harper, 1963.
London: Faber, 1964. (B)

Toronto lawyer Sidney Grant (known as the Gargoyle)
defends the paranoid title character, accused of the murder of his wealthy uncle.   The facetious style and rather
strained humor sometimes irritate, but the trial stuff is
okay.   The gimmick by which Wes is framed is interesting
if far-fetched.   This North-of-the-border Perry Mason
apparently never reappeared.

HART, Frances Noyes (1890-1943)

217. The Bellamy Trial.   Garden City, NY: Doubleday, Page;
London: Heinemann, 1927. (A)

Hart's famous novel has been rightly praised as a classic of
both courtroom and detective fiction.   The scene is Redfield, county seat of New York's Bellechester County,
where Stephen Bellamy and Susan Ives are accused of the
murder of Madeleine Bellamy, found stabbed to death in
the gardener's cottage of an unoccupied property where she
allegedly had come to meet her lover, Patrick Ives. View-

point character is an unnamed red-haired female reporter for the Philadelphia Planet who is covering her first big trial. A male reporter for the New York Sphere fills her in on procedure, and soon romance blossoms. The author drew on her experience of covering the Hall-Mills murder case to give the novel the feel of authenticity.

HAYES, Ralph (1927-   )

218. A Sudden Madness. New York: Tower, 1981. (B)

A police shooting incites racial tensions in a small city and leads to an ethical dilemma for the honest cop assigned to investigate.   The book starts as second-road-company Wambaugh but gathers momentum and reader interest as it goes along. Paperback veteran Hayes' generally competent story-telling does not extend to the unintentionally humorous sex scenes or some dreadfully botched courtroom scenes, covering about forty pages. Among the absurdities is a nurse testifying to the cause of death.

HENDERSON, Donald

See LANDELS, D. H.

HENSLEY, Joe L. (1926-   )

219. The Color of Hate. New York: Ace, 1960. (B)

Sam April, small-town midwestern lawyer establishing the tradition of Hensley heroes to come, defends a black accused of the rape-murder of a white woman. This is a sincere liberal novel reflecting on the race relations of its time, somewhat simplistic perhaps but less so than some similar books. It is also a sound fair-play detective story. The courtroom action (obviously preceding some Warren Court decisions regarding the rights of an accused person) is not as strong as the author would produce later.

220. Song of Corpus Juris. Garden City, NY: Doubleday, 1974. (B)

Series lawyer Donald Robak (of the small midwestern city

of Bington) defends Mary Ann Moffatt, accused of murdering Roger Tuttle while attempting to kill her wealthy and powerful former stepfather Joe Watts. The author seems more interested in exploring local political corruption than trial action, though about 25 pages are spent in court. A circuit judge in Indiana, Hensley only occasionally takes a busman's holiday by putting a trial scene in one of his novels. Attorney Mike Bowen comments that Hensley's is "the only judge I've ever seen in fiction who talks to the lawyers the way judges really talk to lawyers and uses the kind of language judges use when the reporter has her fingers off the keys."

221. Rivertown Risk. Garden City, NY: Doubleday, 1977. (B)

Early in the going, Hensley presents enough characters and plot-lines to support a 500-page blockbuster. In the middle-American town of Riverton, politically powerful Amos Walker (coincidentally a name later used by Loren D. Estleman for a series of novels about a Detroit private eye) is on trial for the murder of his wife, and presiding judge Michael Tostini, appointed to the bench by the defendant, is in an awkward position. Besides his political problems, Tostini's bailiff has been murdered and he is threatened by an escaped convict he'd sent up. Though the trial is going on throughout the novel, most of the action takes place outside. In the less than twenty pages spent in the courtroom, though, Hensley offers some realistic details. In one telling sequence, Tostini admonishes the police guard not to appear too chummy with the defendant and thus unduly influence the jury.

Preview of coming attractions: a forthcoming book (unpublished as of mid-1984) tentatively titled Robak's Cross is Hensley's best courtroom novel to date.

HICHENS, Robert (1864-1950)

222. The Paradine Case. London: Benn; Garden City, NY: Doubleday, Doran, 1934. (¼)

Sir Malcolm Keane is briefed to defend Ingrid Paradine, accused of the poisoning murder of her husband, Col. Paradine, a blinded World War I veteran. In his phlegmatic British way, Keane gradually becomes smitten with his client, to the distress of his gallant but over-protected wife Gay. In a soap opera Old Bailey trial before the sadistic Mr. Justice Horfield, who loves to don the black cap and send accused murderers (women especially) to their deaths, Keane attempts to suggest an alternative murderer in the person of William Marsh, the colonel's faithful valet. Court procedure seems shaky: much mind-reading and purely speculative testimony is allowed in unchallenged, and at one point the judge rules a question irrelevant on the objection of the witness with opposing counsel totally silent! Hichens writes about the same sort of stuffy upper-class people as John Galsworthy (q.v.) but doesn't provide the spark to make them interesting. Ago-nizingly slow-paced and padded, this book is easily the least rewarding of the handful of very famous trial novels. In 1947, it became one of Alfred Hitchcock's lesser films.

HINKEMEYER, Michael T. (1940-   )

223. The Fields of Eden. New York: Putnam, 1977. London: Futura, 1980. (B)

Sheriff Emil Whippletree of Lake Eden, Minnesota, investi-gates the shotgun murder of a local minister's wife and four children. The 35-page climax in the admittedly "casual and freewheeling" court of Stearns County Chief Judge Alphonse Reisinger, where non-lawyer Whippletree takes on the defense of fired church organist Abner Fen-sterwald, belongs to the trial-as-sleuth's-theatre school. The extremely loose procedure is exemplified by the prose-cutor's freedom to argue his case to the jury during interrogation of a witness. This is an excellent small-town mystery, despite its unsatisfactory jurisprudence.

HUGHSTON, Dana

224. You Stand Accused! New York: Hillman-Curl, 1937. (¼)

Wife and medical-student lover accused of murder of husband, whose death is attributed to cholera. Here is a well-intended but truly awful novel of which the trial scenes (though undistinguished) are the least appalling part. Procedure, though, is sometimes shaky: the prosecutor is precluded from asking a leading question on cross-exami-

nation!   The locale is the fictional city of Oakdale,
California.   (Sample dialogue: "...she doesn't look like a gal
who would have a covey of cholera germs around to sic at
people." p. 38)

HUME, Fergus (1859-1932)

225. The Mystery of a Hansom Cab.   Melbourne: Kemp and
      Boyce, 1886. London: Hansom Cab Company; New York:
      Munro, 1888. (B)

      Though undeniably a period piece, this famous Australian
      bestseller is a much better book than sometimes reputed.
      The mystery (the chloroform murder of cab passenger
      Oliver Whyte) is a good one, and the picture of Melbourne
      underworld life is fascinating.   The trial of Brian Fitz-
      gerald, alleged to have been Whyte's fellow passenger, is
      briefly but effectively recounted midway. (Note: Barrister
      Hume's many later books, unexamined by the compiler,
      may well contain other trials.)

HUNT, Kyle

      See CREASEY, John

HUNTER, Evan (1926-   )

226. A Matter of Conviction.   New York: Simon and Schuster;
      London: Constable, 1959. (B)

      Hunter, of course, scored his first major success with The
      Blackboard Jungle.   In the years since, he has become the
      most versatile of popular novelists, but here he returned to
      his juvenile delinquency specialty.   Henry Bell is the rare
      prosecutor-hero in this account of three New York gang
      members accused of murder in the stabbing death of a
      blind Puerto Rican youth.   Bell's doubts about prosecuting
      them lead to some odd behavior at the trial, as he even
      admits to the presiding judge he's throwing the case.
      Albeit well-meaning and rich in liberal pieties, this is one
      of Hunter's weakest books. The trial is baffling and absurd,
      as the D.A. is allowed to call two of the defendants as
      witnesses with no mention made of the possibility of self-

incrimination by judge or opposing lawyer.

227. The Paper Dragon. New York: Delacorte, 1966. London: Constable, 1967. (¼)

In contrast to Hunter's first courtroom effort, this is one of the very best of the Big Trial novels, including over two hundred pages describing a U.S. District Court suit for plagiarism. Arthur Nelson Constantine, an only moderately successful screenwriter, claims his flop Broadway play Catchpole formed the basis for James Driscoll's best-selling novel The Paper Dragon, subsequently a major motion picture. Defendants are Driscoll, his publisher, and Artists-Producers-International, the releasing company of the film. Hunter follows the trial from the beginning, with lengthy flashbacks involving various lawyers and litigants. Though the concerns of the novel may be too specialized for some readers, anyone fascinated with the world of writers and publishers or the machinations of the law will be enthralled. The novel is as interesting on the creative process (novel vs. film) as on the plagiarism question. As readers of Hunter's 87th Precinct novels (written as Ed McBain) know, he is a master of interrogation, and he has written some of the best courtroom give-and-take extant in this book.

228. Lizzie. New York: Arbor House, 1984. (¼)

Here Hunter addresses a question that has fascinated crime buffs for nearly a century: did Lizzie Borden, who before and after lived the life of a respectable New England spinster, really murder her parents with a hatchet one August 1892 day in Fall River, Massachusetts? If she did, why did she? And if she didn't, who did? The author's theory, both ingenious and credible, is new to me but embodies some elements of earlier theories. Hunter alternates testimony from the inquest and trial with a purely conjectural account of Lizzie's 1890 European tour, finishing with a recreation of the crime. As all "faction" writers should (but usually don't) do, Hunter explains in an afterword exactly what is fact and what fancy. In the trial scenes, he uses the exact words of the advocates and witnesses but compresses and reorders them, sometimes presenting them as narration rather than Q-and-A. While this is an effective method of telling the story, it robs the novel of some of its interest as a courtroom drama.

HURWITZ, Ken

See BUGLIOSI, Vincent

IANNUZZI, John Nicholas (1935-   )

229. <u>Part 35</u>. New York: Baron, 1970. (¾)

Allesandro Luca, 31-year-old Italian-American lawyer, defends Luis Alvarado, one of two Puerto Rican drug addicts
accused of the shooting death of a police officer during
commission of a burglary. The novel offers considerable
step-by-step detail on both the preparation and presentation of the case, from jury selection through closing
arguments. A New York trial lawyer like his hero, Iannuzzi
gives the proceedings an undeniable feel of authenticity.
This is a very long book, including over 200 pages in court,
and it is probably too meticulously detailed for anyone who
isn't a dedicated courtroom buff. For one who is, however,
it is a feast. The ending is not quite satisfactory after
such a long trip.

230. <u>Courthouse</u>. Garden City, NY: Doubleday, 1975. (B)

This is more a novel about the criminal justice system in
New York City generally than a genuine trial book, but it
does pop in and out of court at intervals, more often for
bail hearings and sentencings than for full dress trials.
Central character is dedicated criminal lawyer Marc Con-
te, who has the knee-jerk nobility of a TV counsellor.
Several cases are involved, most notably a prison riot in
the Tombs, a poor man accused of attempting to bribe an
officer on receiving a traffic ticket, and a glamorous
society murder case involving the unlikeable rich-bitch
Toni Wainwright. The latter case provides a detective
story plot in one part of the large canvas. Though the
Wainwright trial seems to be coming as the book's logical
climax, it never happens. The book has a strong liberal

stance (now decidedly unfashionable) toward the justice system, and the dialogue (as is often the case in legal fiction) runs to speechifying. Despite the reservations noted, this novel offers an insider's view of a fascinating background, and few readers will lose interest. Iannuzzi's Sicilian Defense (1972) may also include courtroom action.

ILES, Francis

See BERKELEY, Anthony

INNES, Hammond (1913-   )

231. Atlantic Fury. London: Collins; New York: Knopf, 1962. (B)

Though this is an exceptionally fine adventure novel, the few pages of courtroom action (a Board of Inquiry and court-martial arising from the botched evacuation of a remote military installation in the Hebrides) are not especially notable or interesting. They confine themselves to the testimony of narrator Donald Ross, a painter and the brother of defendant George Braddock, actually his supposedly-long-dead brother Iain under a new identity.

Innes is frequently drawn to trial settings. Maddon's Rock (London: Collins, 1948; as Gale Warning, New York: Harper, 1948) includes a court-martial, and The Doomed Oasis (London: Collins; New York: Knopf, 1960) uses a trial as a framing device. North Star (Collins, 1974; Knopf, 1975) also has brief trial action. The Formal Inquiry in The Mary Deare (1956; U. S. title The Wreck of the Mary Deare) is more in the nature of an inquest than a trial.

IRISH, William, pseudonym of Cornell Woolrich (1903-1968)

232. Phantom Lady. Philadelphia: Lippincott, 1942. London: Hale, 1945. (B)

Scott Henderson, accused of the strangling murder of his wife Marcella, tries desperately to find the woman who can provide him with an alibi in one of the finest of the author's many variations on the "lady vanishes" situation.

The dozen pages of trial action early in the book consist of the prosecutor's very able and harrowing closing argument, followed by the verdict and sentencing.

One of the very best writers of pure suspense, Woolrich-Irish only rarely got in the courtroom. Mike Nevins points out "the trial scenes in his novels tend to be both very brief and surrealistic" but suggests two short stories, "Silhouette" (1936), collected in Bluebeard's Seventh Wife (1952, as by Irish) and "The Hopeless Defense of Mrs. Dellford" (1942), reprinted as "That New York Woman" in Violence (1958, as by Woolrich) and later (also as by Woolrich) as "The Town Says Murder" (Manhunt, January 1958). Nevins adds, "Perhaps one should be polite and say that the trial scenes in these stories take place in a courtroom of the mind..."

JACOBS, Harvey (1930-   )

233. <u>The Juror</u>. New York: Watts, 1980. (¼)

Resentful juror Leon Drew, called again and again when
others are passed over, is denied his fifth postponement
(requested on grounds of the critical need for his services
at the advertising agency where he works). Selected for a
jury in the suit of a taxi-driver against the City of New
York for injuries sustained when his cab is crushed between
two buses, Leon gets wrapped up in the case and is
determined to exercise his will (as foreman) on the other
five Civil Court jurors, whom he goes out of his way to
cultivate during the course of the proceedings. Jacobs
presents a comic trial, featuring a fine parade of offbeat
witnesses and climaxing with effective emotional appeals
by the opposing advocates. The whole process exists at one
remove from recognizable real life, and there are numerous absurdist touches, such as Drew's personal crime spree
between court sittings. The jury deliberations, initially
conscientious but ultimately frivolous, present a cynical
view of the workings of justice. An amusing but disturbing
novel.

JEFFRIES, Roderic (1926-   )

234. <u>Evidence of the Accused</u>. London: Collins, 1961. New
York: British Book Centre, 1963. (¼)

Lindy Cheesman dies in a suspicious fall from the top of
the staircase in her expensively-furnished home while her
husband Mark is ostensibly hunting with a friend, Stuart
Tetley. Both hunters are suspected (and in turn tried) for

her murder. Third-person narration alternates with the
first-person account of novelist and family friend John
Waring, a failed barrister who edits a lawyers' periodical.
The trickily constructed novel, including a clever stunt to
defeat justice and a final fairly-foreshadowed surprise, is
one of Jeffries' best. It displays his gift for economical
characterization, especially in the portrait of a bitter,
class-conscious cop determined to score points off the
upper-class suspects.

Jeffries' subsequent novel, Exhibit No. Thirteen (Collins,
1962), never published in the United States, presumably
also involves trial action.

235. The Benefits of Death. London: Collins, 1963. New York:
      Dodd, Mead, 1964. (B)

Novelist Charles Leithan, a stuffy but somewhat sympathetic character, is accused of murdering his obnoxious
dog-raising wife Evadne in order to marry his mistress,
beautiful Pamela Breslow. As in Michael Underwood's
later Hand of Fate (q.v.), he is tried for the killing on
circumstantial evidence, although the body has not been
found. The forty pages of trial are done as expertly as
usual; the Kennel Club set are entertainingly depicted; and
the novel has a satisfactory double-twist ending. In an
interesting reference to his principal pseudonym, Jeffries
sets the events in the town of Ashford.

236. An Embarrassing Death. London: Collins, 1965. New York:
      Dodd, Mead, 1966. (¼)

Bill Stemple, who works in an automobile manufacturer's
publicity department, is accused of the murder of beautiful
secretary Sheila Jones, found clubbed with a tripod following an office party. The novel is unusual in including Bill's
trial and conviction, an appeal hearing, and a second trial,
for part of which he acts as his own counsel at the urging
of his determined solicitor Joshua Tring. The build-up is as
good as ever, but the trial scenes themselves seem unusually loose and ragged compared to the author's best, and the
plot has too many improbabilities. The prosecutor fails to
attack one of the weakest points of Bill's story (his false
claim of having won at the races some money the prosecution believes was profit from pornographic photos of the
victim), and it strains credibility that Bill would refuse to

admit the petty act of industrial espionage that did account for the money, even to save himself from a murder conviction. Tring gets the defendant his new trial by some egregiously unethical trickery. The locale is again the suburban community of Ashford.

237. Dead Against the Lawyers. London: Collins, 1965. New York: Dodd, Mead, 1966. (B)

A widely-hated solicitor is murdered in the chambers of the provincial Hertonhurst Bar. Middle-aged Radwick Holter, Q.C., winds up on trial for the crime and midway acquires a fool for a client. His trumped-up defense is one of the most unlikely in fictional annals. Holter's lack of suspicion of his beautiful young wife and his lethal office collection of potential murder weapons also take some believing. Still, this is an entertaining, nimbly plotted exercise. Included in addition to his trial is a hearing before the Benchers of the Inn of Court on Holter's conduct as a member of the Bar.

(as Jeffrey Ashford)

238. Counsel for the Defense. London: Long; New York: Harper, 1961. (¼)

Barrister David Adams has a special motivation for wanting to get client George Clover off on a charge of bank robbery "with extreme violence": he wants to see his kidnapped daughter Jane alive. The trial runs its full course in some fifty pages of expertly described action, and Ashford (a consummate pro) does a beautiful job of combining suspense thriller with legal drama. The twist by which justice is finally done is as satisfying as it is unexpected.

239. The Burden of Proof. London: Long; New York: Harper, 1962. (B)

Roger Ventnor, hard-pressed playboy of the landed gentry, is about to marry advantageously when he is accused of the murder of a former girlfriend via an overdose of abortion medication, the provision of which to a woman is a crime under the Offenses Against the Person Act of 1961. This is strong, intensely readable Ashford, with about forty pages of diverting courtroom action.

240. Will Anyone Who Saw the Accident.... London: Long, 1963.
     New York: Harper, 1964. (B)

     Steven Predaux, a 25-year-old still treated more or less as
     an adolescent by his parents (and not without justification),
     leaves a drunken party angry and alone in his father's green
     Jaguar. When the car kills a man in a hit-run accident, the
     efforts of solicitor Gerald Predaux to cover up for his son
     bring various miseries to a previously happy suburban
     household. Torrents, the barrister briefed to defend Steven
     in Assize Court, generates a rabbit-out-of-the-hat solution
     somewhat in the Perry Mason manner. In another strong
     performance, Ashford reveals a keen eye for human self-
     destructiveness, as his characters make bad moves to the
     last.

241. Enquiries are Continuing. London: Long, 1964. As The
     Superintendent's Room. New York: Harper, 1965. (B)

     Detective Inspector Don Kerry, of the Bilhurst C.I.D.'s X
     Division, must deal with two major cases plus a difficult
     new superintendent in this modular police procedural. The
     more interesting case involves an alleged sexual assault on
     a 12-year-old girl. What the attack is supposed to have
     involved is treated by Ashford with almost excessive
     discretion. The view seems to be that mystery writer
     Franchot Hamble, the definitely unpleasant but possibly
     innocent suspect, is made a danger to young girls by his
     hinted homosexuality! The case that gets to court, how-
     ever, concerns a factory fire and a murdered constable.
     When two youths named Kraster and Pitts are tried, the
     defense accuses Kerry of obtaining Pitts' confession by
     threat of force, making much of the proceeding more
     Kerry's trial than the defendants'. Best thing about this
     average Ashford is its believable account of the various
     pressures on a police officer of high middle rank.

242. The Hands of Innocence. London: Long, 1965. New York:
     Walker, 1966. (B)

     Ashford begins in court for a change but stays for a scant
     ten pages, as the trial of George Krammer for the torture
     and murder of two young girls draws to a close with the
     judge's charge (peppered by frequent objections from the
     defense barrister) and the guilty verdict. The death
     penalty having been commuted to life imprisonment by the

Home Secretary, Krammer escapes, and the remainder of the book is very effective pure suspense, as the police try to locate the fugitive before he can kill again. Though the novel seems a brief for the reinstatement of capital punishment in Britain, the message never overwhelms the story.

243. <u>Consider the Evidence</u>. London: Long; New York: Walker, 1966. (B)

In the southern coastal city of Frindhurst, Tom Haggard is the vicious mastermind of an armored car robbery that leaves one of the guards brain damaged. Detective Sergeant Albert Miller, an outspoken law-and-order hardliner, is accused at Haggard's Assize Court trial of planting evidence and is himself convicted of perjury. Detective Constable John Craig, Miller's young colleague on the Regional Crime Squad, is determined to prove him innocent. Strong on atomic age <u>angst</u>, with references to Auschwitz and the Bomb, this is a downbeat and ironic novel that examines police ethics. Four brief courtroom sequences are involved, two involving Miller and two Haggard.

244. <u>Forget What you Saw</u>. London: Long; New York: Walker, 1967. (B)

This one starts as a big caper novel but quickly mutates into a pure suspense tale of the "threatened witness" type. A planned bank robbery in the old cathedral town of Repperton depends on the ability of reluctant amateur Andrew Simon to circumvent the alarm system. Young barrister Harry Brissom witnesses the hit-run death of a pedestrian and can identify the driver of the car as Simon. The gang are determined he not talk and deliver threats, but the police (attributing an anti-police bias to Harry) don't believe the threats are real. Simon's preliminary hearing and assize trial are described in about fourteen pages, less than usual for this author. Though padded in spots and having an overly-neat ending, the novel shows the author's ability to make you care about his characters. A somewhat similar American novel is Frank Kane's <u>Key Witness</u> (Dell, 1956), though Kane spends even less time in court.

245. <u>Prisoner at the Bar</u>. London: Long; New York: Walker,

1969. (B)

Barrister Robert Bladen, in love with unhappily married Katherine Curson, goes on trial for the murder of the Curson gardener, a peeping tom allegedly caught in the act at a Lover's Lane where the pair were engaged quite innocently in conversation. (Really, they were.) Bladen does not act as his own advocate in the murder trial but does some cross-examining in the book's finale in a different kind of court. Though Ashford is never less than enjoyable, this is far from his best, presenting some overwrought melodramatic prose, corny dialogue, and a far-fetched plot. The somewhat cruel stunt by which Bladen achieves his victory is hard to accept, and he enjoys amazing latitude from the judge in that final courtroom scene.

Under the pseudonym Hastings Draper, Jeffries/Ashford was also the author of a series of non-mysteries about the legal life, published only in England, all by W. H. Allen: Wiggery Pokery (1956), Wigged and Gowned (1958), and Brief Help (1961).

JOBSON, Hamilton (1914-1982)

246. The Evidence you Will Hear. London: Collins; New York: Scribners, 1975. (B)

This is a sound and suspenseful British police procedural, reminiscent of John Creasey at his best, about the search for missing child Angela Murray, who may prove to be the latest of a series of murdered children in the town of Coolidge. About 25 pages are spent on defendant Mellish's Crown Court trial for murder and abduction, including some sharp Q-and-A. The prosecutor oddly states that his case is unusual in relying on circumstantial evidence. Most recent trial novels stress exactly the opposite.

JON, Montague

247. The Wallington Case. London: Macmillan; New York: St. Martin's, 1981. (¼)

A new series barrister, Steven Kale, Q.C., defends Lady

Ann Wallington, accused of murdering her wealthy husband. Trial action, covering some eighty pages, is good but not exceptional. Unfortunately, the novel ends badly as a detective story-- one of the climactic revelations is based on an incredible error in investigative procedure, and another surprise is badly telegraphed. Jon is, says his publisher, a pseudonymous London barrister "with a large criminal practice."

248. A Question of Law. London: Macmillan, 1981. New York: St. Martin's, 1982. (¼)

At Liverpool Crown Court (a change of venue from Manchester), Dr. Christopher Stirling is tried for the rape of Judy Smith, a housewife noted in the community for giving away her charms. Between the crime and the trial, Stirling's wife June is found strangled to death in their home. Steven Kale, Q.C., surely the most inept of lawyer-detectives, defends his close friend against his better judgement. The judge and opposing lawyer also recur from The Wallington Case. The knowledgeable author offers some interesting points about courtroom procedure and design, but the ingenious plot idea is compromised by too much padding and unconvincing execution.

JONES, Douglas C. (1924-   )

249. The Court-Martial of George Armstrong Custer. New York: Scribner's, 1976. London: Allen, 1977. (½)

General Custer survives the Little Bighorn and, in a political move by Army Commanding General Sherman, is court-martialed on charges of disobedience to orders. A recurring phrase in the charges is "unwarranted loss of animals and men." Jones sets the scene with much descriptive detail and does an excellent job of bringing to life the opposing lawyers: flamboyant civilian attorney Allan Jacobson, representing Custer, and Major Asa B. Gardiner, representing the Army. The trial scenes and the vivid, realistic accounts of cavalry combat are beautifully done. Both points of view on Custer's culpability are given a full airing, and it is not until late in the story that the author's sympathies become obvious. Jones, a retired Army officer of Custer's own permanent rank of Lieutenant Colonel, provides his own illustrations, sketching the participants in the style of a courtroom artist.

This novel belongs to the small sub-genre of imaginary trials of real people. Others (not involving English-speaking jurisdictions): Max Radin's Day of Reckoning (Knopf, 1943), about a post-war trial of Hitler; Philippe van Rjndt's somewhat disappointing The Trial of Adolf Hitler (Summit, 1978); and Alfred Fabre-Luce's The Trial of Charles de Gaulle (Praeger, 1961).

Jones returns to the courtroom in two historical novels about attorney Eben Pay, Winding Stair (New York: Holt, Rinehart, and Winston, 1979; as The Winding Stair Massacre, London: Allen and Unwin, 1980) and Weedy Rough (Holt, Rinehart, and Winston, 1981).

JUDD, Harrison

　　See DANIELS, Norman

KATKOV, Norman

250. <u>Blood and Orchids</u>. New York: St. Martin's/Marek, 1983.
(B)

Set in the Honolulu of 1930 and based on the infamous and
fascinating Massie case, this miniseries-between-covers
should have been a much better novel than it is. There are
some good and compelling scenes but many more trite and
corny exchanges, especially those involving characters of
opposite sexes. Two trials are included: first, four Hawaiian youths are wrongly accused of the rape and beating
of socially prominent Navy wife Hester Ashley Murdoch;
then Lt. Gerald Murdoch (the victim's husband), Doris
Ashley (her mother), and Seaman Duane York are tried for
the shooting murder of one of the youths, Joe Liliuohe.
The first trial is competently done and includes a memorable scene where young defense lawyer Tom Halehone
maneuvers desperately to get at least one native Hawaiian
juror seated. The second trial includes TV-ish histrionics
both in court and in the jury room. In a serious procedural
gaffe, an objection to asking leading questions on cross-
examination is sustained by the judge. Appearing for the
defense in the second trial is Walter Bergman, a lightly
fictionalized version of Clarence Darrow, who also appeared under the aliases of Jonathan Wilk, in Meyer Levin's
<u>Compulsion</u> (q.v.); Martin Brennan, in James Yaffe's <u>Noth-
ing but the Night</u> (q.v.); and Henry Drummond, in the
Jerome Lawrence-Robert E. Lee play, <u>Inherit the Wind</u>.

KEELER, Harry Stephen (1890-1967)

251. <u>The Amazing Web</u>. London: Ward, Lock, 1929. New York:

Dutton, 1930. (¼)

Always generous in verbiage, the incomparable Keeler offers three trials in this ornate masterpiece of unfettered plot-spinning. In Brossville, Kansas, inept young lawyer David Crosby ignores the "not guilty" plea of client and girl friend Lindell Trent and offers a pitiful plea for mercy instead. By the time he defends Chicago clubman Archibald Chalmers, accused of the shooting murder of Rupert van Slyke, he has been transformed into a fighter. Prosecuting is Rudolph "Blue-Bow" Ballmeier, who reputedly never loses when he wears his lucky bow tie. Chalmers' first trial ends in a hung jury, and the second involves virtually all new witnesses. Keeler was a wonderful and unique writer, but he is not a reliable guide to accurate legal procedure. In his alternate-universe courtroom, everything (law, terminology, strategy) is just a little bit off. Objections and legal arguments are nonsensical, and the judge's rulings are even-handedly idiotic. For a detailed account of the novel's wondrous plot, see Francis M. Nevins, Jr.'s "The Worst Legal Mystery in the World" (The Armchair Detective, volume 1, number 3, April 1968, pp. 82-85).

According to Nevins, several other Keeler novels also contain courtroom action. The following titles were published by Dutton: The Defrauded Yeggman (1937), 10 Hours (1937), The Sharkskin Book (1941; British title By Third Degree, Ward, Lock, 1948). First published in Britain by Ward, Lock was The Lavender Gripsack (1941; American title The Case of the Lavender Gripsack, Phoenix, 1944). For the incredibly complicated British and American publishing histories of the first two titles listed above, consult Allen J. Hubin's Crime Fiction, 1749-1980.

KELLEY, Leo P. (1928-   )

252. Cimarron and the Hanging Judge. New York: Signet, 1983. (B)

In a routine, readable "adult" western, with enough detail about frontier life to show the author did his homework, the strong, tall, and silent hero is framed by treacherous Emma Dorset and charged before the notorious Judge Parker (a less interesting character than the title leads one to hope) with killing and robbing a deputy as well as kidnapping and rape. Such is the speed of the frontier court that the whole trial (not an especially notable one) can be presented, complete with opening and closing arguments, testimony, verdict and sentencing, in a mere fourteen pages. The rest of the episodic account deals with Cimarron's escape and efforts to prove his innocence.

An earlier Kelley suspense novel, Deadlocked (Fawcett Gold Medal, 1973), concerns revenge against a jury and the officers of a court that sentenced an innocent man to death but includes no trial action.

KENNEDY, John de N. (1888-   )

253. Crime in Reverse. London: Nelson, 1939. (¼)

When artist Chevalier Eric Ricardo is tried in the Old Bailey for the murder of private detective Joshua Makin, his defense barrister is the real murderer, Nicholas Chetwynd, K.C. Trying to find the truth is an interesting variant on the clerical detective, Rev. John Morton of the charitable institution called Toc H. Kennedy handles the unusual situation expertly through the well-managed trial scenes to the satisfactorily dramatic conclusion. Most notable perhaps is the affecting portrait of Mr. Justice Hawthorne, the hard-working, conscientious, not especially gifted, and certainly far-from-omniscient judge. As the jury deliberates, we see him looking up the sentence of death in his law references, just in case he needs it.

KENNY, Charles J.

See GARDNER, Erle Stanley

L

LACY, Ed, pseudonym of Leonard S. Zinberg (1911-1968)

254. Breathe No More, My Lady. New York: Avon, 1958. (¼)

Like many Avon originals of the period, this one has
dauntingly small print, but if your eyes can stand the
strain, the effort is worth it. Private eye writer Matt
Anthony is accused of the murder of his wife, dead from a
blow to the forehead while fishing in her rowboat. He
claims it was an accident. As the small-town trial
proceeds in the second half of the book, Lincolnesque
defense attorney Jackson Clair paints Anthony as a man of
creative genius, to whom the usual rules of conduct do not
apply. The prosecutor offers the defendant's violent, sexy
novels as evidence of his true nature, plus an article in the
Third Degree (the Mystery Writers of America newsletter)
in which he claims knowledge of "more ways to commit
murder than any killer." Meanwhile, Anthony sits busily
making notes for his proposed book about the trial. Lacy
has a great deal of fun with the situation, quoting Anthony's books in parody of Spillane and other fifties paperback writers and producing a richly ironic surprise ending.

LANDELS, D. H., pseudonym of Donald Henderson (1905-)

255. His Lordship the Judge. London: Paul, 1936. (B)

At Issiter Assize Court (located either in Devon or Somer-
set-- reports differ), Mr. Justice Jantor presides over the
trial of Ann Century for the murder of her husband and
relives a long-ago love affair with the defendant. Also
viewed is a case involving the alleged theft of six pigs.
Less time is spent in court but more in rehearsal than in

many trial novels. Offering much humor and too much dialect, this comic novel doesn't quite fulfill its early promise, but it includes some of the best parody extant of florid courtroom argument. For example, "My lord, my friends, we who know freedom, we who walk daily through fields of waving corn, or fields of yellow buttercups, we who tread beneath our feet the springy turf, the yielding moss, the unaccusing daisy, we do not know the dreadful sound of locks-- much less the sentinel tread of the gaoler who guards us, leads us, to a cruel doom."

LANDON, Christopher (1911-   )

256. Dead Men Rise Up Never. London: Heinemann, 1963. New York: Sloane, 1963. (B)

Accountant Harry Andrews, literary executor for novelist Colin Headly, receives his late friend's last novel for delivery to his publishers. The novel, titled as is Landon's book, appears to accuse Headly's wife of his murder. In three brief but effective courtroom sequences, the widow brings a libel action against the publisher; Harry is charged in Magistrate's Court with being an accessory to the murder; and finally he is tried before a jury in the Old Bailey. This short book is written and plotted with considerable style.

LEE, Elsie (1912-   )

257. Cast the First Stone. New York: Lancer, 1963. (¼)

This novelization of an Ellis Marcus script from the Sam Benedict TV series is credited on the cover to Norman Daniels (mistakenly) and on the title page to Lee. Sam, patterned on San Francisco lawyer J. W. Ehrlich, here defends a cop accused of homicide in the resisting-arrest death of a rich man's son. The prosecution's case in the preliminary hearing, based on the uncorroborated testimony of one witness, never seems formidable enough. The somewhat simple-minded accused cop and his good-as-gold wife are exceedingly hard to take. In summary, this is an altogether unconvincing exercise. First Howard Oleck and later Ehrlich and collaborator Brad Williams (q.q.v.), produced some hardcover novels about Benedict several years after the TV show went off the air.

LEE, Harper (1926-   )

258. To Kill a Mockingbird.   Philadelphia: Lippincott; London:
     Heinemann, 1960. (B)

     One of the great novels about childhood, this Pulitzer Prize
     winner also delivers impressively in its forty-plus pages of
     courtroom action. The setting is the small Alabama town
     of Maycomb, the time deep in the Great Depression.
     Through the eyes of his young daughter Scout, we see
     lawyer Atticus Finch defend Tom Robinson, a black ac-
     cused of raping the daughter of a poor white family. Lee
     beautifully conveys the atmosphere of a rural court as well
     as the unenviable position of a black accused of a crime
     against a white in the deep South. Finch, an exceptional
     man as his children gradually come to understand, has a
     confidence in eye-witness testimony and suspicion of cir-
     cumstantial evidence that is unusual among recent fic-
     tional lawyers.

LEVIN, Meyer (1905-1981)

259. Compulsion.   New York: Simon and Schuster, 1956. Lon-
     don: Muller, 1957. (B)

     Levin's most famous novel is closely based on the case of
     Nathan Leopold and Richard Loeb, two highly gifted 18-
     year-olds from wealthy Chicago families who were tried
     and convicted for the "thrill killing" of a small child, Bobby
     Franks. Leopold and Loeb become Judd Steiner and Artie
     Straus, permitting the author more freedom to fictionalize
     and apply Freudian analysis. In a foreword Levin acknow-
     ledges using direct quotes from press reports of the case,
     most notably the closing defense speech of Clarence Dar-
     row (here called Jonathan Wilk), an enormously eloquent
     plea against capital punishment that is one of the high
     points of the book. Levin, assigned to the case as an 18-
     year-old reporter, makes himself a character as Sid Silver,
     an acquaintance of the defendants.

     Levin captures the circus atmosphere of the trial very
     effectively. The defendants having changed their plea to

guilty, Wilk desperately trying to prove mitigation while avoiding the claim of insanity that would force a jury trial, the jury box in the crowded courtroom is occupied, appropriately, by members of the press. Though much testimony, mostly psychiatric, is quoted, a majority of the hundred-plus pages of trial action is taken up by the lawyers' closing arguments to the judge. This is a classic of legal fiction (or, in the current term, faction).

LEWIS, Roy (1933-   )

260. A Fool for a Client. London: Collins, 1972. (¼)

While his wife is away, a middle-aged barrister innocently acquires a young female protégée. He winds up defending himself on a charge of murdering her in the latter half of the novel. Most memorable aspect of this book is its plot, which seems to follow point by point that of Patrick Quentin's Black Widow (1952), a non-courtroom book in the Peter Duluth series.

261. A Wolf by the Ears. London: Collins, 1970. New York: World, 1972. (B)

Stephen Kirk, whose parents have died in a fire leaving no will, hires David Centre, a newly qualified solicitor with time on his hands, to defend him against a charge of illegitimacy that would invalidate his claim to the estate. This neatly plotted detective novel, intimately involved with points of law, offers the buff three separate courtroom proceedings: a drunk driving trial in Magistrate's Court, which solicitor Centre wins on a technicality; a Chancery hearing turning on obscure points of Austrian marriage law; and finally a preliminary hearing on a murder charge against Kirk. The title is from Robert Burton's Anatomy of Melancholy: "He who goes to law holds a wolf by the ears."

262. Dwell in Danger. London: Collins, 1982. New York: St. Martin's, 1983. (B)

Lewis' recent books feature solicitor Eric Ward, a former policeman and glaucoma sufferer with more problems than his law practice brings him. Here he becomes involved in intra-family litigation over the conveyance of farm property. The Crown Court case of Saxby v. Saxby is expertly described in ten pages early in the book, before the family squabble culminates in murder. A solid entry in a strong series of legal mysteries, most of which eschew the courtroom.

LIPSKY, Eleazar (1911-   )

263. Murder One. Garden City, NY: Doubleday, 1948. (B)

In a brief, tough novel with the atmosphere of forties film noir, New York Assistant D.A. Esau Frost prosecutes aging prostitute Alice Williston and gambler Frank Albany on a charge of murdering James Madena. Though Frost abhors physical abuse of suspects and witnesses, any other kind of abuse is okay. The novel is at its best conveying the behind-the-scenes legal maneuvering that goes on outside the courtroom. Everyone, including her own lawyer, believes Alice guilty and wishes she would cop a plea. The finish is typical of forties psychological mysteries. An interesting novel, but there was better to come from Lipsky.

264. The People Against O'Hara. Garden City, NY: Doubleday, 1950. London: Wingate, 1951. (B)

Manhattan lawyer James Curtayne represents a familiar figure in legal fiction: the brilliant, flamboyant defender, slowed by health and/or drinking problems, attempting a comeback. Twenty-one-year-old Johnny O'Hara is accused of the shooting murder of William Sheffield, his employer at the Carney Street Fish Market, during the course of a robbery. Curtayne blows the case in some 45 pages of suspenseful trial action. His detection after the verdict results in an even more exciting action finish outside the courtroom.

265. Lincoln McKeever. New York: Appleton, 1953. London: Deutsch, 1954. (B)

The novel opens with famed defense lawyer McKeever addressing the U.S. Supreme Court on one of his customary lost causes. But the widowed lawyer, whose young and ailing son needs a change of climate, gives up practice to move to Denver. He comes out of retirement to accept a case in New Mexico Territory, where Don Carlos de Niza is accused of hiring Tom Canty to murder the elderly Judge Douglas Hanna, an adversary of Don Carlos in the Anglo-Hispanic strife over Spanish land grants. In Hogarth County, it seems doubtful Don Carlos can get a fair trial, and McKeever is up against a blatantly biassed judge, a nearly-all-Anglo jury, and a proud, uncooperative client. Trial action totals about sixty pages, including a good scene in which McKeever challenges the legality of his client's extradition from Mexico and an extremely eloquent summation under painful circumstances. (Did Lipsky visualize Spencer Tracy playing McKeever on the screen as he earlier had the lawyer-hero of The People Against O'Hara?) Oddly, the key prosecution testimony of killer Canty occurs off-stage. A jailhouse mock trial, in which Don Carlos acts as defense attorney, is also described briefly. Though Lipsky is generally better in a contemporary setting, this semi-western ranks as one of his better books. In apparent homage to an earlier specialist in legal fiction, Lipsky names a deputy sheriff Art Train.

266. The Scientists.   New York: Appleton; London: Longmans, 1959. (B)

Prof. David Luzzatto, celebrated discoverer of the wonder drug biocin, is accused of usurping credit for the idea by his former mentor Prof. Victor Ullman, who brings an action claiming rights to the biocin patent. The situation seems cut-and-dried at first but (like many legal problems) becomes more and more complicated as resolution is sought. The case is scheduled for trial in the Supreme Court of Merton County, New York, but the 32 pages of courtroom action here involve the preliminary taking of depositions, sometimes with and sometimes without the judge presiding. Lipsky devotes another 27 pages to the quasi-judicial arbitration hearing, before an old and respected Scottish scientist, that ultimately decides the issue. The final confrontation of the opposing professors somewhat recalls the testimony of Captain Queeg in Wouk's The Caine Mutiny (q.v.). In what may be his best novel, Lipsky presents an all-too-believable account of academic/scientific political infighting and ethical pondering, recommended to the same readers who enjoyed C. P. Snow novels like The Search and The Affair.

267. The Devil's Daughter. New York: Meredith, 1969. (B)

The background of San Francisco in the 1880's is colorful, and Lipsky's research and legal knowledge seem impeccable, but some spark is missing from this slow-moving and overblown historical. Even the trial scenes do not cause the tale to catch fire. Based on an actual case, the novel tells of the divorce action brought by the ill-reputed beauty of the title against a former senator who denies they were ever married. It's scandalous as all-get-out but also rather boring.

268. Malpractice. New York: Morrow, 1972. (B)

In Huron County, New York, former D.A. Will Mahler appears for Manya Schroeder in her malpractice suit against Lewiston Central Hospital, where she allegedly had unnecessary brain surgery at the hands of Percy Tatum, a black surgeon who subsequently left the area. The novel conveys a strong sense of the tension and rivalry between legal and medical professionals and includes a detailed description of brain surgery that seems as authentic as the courtroom scenes. The emotionally-charged trial may leave the reader nearly as wrung out as it does the participants. The two sides in the case are presented even-handedly, and only in the final lines of the book does the reader learn who was right. This is either Lipsky's best or a close second to The Scientists. James P. Curtayne, the hero of The People Against O'Hara, recurs in a supporting role as a member of Mahler's firm.

Lipsky was also the author, in collaboration with science fiction writer Robert Silverberg, of the paperback original western Frontier Lawyer (Pocket Books, 1961), published under the joint pseudonym Laurence L. Blaine.

LOCKRIDGE, Richard (1898-1982)

269. Something Up a Sleeve.   Philadelphia: Lippincott, 1972. London: Long, 1973. (¼)

How can you have both a courtroom drama and a whodunit when your hero is the D.A.? The challenge is met in this originally structured novel. Bernie Simmons is prosecuting J. Stanley Martin for the murder of his wife. His opponent and old friend, defense attorney Abe Levinsky, seems to have some secret answer to the state's apparently powerful case. (One indication: he doesn't even bother to make the traditional motion for directed acquittal at the end of the state's evidence.) At the beginning of the novel, Levinsky has been murdered, and Bernie spends a good portion of the book studying the trial transcript looking for clues to the lawyer's death. This is a typically smooth Lockridge product and (to my knowledge) the author's one venture into the courtroom, where he seems very much at home.

LONDON, Ephraim, ed.

270. The World of Law. Two volumes. New York: Simon and Schuster, 1960. (C)

The first volume of this splendid anthology, The Law in Literature, is devoted to fiction and drama (world-wide in scope) with legal backgrounds, most selections spending at least some time in court. Short stories and excerpts falling within the English-speaking-jurisdiction stricture of the present volume include two Dickens selections ("The Trial of Bardell v. Pickwick" from The Pickwick Papers and "In Chancery" from Bleak House); Lewis Carroll's "The Trial of the Knave of Hearts" from Alice's Adventures in Wonderland; Jack London's "The Benefit of the Doubt"; John Galsworthy's "Manna"; Frank O'Connor's "Counsel for Oedipus"; Agatha Christie's "The Witness for the Prosecution" (short story version); Arthur Train's "The Dog Andrew"; Mark Twain's "Science vs. Luck"; Herman Wouk's "The Court-Martial," from The Caine Mutiny; A. A. Milne's "The Barrister"; William Faulkner's "Tomorrow"; Twain's "Act of God in Nevada"; Sir Walter Scott's "Alan Fairford's First Cause," from Redgauntlet; two fables by Theobald Mathew ("The Blushing Beginner and the Bearded Juryman" and "The Witty Judge and the Bronchial Usher"); W. Somerset Maugham's "The Happy Couple"; Bret Harte's "Colonel Starbottle for the Plaintiff"; Ben Hecht's "Crime Without Passion"; and Joseph Sheridan LeFanu's "Mr. Justice Harbottle." Dramatic selections include Terence Rattigan's "The Winslow Boy" (which is all about a trial but has no scenes in court); W. S. Gilbert's "Trial by Jury"; and John Mortimer's "The Dock Brief." Among the world literary figures represented are Cervantes, de Maupassant, Chekhov, Pirandello, Sholom Aleichem, Anatole France, Balzac, and Rabelais. The volume closes with a comic essay by

Robert Benchley, "Take the Witness." The second volume, The Law as Literature, is devoted to non-fiction, including journalistic accounts, essays, judicial opinions, and excerpts from trial transcripts.

LUSTGARTEN, Edgar (1907-1978)

271. A Case to Answer. London: Eyre and Spottiswoode, 1947. (As One More Unfortunate, New York: Scribner's, 1947.) (½)

Respectable businessman Arthur Groome is accused of the mutilation-murder (by both knife and blunt instrument) of Kate Haggerty, a Soho prostitute, in circumstances that recall Jack the Ripper. Lustgarten, a first-rank true crime writer as well as a powerful novelist, presents a complete trial that is one of the most enthralling and meticulously detailed in fiction. Many of the parties to the case-- judge, advocates, witnesses-- are explored in depth, but the jury, in whose hands Groome's ultimate fate lies, are faceless. This is an anti-capital punishment novel but in no sense a tract, as Tom and Enid Schantz point out in their excellent introduction to the 1980 Gregg Press reprint.

Other Lustgarten novels with trial action include Game for Three Losers (London: Museum Press; New York: Scribner's, 1952) and Blondie Iscariot (Scribner's, 1948; Museum, 1949).

MCMAHON, Thomas Patrick

272. The Hubschmann Effect. New York: Simon and Schuster, 1973. As The Little Victims, London: Constable, 1974. (A)

Brief documentary novel in the form of grand jury testimony. The case involves the terrifying side effects of an oral contraceptive known as Panesterol, its makers charged with selling the product knowing it was "adulterated, diluted, and/or tainted." The proceedings are precipitated by the attacks on several children (by parents or school friends) because they are "different." This is a science fictional mystery with a fascinating theme rich in legal and moral ramifications.

MCNEISH, James (1931-   )

273. The Glass Zoo. London: Hodder and Stoughton; New York: St. Martin's, 1976. (B)

This belongs to a long line of education novels depicting the relationship of a dedicated teacher with a promising but difficult student. Fourteen-year-old schoolboy John Marsh is tried for the murder of schoolmaster Douglas Page, who was struck by a piece of masonry dislodged from the roof at a school building. The narrator is New Zealander Ralph Stanton, Page's replacement at the Coldstream Park School in a fictitious South London slum area. The sixty pages of trial action are as effectively done as the classroom sequences.

MASUR, Harold Q. (1909-   )

274. The Attorney. New York: Random House, 1973. London: Souvenir Press, 1974. (¼)

Though Masur's lawyer-sleuth Scott Jordan rarely appears in court except in short stories, this non-series novel is a fine specimen of the Big Trial Book. New York lawyer Paul Slater represents his wife's cousin, law student Ken Sheridan, accused of strangling actress Dolly Wayne, mother of his pregnant girl friend (and, secretly, wife). The trial is very expertly done from the detailed description of jury selection (including reference to a juror training film that makes them "no more expert on the subject of jury service than the GI had become on the subject of gonorrhea") to the dramatic conclusion. One question: are there a bit too many surprise witnesses in a case that surely must take place under current discovery rules? The level of adversarial sniping, which reads well in a novel but seems unlikely in real life, also involves some artistic license.

MATTHEWS, Clayton (1918-   )

275. The Power Seekers. Los Angeles: Pinnacle, 1978. (B)

Tennessee lawyer King Hanratty, defending Senatorial candidate Adam Starke, who is accused in the shooting death of his wife, has an unconventional way of preparing his case: researching his client's family tree. The contemporary case is presented in alternate chapters with the saga of the powerful Starke family, beginning in 1845. Matthews, an old pro, keeps up the reader's interest in both story lines, and the sixty-plus pages of trial action (beginning with an account of jury selection) are effectively done. The lawyers, though, seem less well-prepared than real-life advocates, tending to miss things the reader picks up on. And at one point Hanratty, with no objection from his adversary, is allowed to bring in new matter on cross-examination. The prosecutor enters an exception at one point, pointless since the prosecution cannot appeal in a criminal case. Cavils aside, this is a fast-reading and enjoyable courtroom-historical hybrid.

Matthews' early novel The Mendoza File (1969) is a trial-aftermath novel that spends only a brief interlude or two in the courtroom.

MIEDANER, Terrel

276. The Soul of Anna Klane. New York: Coward, McCann, and
Geoghegan, 1977. London: New English Library, 1979. (¾)

In one of the most unusual fictional murder trials, defense
attorney Jason Hunt must prove the existence of the soul
to save his client, Anatol Klane, accused of being "an
accessory to the premeditated death" of his daughter Anna,
a crime that carries the same penalty as premeditated
murder. Believing Anna lost her soul during brain surgery,
Klane has provided her with a revolver and urged her to kill
herself. The setting is Madison, Wisconsin. The case runs
its full course with some effectively presented legal,
religious, and philosophical arguments. This is easily the
best of the occult/supernatural trial novels that became an
off-beat sub-genre in the seventies. For other examples,
see Frank De Felitta's Audrey Rose (reincarnation) and
Gene Thompson's Lupe (witchcraft).

MILLAR, Margaret (1915-   )

277. Beyond this Point are Monsters. New York: Random
House, 1970. London: Gollancz, 1971. (¾)

Devon Osborne brings a non-adversary probate action in
San Diego to have her husband, wealthy fruit-grower
Robert Osborne, declared legally dead and herself declared
administrator of his estate. Her lawyer argues that he was
murdered the night he left their ranch house in search of
his missing dog, and California's celebrated L. Ewing Scott
case is used as a precedent for proving death in the
absence of a body. Millar, a long-time Santa Barbara
court-watcher, writes effective trial scenes, as well as
providing insights into Anglo-Chicano relations near the
U.S.-Mexican border and orchestrating a fine finishing
surprise. Millar told an L. A. Times interviewer in 1983
that her next novel would include extensive trial action.

MOORE, Robin (1925-   ), with Henry ROTHBLATT

278. Court-Martial. Garden City, NY: Doubleday, 1971. London: Harrap, 1972. (¼)

Non-military lawyer Hank McEwan appears for the defense in the court-martial of Major Richard Becker and Captain Lewis Marone, two of five Green Beret officers accused of the murder of Tran Van Troc, a Vietnamese civilian believed to be a double agent. After a couple of preliminary hearings, the near-hundred-page trial takes place at the Pentagon, with angry demonstrations going on outside. Villain of the piece is a general who hates the Green Berets. This is a polemical novel with much hawkish propaganda, but thanks to Rothblatt's expertise it provides an interesting and detailed look at the military justice system. Rothblatt also lent his legal knowledge (with more impressive results) to Robert L. Fish in A Handy Death (q.v.).

MORTIMER, John (1923-   )

279. Rumpole of the Bailey. Harmondsworth, England: Penguin, 1978. New York: Penguin, 1980. (C)

Six short stories are told by aging, poetry-quoting junior barrister Horace Rumpole, the character played so memorably on television by Leo McKern. There are at least three common problems with adaptations of movies and TV shows into novels and short story collections: 1) the adapter is usually not the original screenwriter, and making the characters conform to someone else's concept renders them lifeless; 2) the style is usually third-person pedestrian; and 3) a screenplay or TV script is not the same thing as a short story or a novel. Mortimer's adaptations of his own scripts eliminate at least the first two complaints: he is the original creator and he writes in Rumpole's voice, delightfully. The stories could easily stand on their own for a reader unacquainted with the small-screen Rumpole.

There are continuing appearances by his interestingly assorted colleagues in Chambers and his wife Hilda, a.k.a. She Who Must Be Obeyed. And there are recurrent references to the young Rumpole's two unforgettable triumphs, the "Penge Bungalow Murder" and the "Great

Brighton Benefit Club Forgery." Best of the six tales (and probably of the whole series) is "Rumpole and the Honourable Member," wherein he defends (in court) a Labour M.P. on a rape charge and (in Chambers) senior clerk Albert on charges of cooking the books and robbing the petty cash. The conclusion conveys not the easy irony of a situation comedy but the uncertainty and ambivalence of real life. Most like a sitcom episode (albeit a very good one) is "Rumpole and the Married Lady," in which he takes on a rare divorce case. Other cases concern robbery, marijuana possession, safecracking, and murder.

Rumpole is one of the few series lawyers in fiction who gets into court in every adventure, and his appearances are always lively. But his ability to sneak in a comment when examining witnesses and his tendency to be rude to judges, somewhat more noticeable in the TV version, led me to write to author Mortimer and ask him how much dramatic license he was taking. The answer: not much. In a 1981 letter, Mortimer wrote, "The truth is that brave advocates (and Rumpole is very brave) can almost get away with what he does, and I have got quite near it myself. You can't, of course, do as much in examination in chief, but in cross examination you can squeeze in a comment. As for being rude to the Judge, F. E. Smith (later Lord Birkenhead) was much ruder to Judges than ever Rumpole was."

280. The Trials of Rumpole. Harmondsworth, England: Penguin, 1979. New York: Penguin, 1981. (C)

The second gathering of six tales is not quite up to the standard of the first but still very entertaining. The prose is as well-wrought as ever, and only an occasional repetitiousness suggests a too quick execution. Best of the group is "Rumpole and the Fascist Beast," wherein right-winger Captain Rex Parkin is charged for inciting a crowd under the Race Relations Act, and an Indian barrister is welcomed (sort of) into Chambers as Rumpole's pupil. A key story in the saga is "Rumpole and the Age for Retirement," wherein pressure begins from family and colleagues to force the Old Bailey war-horse to retire to America. Meanwhile, the ungodly Timson clan (whose various misdeeds have helped to support the Rumpole family for many years) plot to farm out their past-his-prime family fence. The last line of the tale gives this second volume a memorable close. Other cases involve a vicar accused of shoplifting, murder in an acting troupe, and a schoolmaster accused of a sex offense.

281. Regina v. Rumpole.   London: Allen Lane, 1981.   As Rumpole for the Defence, New York: Penguin, 1984. (C)

The seven adventures here are better on average than the second collection if not up to the high level of the first. In some of them there is a closer approach to conventional detective fiction than in earlier stories. "Rumpole and the Expert Witness," about a doctor accused of wife murder, may be the best Rumpole tale of all from a standpoint of pure mystery story plotting.   "Rumpole and the Boat People" takes a better-worn path to its somewhat telegraphed final surprise. "Rumpole and the Dear Departed," concerning a will contest, describes his only appearance in the Chancery Division as well as his one recorded brush with the occult.   Among the other clients are a college gardener accused of blackmailing a professor and a policeman accused of soliciting a bribe.

282. Rumpole's Return.   Harmondsworth, England: Penguin, 1981. New York: Penguin, 1982. (B)

The first Rumpole novel begins in Florida, where he and She Who Must Be Obeyed have moved in with their professor-son and family. A long losing streak in the court of the obnoxious Judge Bullingham has nearly convinced Rumpole he is past it. However, he soon flees retirement to return to London and re-establish himself as a "squatter" in a Chambers that, assured he was gone for good, has made other arrangements. The episodic novel sees Rumpole in action twice, first (briefly) in an obscenity trial, where his high-minded freedom-of-speech defense leads to another loss, then to a murder trial in the court of that same Judge Bullingham with predictable results. Entertaining as Mortimer's writing is, this book does not entirely allow the reader to forget it is a novelized TV serial. On the whole, it is less impressive than the shorter Rumpole tales.

MURPHY, Warren B. (1933-   )

283. Leonardo's Law. New York: Carlyle, 1978. (B)

Here is a latter-day attempt to create a Great Detective
in the Holmes-Vance-Queen-Wolfe mold. Prof. David Vincent Leonardo, who teaches college mathematics but is
brilliant in numerous other fields, is requested by his
Watson (Lt. Jezail of the Walton, Connecticut, police,
whose name will be appreciated by Sherlockians) to look
into the locked room murder of mystery writer Barry
Dawson. The plot is ingenious if far-fetched, and Jezail,
who has a prejudice for every occasion, provides some of
the laugh-out-loud funniest narration in the mystery genre.
The courtroom sequence is an odd one: it takes place on a
Sunday, and although it is expected to be a routine
arraignment, all the prosecution witnesses are present and
ready when the defense attorney insists on a full hearing.
The hearing is basically used as a theatre for Leonardo's
summation.

NIVEN, Larry (1938-   )

284. The Patchwork Girl.   New York: Ace, 1980.   London: Orbit/Futura, 1982. (B)

This adventure of future detective Gil (the ARM) Hamilton is one of the rare science fiction novels with measurable courtroom action. It concerns the attempted murder of a delegate to a Lunar Law Conference being held on the moon. With one glass wall overlooking a garden, Niven's courtroom must be one of the most beautiful in fiction. Despite seven-foot "lunie" advocates on both sides, the court scenes are unremarkable as well as brief (about ten pages not counting illustrations). As a detective story, the novel is less successful than the novelette collection The Long ARM of Gil Hamilton (1976), acquaintance with which is desirable to understand some of the events and circumstances referred to here.

O

OLANDER, Joseph D.; and GREENBERG, Martin Harry, eds.

285. <u>Criminal Justice Through Science Fiction</u>. New York: New Viewpoints/Franklin Watts, 1977. (C)

To my knowledge, there is no anthology entirely devoted to science fiction courtroom stories. The four such tales included in this broader collection may give an idea of why: the pickings are pretty slim. Arthur Porges' "Guilty as Charged" is a stunt tale in which a 1956 time travel researcher is able to view a trial in 2183 Massachusetts. Since he gets picture only, no sound, a circumstance essential to Porges' twist, there is no Q-and-A. J. Francis McComas's "Shock Treatment" shows us a new (and highly simplified) court system developed by settlers on a distant planet. His basic message is opposition to capital punishment. Pg Wyal's "A Jury Not of Peers" also gives us a simplified system, one where a "judging machine" is employed. Alexander B. Malec's "10:01 a.m.," involving the hit-and-run killing of a child by two "null-vehicle" hot rodders, has the briefest trial of the lot. For s.f.novels with court scenes, see Harness, McMahon, and Niven.

OLECK, Howard (1911-)

286. <u>A Singular Fury</u>. Cleveland: World, 1968. (B)

The first hard-cover novel about TV lawyer Sam Benedict appeared several years after the program, based on the career of San Francisco attorney J. W. Ehrlich, left the air. Though the novel was called the first in a series, lawyer Oleck never produced a second. Ehrlich and Brad Williams (q.v.) co-authored two more hardbound Benedicts,

with much greater success. In the more important of the
two cases covered here, Sam (a much stodgier figure than
in other incarnations) defends Janet Porter, daughter of a
famous legal scholar, who is accused of bludgeoning her
law-professor husband to death with a bronze statue of
justice. The characters recite essays to each other; dream
sequences flashing back to Sam's service career are highly
intrusive; and the unintendedly risible courtroom climax
reminded me of a Nichols and May psychiatric parody.

OURSLER, Will (1913-)

287. The Trial of Vincent Doon. New York: Simon and Schuster,
     1941. London: Museum, 1943. (A)

Somewhat in the spirit of the recently-revived "crime file"
dossiers of the late thirties, this is a novel in the form of a
trial transcript. Artist Doon is accused in the Court of
General Sessions, County of New York, of the stabbing
murder of Edwin Hallett in the home of the wealthy Van
Eyck family. The victim was engaged to Betty Van Eyck,
whom Doon wanted to marry. The defenders are the firm
of Strong and Matthews. The latter serves as editor of the
transcript, filling in physical descriptions and personal
details in some Van Dine-ish footnotes. The account is
illustrated with line drawings of witnesses and photographs
of evidence. Beyond the gimmick, the novel is a traditional closed-circle whodunit. Some liberties are taken
with procedure to accommodate the plot: Strong is allowed
to bring in on cross-examination matters not covered on
direct, and he tries to cast suspicion on each prosecution
witness in turn. At one point, a police witness leaves the
stand to pursue a young woman who has fled the courtroom, returning later to report on his pursuit as part of
cross examination. All in all, an enjoyable experiment.
(The novel's sequel, the 1942 Folio on Florence White, is
also in documentary format from the Strong and Matthews
files but includes only about six pages of actual courtroom
action.)

PALMER, Stuart (1905-1968)

288. The Penguin Pool Murder. New York: Brentano's, 1931. London: Long, 1932. (B)

The first novel about schoolteacher-sleuth Hildegarde Withers, concerning a hatpin murder in the New York Aquarium's penguin enclosure, has only a very brief courtroom scene in the penultimate chapter. But the denouement, with Miss Withers on the witness stand, is sufficiently unusual in fictional trial annals to demand inclusion here. (No more can be said.)

PHILLIPS, Steven

289. Civil Actions. Garden City, NY: Doubleday, 1983. (B)

Four former law school classmates are involved in different capacities in a controversial case: a Vietnam veteran wants to collect damages from the Army for allegedly giving him pills (ostensibly to prevent tropical diseases) that caused his terminal cancer. After introducing an interesting case, Phillips backtracks to law school days and follows the careers of his four main characters up to the present. The disappointingly sparse trial action (totalling less than twenty pages) includes a law school moot court sequence, oral arguments on the right of the plaintiff to sue the Army in a Federal court, the taking of the dying plaintiff's deposition, and (very briefly) a criminal trial of one of the principals at the end of the book. Though the characters are not terribly striking, the background is knowledgeable, and the total effect is a readable legal novel that still was not all it could have been.

PHILLPOTTS, Eden (1862-1960)

290. The Jury.   London: Hutchinson; New York: Macmillan,
     1927. (A)

     Phillpotts' novel was the first to concentrate its action in
     the jury room, as a panel of ten men and two women
     consider the evidence against Lady Heron, a Spanish fenc-
     ing champion accused of the stabbing murder of her
     husband Sir Philip. It is a small-town case in Redchester
     Assize Court, and many of the jurors already know each
     other and some of the parties involved. The differences
     from contemporary practice are striking: the jurors are
     locked up in a very narrow and unpleasant room and denied
     food until a verdict is reached. They talk among them-
     selves in groups of two or three rather than assuring that
     everyone hears all deliberations. There is some sly satire in
     the efforts of the majority to convince the single hold-out
     for acquittal. They invoke God and when that fails resort
     to less relevant argument. When convinced, most of the
     jurors' conversation gets off the case and on to other
     matters. They make no attempt to reach a real solution
     like the characters in Reginald Rose's TV play "Twelve
     Angry Men" or in George Goodchild and Bechhofer Roberts'
     The Jury Disagree (q.v.). In the end, the truth of the
     matter is presented, but ultimately this strongly written
     and characterized novel belongs more with Phillpotts'
     mainstream fiction than with his detective stories.

POST, Melville Davisson (1871-1930)

291. The Strange Schemes of Randolph Mason.   New York:
     Putnam, 1896. (C)

     Post practiced law in West Virginia, and many of his short
     stories turn on legal points. His first collection contains
     seven stories about the villainous lawyer (later to reform
     somewhat) who finds loopholes in the law to help his clients
     defeat justice. The courtroom action, present in only two
     of the longer tales ("The Corpus Delicti" and "The Men of
     the Jimmy"), is made up of speechifying by counsel and
     judge rather than Q-and-A. Purely as works of fiction,
     these floridly-written tales are less successful than much
     of Post's later work, particularly the Uncle Abner stories
     (of which only the classic "Naboth's Vineyard" involves a

trial), but the explorations of legal technicalities of the time are fascinating.

In an irony pointed out by Ellery Queen, the surname of Post's "criminal" lawyer was the same as that of Perry Mason, the ultimate good-guy lawyer created by Erle Stanley Gardner nearly forty years later. Squire Hezekiah Mason, another villainous character, is the courtroom adversary of Mr. Tutt in some of Arthur Train's short stories. Why so many fictional attorneys named Mason? Because the doings of lawyers are sometimes as mysterious and impenetrable to the layperson as the rites of Free-masons?

292. The Man of Last Resort; or The Clients of Randolph Mason. New York: Putnam, 1897. (C)

The sub-title is apt, for "criminal" lawyer Mason's in-person appearances in this second collection are very brief indeed. In the first story, "The Governor's Machine," a tale as dry as a law report with only a judge's address in the courtroom scene, Mason does all his work from off-stage. He fails to appear at all in the last of the five stories, "The People Against Carper," which includes a shock ending possibly intended to appease those who doubted the ethics or morality of Post's approach to exposing loopholes in the law. "Carper" begins with a brief courtroom sequence. The only other story with trial action is "Once in Jeo-pardy," involving murder and insurance fraud and hinging on a rather obvious point to most experienced readers of legal fiction. Again, adversarial thrust-and-parry is mostly absent in a group of stories less enthralling than the first Mason volume.

293. The Corrector of Destinies. New York: Clode, 1908. (C)

In the third volume, we see more of Mason, no longer a scoundrel but now obsessed with rooting out injustice. Only two of the thirteen tales have trial scenes: "The District-Attorney," the rather dry account of a techni-cality in a bank fraud case; and "The Virgin of the Mountain," about the murder trial of an Italian Marquis for killing an art collector, an overblown story turning on a simple point regarding dying declarations.

294. The Silent Witness. New York: Farrar and Rinehart, 1929.
(C)

The thirteen tales of the flamboyant Colonel Braxton, a
much more attractive advocate than Randolph Mason, are
set in nineteenth-century Virginia and are very similar in
flavor to the Uncle Abner series. The title refers to
physical evidence presented by Braxton, who customarily
astounds the court by the announcement that he will call
no witnesses. A recurring theme is the contention that a
Virginia lawyer of the time needed to know his Bible, the
one book the common people were familiar with, as well as
his Blackstone. The first story, "The Metal Box," gives a
prime example of the seemingly irrelevant question on
cross-examination that proves central to Braxton's case in
a will contest-- something about plowing fields. Other
tales with court action include "The Survivor," "The Cross-
Examination," "The Guilty Man," "The Mark on the Window," "The Mute Voices," and "The Leading Case." As
legal essays, they are less interesting than the Randolph
Mason stories, but as courtroom drama they are superior.

POSTGATE, Raymond (1896-1971)

295. Verdict of Twelve. London: Collins; Garden City, NY:
Doubleday, Doran, 1940. (¼)

Here is one of the best and most famous of that group of
trial books (including among others Gerald Bullett's The
Jury, Eden Phillpotts' The Jury, George Goodchild and
Bechhofer Roberts' The Jury Disagree, Michael Underwood's Hand of Fate, Harvey Jacobs' The Juror, and John
Wainwright's The Jury People, qqv.) that emphasize the
viewpoint of the jurors and their deliberations. We open
with the Clerk of Assize swearing them in, with lengthy
flashbacks establishing the background of each. There
follows a section about the case to be tried: Rosalie van
Beer is accused of the poison murder of a child, her nephew
Philip Arkwright. The jurors' reactions are recorded
throughout a 40-page description of the trial proper. During the section on their deliberations, the jurors' minds are
likened to a dial of a car's dashboard, with a quivering
needle registering negative or positive more or less deci-
sively. Following the verdict, Postgate reveals the truth in
a chilling conclusion.

PRESCOT, Julian, pseudonym of John Budd

296. Case for Court. London: Barker, 1964. (¾)

Narrator Prescot tells of the feud of two solicitors in a
small English city: Weld, the young and capable newcomer,
and Major Matheson, the self-important, well-entrenched
older advocate. The novel gives a fascinating picture of
English legal life and a telling commentary on contrasting
courtroom styles, demonstrating how flamboyant inepti-
tude can impress lay observers (including members of the
press) more than quiet competence. Five court proceedings are visited, including a licensing hearing, an accusation of "sheep-worrying" against an Alsatian dog, a larceny
charge against a mentally disturbed poison pen writer, a
jewelry store robbery-with-violence case against a long-
time felon, and the climactic murder case, in which Mr.
and Mrs. Sorensen are accused of killing for gain the
wealthy and elderly Mrs. Skeet. Matheson and Weld are
ostensibly on the same side, representing the husband and
wife respectively, but they go about their tasks quite
differently. The conclusion is genuinely surprising and
truer to real life than to fictional formula.

Prescot, whose novels have never been published in the
U.S., offers more careful carpentry than soaring brilliance.
There are traces of padding, and the dialogue suggests
expository prose more than speech. He will certainly
please hard-core legal buffs, but he is less likely to win
non-buff readers than writers like Henry Cecil or Roderic
Jeffries (q.q.v.). Other titles, all published by Barker,
include Both Sides of the Case (1958), The Case Continued,
(1959), Case Proceeding (1960), Case for the Accused
(1961), Case for Trial (1962), Case for Hearing (1963), and
The Case Re-Opened (1965).

Q

QUEEN, Ellery (pseudonym of Frederic Dannay, 1905-1982, and Manfred B. Lee, 1905-1971)

297. Halfway House. New York: Stokes; London: Gollancz, 1936. (B)

Joseph Kent Gimball led a double life, maintaining households under his own name in New York and as Joseph Wilson in Philadelphia, using a house in Trenton, New Jersey, to change identities. He is found dead there, stabbed with a paper-cutter, and his Philadelphia wife Lucy is tried for the crime in the Mercer County Courthouse midway through this superlative novel from the Golden Age of detective fiction. When Ellery Queen's testimony fails to turn the tide for the defense. she is found guilty, and Ellery must find the real killer to exonerate her. The 50+ pages of trial, partly told through press accounts from various papers, are dramatic and enthralling. The Queen team were very good at witness-stand give-and-take.

Though the trials in the Queen novels rarely contain procedural errors obvious to the lay reader, Queen expert (and law professor) Francis M. Nevins, Jr., writes in The Sound of Detection: Ellery Queen's Adventures in Radio (Brownstone Books, 1983) that "Fred and Manny were never terribly convincing when they introduced elements from the world of law and lawyers." He cites as a particularly horrible example the radio play, "The Meanest Man in the World" (Ellery Queen's Mystery Magazine, July 1942), which "opens with the kind of situation that makes so many mysteries laughable to lawyers: Ellery and Nikki (Porter, his secretary) are empaneled side by side as jurors in the same murder trial....Ellery reads the evidence differently, jumps out of the jury box, cross-examines witnesses himself, and extracts a confession in open court from the real murderer."

298.   Calamity Town. Boston: Little, Brown; London: Gollancz, 1942. (B)

This is one of the best Queens and thus an automatic inclusion on any list of detective novel cornerstones. All mystery fiction logic tells us that Jim Haight, accused of the murder of his sister via a poisoned drink apparently intended for his wife, must be innocent, yet he faces one of the most damning circumstantial cases imaginable. This was the first of Queen's Wrightsville novels, and the small New England town comes to life. The tale is explicitly set in the 1940-41 period, before America's entry into the war, with references to the draft lottery and Roosevelt's election to a third term. Jim's trial occupies some fifty pages and is expertly done, with Ellery's appearance as a witness particularly interesting. (One question, though: would the judge wait until mid-trial to begin admonishing the jury not to discuss the case at the end of each session?)

299.   The Glass Village. Boston: Little, Brown; London: Gollancz, 1954. (¾)

This celebrated novel, an impassioned and courageous plea against the anti-Communist witch hunt of the early fifties as well as an excellent formal detective story, contains Queen's longest, best, and (paradoxically) worst trial. Aunt Fanny Adams, an elderly painter along the lines of Grandma Moses, is the most famous and beloved citizen of the New England village of Shinn Corners. When she is beaten to death with a poker, tramp Josef Kowalczyk is accused by a citizenry hungry for blood. To avert lynch justice, Judge Shinn must preside over a phony trial where everything is intentionally done wrong, certain of reversal but still convincing enough to satisfy First Selectman Hube Hemus, leader of the angry townspeople. Beginning the case on the desired wrong foot, a jury of biassed, unqualified people, many of whom are also witnesses in the case, is empanelled. The village is so small, there are still not enough to make up the required twelve, and the judge's visiting nephew, Korean War veteran Johnny Shinn, is added. This was one of the few hardcover Queen novels in which Ellery the character does not appear.

300. The Fourth Side of the Triangle.   New York: Random
     House; London: Gollancz, 1965. (B)

     This latter-day Queen novel verges on self-parody, inclu-
     ding the kind of contrived plot twists Dannay and Lee
     might have come up with for their "Author! Author!" radio
     show of the late thirties. Still, it's a great deal of fun and
     includes technical trickery of a sort few authors were
     attempting at the time it was published. There are two
     trials in the murder of a fashion designer, as millionaire
     Ashton McKell and his socialite wife Lutetia are accused in
     their turn. Son Dane is subsequently arrested, but his trial
     is not described. The courtroom action is rather brief and
     less notable than in other Queen novels. Ellery (laid up
     from a skiing accident) is offstage much of the time.

301. Face to Face. New York: New American Library; London:
     Gollancz, 1967. (B)

     In the briefest courtroom scene in a Queen novel (about ten
     pages), Lorette Spanier is tried for the murder of thirties
     singing star Gloria Guild. Most of the space is taken with a
     colorful defense witness who establishes her alibi. Overall,
     this is one of the strongest of the later EQ efforts.

(as Barnaby Ross)

302. The Tragedy of X.   New York: Viking; London: Cassell,
     1932. (B)

     The first of four novels about Drury Lane, a deaf retired
     actor based on the famous portrayer of Sherlock Holmes,
     William Gillette, is one of the finest pure detective novels
     of the thirties. It also contains the first Queen courtroom
     scene under any byline. In New York's Criminal Courts
     Building, stockbroker John O. DeWitt is tried before the
     aptly-named Judge Grimm for the murder of Charles Wood,
     killed when thrown from a ferry. (This is a secondary
     crime, the novel's first and main murder being that of
     Harley Longstreet, poisoned while riding a streetcar.) The
     successful case for the defense is presented in some fifteen
     pages of interesting action.   District Attorney Bruno
     expresses astonishment that the defense lawyer puts his
     client on the stand, giving the prosecution a chance for
     cross-examination, but the reader is only told that Bruno
     "viciously assailed" DeWitt, with none of that part of the

testimony quoted. A later Lane novel, <u>The Tragedy of Z</u> (1933), includes a mostly-summarized trial of only about seven pages.

R

REED, Barry (1927-)

303. <u>The Verdict</u>. New York: Simon and Schuster, 1980. London: Granada, 1982. (¼)

There is some splendid courtroom give-and-take in this account of a maverick Boston lawyer taking on the establishment in a massive medical malpractice suit. The author, himself a trial lawyer specializing in legal-medical cases, does not avoid the clichés of lawyer fiction but gives them a solid enough undergirding to sustain credibility. The odd romance between hero Frank Galvin and a double-agent female lawyer for the other side is far less convincing and interesting than the case. Anyone who saw the somewhat disappointing film version with Paul Newman should read the novel to find out what was really going on.

REED, David V., pseudonym of David Vern (1924-)

304. <u>I Thought I'd Die</u>. New York: Green Dragon, 1946. (B)

This documentary psychological novel, which is definitely a detective story and may or may not be science fiction, includes excerpts (not always in order) from the transcript of Elliot Hammond's trial for the mutilation-murder of three women. Hammond's diary blames the deaths on a literature-quoting metal swamp creature, who lives in a scrapyard occupied by Hammond's friend, writer Jim Shilling. The trial (about 35 scattered pages) is used as a vehicle for exposition and theorizing. Though this is a literate and ambitious novel, it gives the reader too little to hang onto in the way of character and incident and is ultimately very hard going. There's a nice reference for

mystery fans, though, when author Reed (himself a character) at one point consults the Continental Detective Agency! The novel was reprinted under the lurid title (with
cover to match) of The Thing That Made Love (Unibook,
1951). The author's Murder in Space (New York: Galaxy,
1954) qualifies as a science fictional trial mystery.

RICHLER, Mordecai (1931-   )

305. St. Urbain's Horseman. London: Weidenfeld and Nicolson;
New York: Knopf, 1971. (B)

Canadian film and TV director Jake Hersh is the protagonist of this well-written and thought-provoking satirical
novel. Following a childhood in Montreal's Jewish community, he migrates to London, marries, and is phenomenally
successful. But he seems determined to undermine his
success by his association with sleazy accountant Harry
Stein and his search for his cousin Joey, the symbolic
horseman of the title. Near the end of the book, he is on
trial with Stein in the Old Bailey on charges of aiding and
abetting sodomy, indecent assault, and possession of canna-
bis. The supposed victim is German au pair girl Ingrid
Loeber. The 24-page trial is effective enough, though not
one of the best parts of the novel. The book was inevitably
compared to Philip Roth's Portnoy's Complaint and would
offend and outrage and delight some of the same readers.

RINEHART, Mary Roberts (1876-1958)

306. The Case of Jennie Brice. Indianapolis: Bobbs-Merrill,
1913. London: Hodder and Stoughton, 1919. (B)

Narrator Elizabeth Pitman, who runs a theatrical boarding
house in Pittsburgh, becomes involved in the case of Philip
Ladley, accused of the murder of his wife, actress Jennie
Brice, whose body may have been the one washed ashore
during a flood. The court action is efficient enough but
less memorable than the vividly described flood.

ROBERTS, Bechhofer

See GOODCHILD, George

ROGERS, Garet

307. <u>Scandal in Eden</u>. New York: Dial, 1963. London: Putnam, 1964. (B)

Though set slightly later in time (around 1930) and in Los Angeles rather than San Francisco, the events of this novel are obviously based on the Fatty Arbuckle case. Motion picture comic Archibald Forbes (the Feeb), an obnoxious figure guilty or innocent, is accused of raping and causing the death of Muffin Naismith. Drunken lawyer Mark D'Andor defends, though Muffin was once his mistress. An unpleasant, exploitative book that adds to the probably unjust vilification of Arbuckle, this longish novel nevertheless offers some seventy pages of enthralling courtroom combat, with prosecutor T. Amos Slake matching D'Andor for flamboyance. Besides the Feeb's trial, there is a preliminary hearing on Dr. Snowden, a black-passing-for-white initially accused of the murder-by-abortion of Muffin.

ROLLS, Anthony

See VULLIAMY, C. E.

ROSCOE, Theodore

308. <u>Only in New England</u>. New York: Scribners, 1959. (B)

The author claims this is a fictionalization of a real (but heavily disguised) turn-of-the-century case. Roscoe is his own first-person hero, doing research in the town of Quahog Point into the murder (by clubbing with a bag of shot) of family patriarch Abby Bridewell. The accused is her son Earnest, a State Senator in an unnamed New England state who was always at odds with the victim over money. The novel is a deliberate period piece, set in 1911 and rich in details of everyday life, including many references to the books, music, and amusements of the day. The style is somewhat similar to that employed years later by Jack Finney in the non-fiction <u>Forgotten News</u>. In a good period trial of 30+ pages, some of the testimony is identified in footnotes as coming verbatim from the transcript of the real case, and many of these quotes are infelicitous and awkward enough to be real. The style gets a bit cute at times, and the solution in the last chapter is something of a letdown, albeit ingenious. The side issues are more interesting than the central case, but this is a highly readable and unusual fact-fiction hybrid.

309. To Live and Die in Dixie. New York: Scribners, 1961. (B)

The second of Roscoe's gaslight murder mysteries is every bit as captivating in its nostalgia and social history as its predecessor, as well as being a better detective story and including a lengthier (64 pages) and more interesting trial. We begin in the present, with New York journalist Sherman Grant reluctantly accepting his editor's assignment to investigate a 1902 case in Amityburg, Virginia: the trial of wide-ranging ladies' man Wade B. Brodie, a model of Victorian hypocrisy, for the murder of his wife Effie May Brodie, battered with an Indian club and dumped in a boiling bath. There is less shifting back and forth in time, however, with only the prologue and last section concerning Grant. There's a beautiful bit on the swearing in of a "Free Thinker" witness, presumed to be an atheist.

ROSS, Barnaby

See QUEEN, Ellery

ROTHBLATT, Henry

See FISH, Robert L.; MOORE, Robin

SAYERS, Dorothy L. (1893-1957)

310. Clouds of Witness. London: Unwin, 1926. New York: Dial, 1927. (B)

The Duke of Denver is accused of the murder of his sister's fiancé, Denis Cathcart. The Duke's brother, Lord Peter Wimsey, in the second venture of his illustrious career, searches desperately for evidence that will permit the brilliant advocate Sir Impey Biggs to get the Duke off in a colorful trial before the House of Lords. Though Sayers writes entertainingly (when not trying to reproduce dialect), this is neither one of the most notable fictional trials nor (with its inevitably disappointing solution) one of the better Wimsey novels.

311. Strong Poison. London: Gollancz; New York: Brewer and Warren, 1930. (B)

This novel is a landmark in detective fiction, describing the first meeting of gentleman-detective Lord Peter Wimsey and mystery writer Harriet Vane, on trial for the murder of her lover, Philip Boyes. Principal courtroom interest comes in the first two chapters, where Sayers lays out the basic case against Harriet via a very well-wrought charge to the jury by the presiding judge. When a hung jury necessitates a new trial, Lord Peter swings into action. Thanks to his efforts, the new trial is brief to the vanishing point.

SHERRY, Edna (?-1967)

312. Call the Witness. New York: Dodd, Mead, 1961. London:

Hodder and Stoughton, 1962. (¼)

Britain's Julia Wallace case is updated and set in a small (and very insular) American city where outsider-lawyer Bartley French is accused of the murder of his socially prominent wife. Included is that staple of trial fiction: the prosecutor with his eye on the governor's mansion. The courtroom action is capably done, with some of the testimony borrowed from the Wallace case, and the solution is a clever one. There seems to be too big a hole in the killer's elaborate plan, though, one that is not discovered sooner only through extremely fortuitous circumstances.

SIMPSON, Helen

See DANE, Clemence

SMITH, H(arry) Allen

313. Rhubarb. Garden City, NY: Doubleday, 1946. (B)

The title character is a cat who inherits the New York Loons baseball team from his eccentric millionaire owner, Thad Banner. The deceased's daughter Myra Tatlock challenges the will, thus a burlesque trial in Surrogate's Court. Adversarial insults between opposing lawyers Orlando Dill and P. Duncan Munk fly freely to the delight of Judge Phidias Loudermilk, an odd jurist whose favorite pastime is translating Faith Baldwin novels into Greek. Team manager Len Stickles, formerly a great southpaw pitcher, insists on swearing with his left hand. Smith provides many laughs and absolutely no semblance of accurate procedure. Son of Rhubarb (1967) also logs some court time.

SMITH, Kay Nolte (1932-   )

314. The Watcher. New York: Coward, McCann, and Geoghegan, 1980. London: Gollancz, 1981. (B)

This Edgar-winning first novel is an absorbing though somewhat unbelievable tale. The murder victim is Dr. Martin Granger, think-tank social scientist who gets his

kicks by derailing people from their chosen life's work.
The defendant is a journalist, the wife of one of Granger's
subjects, who is anxious to expose him. Also involved is an
old flame of the defendant, a cop with a law degree. This
is a message novel, and like most such it entails some card
stacking. Some of the courtroom dramatics are unlikely,
and a certain humorlessness detracts from the book's
effectiveness. The finale is a decidedly soggy one. Still,
interest and readability are not in question.

SMITH, Edgar (1934-   )

315. A Reasonable Doubt.   New York: Coward-McCann, 1970.
     (¼)

The author was a Death Row convict whose case for
freedom, told in his non-fiction book Brief Against Death
(1968), was championed by William F. Buckley, Jr., among
others. His one novel displays two attributes: 1) considerable self-taught legal knowledge, and 2) a remarkable lack
of bitterness (from one in his position) about the judicial
process. The ending is somewhat abrupt and unsatisfactory. Two young men are accused of the rape-murder of a
teenage girl in a small New Jersey town.

SNOW, C(harles) P(ercy) (1905-1980)

316. Strangers and Brothers.   London: Faber, 1940.   New York:
     Macmillan, 1958.   (B)

In the first (and title) novel of Snow's justly famous eleven-
book sequence on life in twentieth-century Britain, George
Passant, charismatic guru of a group of young free-think-
ers, is tried along with two of his followers, Olive Calvert
and Jack Cotery, on charges of conspiracy to defraud and
obtaining money under false pretenses in seeking investors
in the Passant group's farm and advertising agency. The
events take place in the unnamed provincial town where
series protagonist Lewis Eliot grew up. Barrister Eliot
defends his old friend Passant in tandem with Herbert
Getliffe, whose closing speech for the defense is an especially effective one, though disagreeable to Passant.
Major events of the book take place in 1929 and 1930.

317. <u>The Sleep of Reason</u>. London: Macmillan, 1968. New
York: Scribners, 1969. (B)

In 1963-64, Eliot returns to the provincial town for another
trial, this time as an observer, the role he usually played in
the series. Cora Ross (niece of George Passant) and Kitty
Pateman are accused of the torture-murder of eight-year-
old Eric Mawby, and their attorneys offer a diminished-
responsibility defense. The crime is based on the notorious
Moors Murders, which Snow's wife, Pamela Hansford Johnson, discussed non-fictionally in <u>On Iniquity</u> (1967). Snow's
trial scenes are extremely effective. Eliot reflects on
changing styles in advocacy since his own days at the Bar
in the twenties and thirties. (Another excellent novel from
the sequence, 1960's <u>The Affair</u>, includes an academic trial
before the Court of Seniors in Eliot's college, technically
disqualified for our purposes here.)

SOLMSSEN, Arthur R. G.

318. <u>Rittenhouse Square</u>. Boston: Little, Brown, 1968. London:
Hodder and Stoughton, 1969. (B)

Young Philadelphia lawyer Ben Butler is volunteered by his
prestigious firm to spend a month in the Public Defender's
office, a month that causes him to question the course of
his career. The very effective 32-page account of his first
jury case, involving the alleged theft by a maid of a pricey
call girl's diamonds, is the novel's principal courtroom
action. This is a very pleasant and readable novel of the
legal life which contrasts criminal and corporation law
tellingly.

SPARK, Muriel (1918-)

319. <u>The Bachelors</u>. London: Macmillan, 1960. Philadelphia:
Lippincott, 1961. (B)

Comic novel of a group of London bachelors, culminating in
the forgery trial of phony medium (and potential murderer)
Patrick Seton. Central character is graphologist Ronald
Bridges, one of whose epileptic seizures is mistaken for the
beginning of a psychic trance. Spark's wit is sharp and
malicious, and in the 25-page trial, justice is entertainingly
done.

STERN, Richard Martin (1915-   )

320. The Will. Garden City, NY: Doubleday; London: Secker and Warburg, 1976. (B)

This is the semi-saga of a family will contest that is made to order for a TV miniseries. There is plenty of conflict (L.A. vs. San Francisco; youth vs. middle age), and much inside information on the wine, aircraft, and banking businesses. The two sides are presented with almost equal sympathy, a rarity in fictional trials, where the reader is usually told pretty clearly whom to root for. (Is it naive to believe that at least some of the jurors would observe the judge's charge not to discuss the case? Stern gives the impression that none do.)

STRANGE, John Stephen, pseudonym of Dorothy Stockbridge Tillett (1896-   )

321. All Men Are Liars. Garden City, NY: Doubleday/Crime Club, 1948. As Come to Judgment, London: Collins, 1949. (¼)

Strange, whose novelistic career extended from 1928 (with formal detective novels typical of the time) all the way to 1976, developed a trial specialty midway in her career and wrote some extremely effective courtroom scenes. Here dying garage owner Andy Newcomb names playboy Lester Ward as his killer, and eyewitness testimony backs up the ID. Needless to say, things are not what they seem, and Strange's series cop George Honegger sorts matters out. The defense lawyer takes exception to the judge's rulings (on rather routine matters) at an almost record clip, and Gardner's three I's make an appearance.

322. Reasonable Doubt. Garden City, NY: Doubleday/Crime Club; London: Collins, 1951. (¼)

Children's book author-illustrator Ruth Purdy is tried for the murder by nicotine poisoning of her husband. This belongs to that small group of books in which the trial is the initial incident rather than the climax. Ruth's acquittal has a shadow on it. Lawyer Arnold Bricker marries the defendant and tries to forget the case, but he gets repeated reminders. An emotional mystery with a mood similar to that of Vera Caspary's Laura, this has a neat plot, but the "boy-loses-girl" section is very hard to take.

323. Let the Dead Past. Garden City, NY: Doubleday/Crime Club, 1953. As Dead End, London: Collins, 1953. (A)

This novel has Strange's most extensive trial action, with all but about forty pages taking place in court. The viewpoint character is Judge Bardoley, who knew and once loved the defendant (many-times-married Valentina Abbott, a Frenchwoman accused of killing her ex-husband seventeen years before the trial). For some reason, the judge, emotionally numb from the recent death of his wife, does not choose to disqualify himself. The very capably described trial has a minimum of hokey dramatics until the likely-unique climax, an audacious stunt even if it doesn't quite come off.

SYMONS, Julian (1912-   )

324. The Progress of a Crime. London: Collins; New York: Harper, 1960. (B)

A sharp observer of post-World War II British life, Symons also does a very good job of depicting and explicating the judicial process. Young small-town reporter Hugh Bennett investigates the Guy Fawkes Night stabbing of a tavern-keeper, seemingly the work of a motorcycle gang the dead man had crossed. Two members of the gang, John Garney and Leslie Winter (with whose sister Hugh has become romantically involved) are charged with the crime in Assize Court. Their trial covers some 35 pages of realistic give-and-take. A fine novel from the middle period of Symons' distinguished career, this is more a straight crime-suspense novel than a mystery or detective story.

325. The End of Solomon Grundy. London: Collins; New York: Harper, 1964. (¼)

Some of the inhabitants of the Dells, a suburban London community, react badly to the presence in their midst of a new black neighbor, Tony Kabanga-- their excuses (lowering of property values and all that sort of thing) are quite familiar to Americans. Cartoonist Grundy is tried in the Old Bailey for the strangulation murder of Sylvia Gresham, a white woman who was Kabanga's mistress. The trial, partly in transcript form, is Symons' most extensive and very effectively done. The author's view of his country's race relations, a subject few British writers were comfortable with even a decade later, is especially interesting.

326. The Man Whose Dreams Came True. London: Collins, 1968. New York: Harper, 1969. (B)

Symons tells the story of Tony Jones, a.k.a. Scott-Williams and Blain-Truscott, a charming roulette-playing rogue who is sucked into a James M. Cain situation, British-style. Tony's lover, Jenny Foster, expounds a plot to kill her wealthy but useless husband Eversley and flee to Venezuela with Tony. But a doublecrossed Tony is charged with the crime in Magistrate's Court and the Old Bailey. Not the author's best book but readable as ever.

327. The Blackheath Poisonings. London: Collins; New York: Harper, 1978. (B)

In the style of a true crime commentator, Symons tells of an upper-class Victorian murder case involving two households in Blackheath. Though several mysterious deaths take place, Isabel Collard can be tried for only one, the arsenic poisoning of Roger Vandervent. The thirty pages of trial action are excellent, as are the fine sense of period, the expert characterization, and a cunningly clued fair-play puzzle.

328. Sweet Adelaide. London: Collins; New York: Harper, 1980. (B)

Continuing in his new historical vein, Symons fictionalizes the life of Adelaide Bartlett, tried in the Old Bailey in 1866 for the chloroform poisoning of her grocer husband George. The trial action, which comes directly from transcripts and contemporary accounts with only the details of jury deliberation imaginary, is mostly summarized in some seventeen pages. Symons is able to bring the historical figures to life as characters and offers a credible theory about how and by whom the crime was committed. The postscript, in which Symons spells out exactly what is real and what invented in the novel, should be obligatory for all writers of "faction."

TEY, Josephine, pseudonym of Elizabeth Mackintosh (1897-1952)

329. The Franchise Affair. London: Davies, 1948. New York: Macmillan, 1949. (B)

In her most famous novel aside from The Daughter of Time, Tey updates the circumstances of the eighteenth-century Elizabeth Canning case. In Norton Assize Court, Marion Sharpe and her mother, inhabitants of the Milford house known as the Franchise, are accused of the kidnapping and imprisonment of fifteen-year-old Betty Kane. Their champion is solicitor Robert Blair, with Tey's series sleuth Alan Grant playing a secondary role. The twenty pages of courtroom give-and-take are presented with a dramatist's flair.

THAYER, Lee (1874-1973)

330. The Prisoner Pleads "Not Guilty". New York: Dodd, Mead, 1953. London: Hurst, 1954. (¼)

American private investigator Peter Clancy and his quasi-Wodehousian valet Wiggar find the drowned body of "(i)nfernal bounder" and "insufferable cad" Edward Graham while vacationing at a Bermuda resort hotel. The dead man proves to be a victim of murder by croquet mallet. Unjustly accused American visitor Dennis Macilroy, a rival for the affections of Irish hotel hostess Kerry Killeen, goes on trial before the Supreme Court at about the halfway point of the novel. The trial runs its full course, complete with closing arguments, judge's charge, and verdict, over most of the next hundred pages. Clancy presents his solution after the trial is done, setting the stage for a melodramatic action denouement typical of the author.

Trial tactics and counsel-witness exchanges, competent but unscintillating, take second place to atmosphere and emotion here. "What was freedom to a man, however innocent, while the black cloud of suspicion would now, and perhaps forever, cloud his horizon?" (p. 220) Though not a high priority for trial buffs, this is a better than average example of Thayer's florid but enjoyable old-fashioned detective novels, which she continued to produce into her nineties, setting a longevity record for mystery writers.

THOMPSON, Gene (1924-   )

331. Lupe. New York: Random House, 1977. London: Raven, 1978. (¾)

Thompson combines two popular genres to create an occult courtroom novel, describing a witchcraft trial in the incongruous atmosphere of contemporary San Francisco. About fifty pages of trial scenes are effectively done, and the fusion proves much more successful than Frank De Felitta's reincarnation case in Audrey Rose (q.v.). Buffs may regret, though, that the odd case is not allowed to finish.

THOMPSON, Thomas (1934-1982)

332. Celebrity. Garden City, NY: Doubleday; London: Lane, 1982. (B)

A trio of Fort Worth high school seniors who call themselves the Three Princes are involved in the possible rape-murder of a teenage girl, cover it up, and share a guilty secret for the next quarter century. Each of them becomes famous, Mack Crawford as an athlete and actor, Kleber Cantrell as a journalist, and finally T. J. Luther, the villain of the piece and least interesting of the three until he achieves his own brand of celebrity in a surprising occupation that could not be more ironic. The narrative jumps around considerably in time between 1950 (and occasionally earlier) and the 1970's. The main present-day character is D.A. Calvin Sledge, building a case though for a long time the reader has no idea for what against whom. Since the secret of what is going on is so central to the story, I should only reveal that the novel does climax in a murder trial with Sledge opposing defense ace Otto Leo in the court of Judge Carlos Mustardseed. One of the highlights of the brief but expertly described trial (covering only about 44 of the novel's 560 pages) comes during jury selection, when the judge pulls the plug on the defense computer.

The book starts and finishes strong, with a fairly foreshadowed shock ending to the trial and a Hollywood ending for the novel. There is only a slight sag in the middle. Like many blockbusters, it is far too long and would be more effective at about two thirds the length. There are too many sidetrips to events of the time (for example, the J.F.K. assassination) that have little bearing on the story. On balance, though, this is a fine novel. Thompson's singing prose puts him above the level of most best seller writers.

TOUSTER, Irwin, and CURTIS, Richard

333. The Perez Arson Mystery. New York: Dial, 1972. (B)

Set in a suburban city in an unspecified state, this is a possibly-unique courtroom juvenile, designed to educate about the workings of the criminal justice system. Unpopular Puerto Rican Antonio Perez is accused of torching his former employer's store, partly on the testimony of teen-age science whiz Vernon Stevenson. The extent to which Vernon and two friends are allowed to get involved in the case is unlikely but essential to the story. The trial action is well done, if sometimes necessarily over-simplified-- the defense lawyer is allowed to testify and argue her case a little bit too much in questioning. The novel is basically a success, including some good low-key humor. The tone of the book is very liberal and quite different from the kind of book that might find favor in the current climate.

TRAIN, Arthur (1875-1945)

334. McAllister and his Double. New York: Scribner's; London: Newnes, 1905. (C)

Train's first book contains eleven short stories, the first

seven about New York clubman "Chubby" McAllister, an unsympathetic character who believes "(o)ur tenements are all right and so are our prisons," until he spends a night in the Tombs when mistaken for the notorious Fatty Welch. In "McAllister's Christmas," the first story in the book, he gets a detailed introduction to the lot of a suspected felon (a fascinating depiction of the course of criminal justice of the time), including an arraignment in police court. The final four tales-- "The Jailbird," "The Course of Justice," "The Maximilian Diamond," and "Extradition"-- concern young assistant D.A. John Dockbridge, and include most of the volume's trial action. Most interesting of the four is "Extradition," involving a clash of U.S. and Canadian law and including a court session in a railway baggage car-- the ending, though, takes some swallowing. Train was already an entertaining writer, though not as skilled as he would be when he embarked on the Mr. Tutt series years later.

335. The Confessions of Artemas Quibble. New York: Scribner's, 1911. (B)

This fictional autobiography, a nearly definitive account of the shyster at work, has been listed as a short story collection but is better categorized as an episodic novel. There is little court action save for two scenes totalling about ten pages: early in the book when thoroughly amoral narrator Quibble sees "criminal" lawyer Gottleib in action swindling a friend and decides to take up the law profession himself ("My objects were practical-- my ambition to get the largest financial return consonant with the least amount of work") and late in the book when the firm of Gottleib and Quibble themselves go on trial and receive their just deserts. En route the team come up with an interesting legal interpretation that would put many confidence men outside the reach of the criminal or civil law.

336. Tutt and Mr. Tutt. New York: Scribner's, 1920. (C)

Lincolnesque attorney Ephraim Tutt, who usually operates in New York City with sidetrips to the upstate town of Pottsville, is the creation for whom Arthur Train is best remembered. The long-running Saturday Evening Post character is known as Mr. Tutt to differentiate him from his younger partner, Samuel Tutt, known simply as Tutt, who is no relation. Although continuing-character short

stories in the slicks were the equivalent of today's TV
series, they often had considerably more substance. Train
and the SEP editors did not insult the intelligence of their
readers by assuming they couldn't (or wouldn't) follow
stories that often hinged on rather subtle points of law.
The firm of Tutt and Tutt specialize in criminal practice,
doing their best to save clients from the worst abuses of
the justice system while sometimes skating on ethical ice
as thin as Perry Mason would in later years. In the early
stories, full of fascinating legal conversations between the
two partners, matters of right and wrong are seldom cut-
and-dried, and the Tutt clients are not always the mistakenly accused.   Later tales in the series, though still
fascinating in their exploration of quirks in the statutes,
would become increasingly formulaic.

Five of the seven tales in the first Tutt collection get into
court.   In "The Dog Andrew," a beachfront boundary
dispute results in litigation when Mr. Appleboy is accused
of assaulting neighbor Tunnygate by sicking on him a newly
acquired dog.   An essay in dialogue on the subject of
animals-as-defendants is one of the best Tutt-Tutt conversations. "The Human Element," in which Mr. Tutt's client
gets off despite an air-tight case and without any legal
tricks, and "The Hepplewhite Tramp," with much interesting talk about the relationship of crime to progress and an
astonishing and ambiguous ending, show how far removed
the early Tutts were from black-and-white melodrama. In
"Lallapaloosa Limited," an expose of stock manipulation,
Mr. Tutt tries in Federal District Court to halt the
reorganization (for the directors' benefit) of the Horse's
Neck Mining Company, pointing out that some actions
called "high finance" in Wall Street would be called grand
larceny in a criminal court.   In "Mock Hen and Mock
Turtle," an unpleasantly racist story set in New York City's
Chinatown, Mr. Tutt's client is accused of a Tong War
murder.   Words like "Chinaman" and "Chink" in third-
person narration grate on the modern ear, and Train's
humor falls flat.

337. The Hermit of Turkey Hollow. New York: Scribner's, 1921.
      (¾)

Skinny the Tramp (originally known as James Hawkins) is
accused of the shooting murder of his friend the title
character, who lived in a cabin three miles northeast of

Pottsville. The villainous Squire Hezekiah Mason, Mr.
Tutt's most frequent and entertaining recurring adversary,
is a newly-appointed prosecutor with his eye on the governor's mansion. He goes after Skinny despite a glaring
conflict of interest as trustee of the tramp's money. The
Brotherhood of Abyssinian Mysteries Lodge #948, whose
ranks Squire Mason has consistently been blackballed from
joining, secures lapsed member Hawkins counsel in the
person of Mr. Tutt, a brother Sacred Camel. The small-
town color is good, and Train's courtroom action is typically diverting. The puzzle of why the jury stayed out so long
has an amusing answer. But the single Tutt novel, wordy
and padded in parts, might have worked better as another
short story.

338. By Advice of Counsel. New York: Scribner's, 1921. (C)

Again, five out of seven tales wind up in court. In the title
story, involving a bigamy case, Mr. Tutt gets his client off
on a technicality that shows up the verbose indictment
specialist of the D.A.'s office. "The Shyster" is a hard-
nosed expose of abuses by lawyers. The title character,
slick but unsavory Raphael P. Hogan, defends a poor youth
involved in a window smashing with more interest in self-
enrichment than guilt or innocence. "Beyond a Reasonable
Doubt" sees Mr. Tutt defending an old horseman entrapped
for practicing veterinary medicine without a license.
Highlights include a funny jury room scene and a prosecuting attorney who may be unique in the annals of fiction
(and as far from Hamilton Burger as could be imagined).
"Contempt of Court" features an elderly society lady who
hears an accused murderer's confession but refuses to
testify to it in court. The volume's booby prize goes to
"The Kid and the Camel," involving murder in New York's
Syrian community. Train's quasi-benign xenophobia renders
the tale far less funny than he intended.

339. Tut, Tut! Mr. Tutt. New York: Scribner's, 1923. London:
Nash, 1924. (C)

The third Tutt collection is a strong one, with five out of
eight stories involving courtroom action. The title of "The
Bloodhound" refers to assistant D.A. William Francis O'Brion, a recurring Tutt nemesis and one of the most villainous
prosecutors in fiction. Mr. Tutt, assigned to defend a
burglary suspect, gets a chance to cross-examine

O'Brion and gives him a taste of his own tactics. "Hocus-Pocus," in which Mr. Tutt seems (incredibly) to have lost or mislaid a will, includes one of his most blatant acts of professional misconduct-- in a worthy cause, of course. Another satisfying probate story, "In Witness Thereof," sees Mr. Tutt foiling a wife's attempt to add a codicil to her ailing husband's will. "The Twelve Little Husbands," in which client Don Antonio Castinados is accused of the attempted poisoning of a lady friend's wealthy husband, is marred by another of Train's patronizing looks at comic foreigners but features an extraordinary and probably unique defense. The amusing title tale, involving the Jiggs-and-Maggie-like Pumpellys, gets in court only very briefly.

340. Page Mr. Tutt. New York: Scribner's, 1926. (C)

This time only three of nine see courtroom action, two of them ("Nine Points of the Law" and "The Maiden and the Tar") very briefly. The third, "The Acid Test," is a neatly plotted detective story and one of the few Tutts to take place entirely in court. Mr. Tutt represents the insurance company at the sentencing of an accused forger, who pled guilty to forging a company endorsement on a check from his firm.

341. When Tutt Meets Tutt. New York: Scribner's, 1927. (C)

The title story is a dandy, with lots of humor, a good surprise twist, and some of the most talkative jurors in fictional annals. The firm is temporarily broken up when the Tutts appear on opposite sides of a will contest in the court of J. Waterbird Maloon. Was the late Commodore Lithgow crazy as his disgrunted heirs believe? Of the other four stories, only "The Meanest Man," a Pottsville tale showing Squire Mason at his most satisfactorily villainous, gets in court.

342. Tutt for Tutt. New York: Scribner's, 1934. (C)

Half of these ten get in court, not including the title tale, a fishing yarn. Mr. Tutt has two lengthy duels with Squire Mason in "Mr. Tutt Swandangles the Squire" (a rare jury trial in a forclosure proceeding) and "Mr. Tutt Takes a Chance," more of a detective story than most, in which a will case allows the elderly lawyer to express his low opinion of Horace Walpole's The Castle of Otranto. "Mr. Tutt Plays it Both Ways" shows the lawyer at his most Randolph Mason-ish (albeit in a good cause), playing musical jurisdictions in a bootlegging-related murder case. Others with courtroom action are "Mr. Tutt, Father-in-Law" and "Mr. Tutt Has a Hunch."

343. Mr. Tutt Takes the Stand. New York: Scribner's, 1936. (C)

Seven out of ten have courtroom action. In "Mr. Tutt, Take the Stand!," the elderly lawyer's cook Mandy (a stereotype in the Aunt Jemima tradition) confronts a burglar. Wanting the poor hungry man to get off, Mr. Tutt appears as both counsel for the defense and chief prosecution witness and cross-examines himself quite tellingly in one of Train's most entertaining and inventive trials. "Take the Witness" is not one of his best but a structural experiment, all taking place in court and nearly all devoted to the cross-examination of the plaintiff, a show girl bringing a breach of promise action against Mr. Tutt's wealthy client. "Prohibition" has a lot of fun with the widespread flouting of the dry law but a rather obvious surprise ending. "Life in the Old Dog Yet," in which a youth is accused of shooting a pawnbroker, has some neat legal finagling. The other three involve Pottsville and the dreaded Squire Mason: "Mr. Tutt Collects a Bet," "The Last Shall Be First," and "That Old Gray Mare," the latter featuring a glimpse of frivolous jury deliberations by a pack of Sacred Camels.

344. Old Man Tutt. New York: Scribner's, 1938. (C)

In "Tootle," the most unusual tale in this collection of eleven (seven of which have courtroom action), Train plays games with Mr. Tutt's alleged dual citizenship as real person and fictional lawyer, somewhat foreshadowing the mock autobiography, Yankee Lawyer (Scribner's, 1943). A writer named Jasper Gilchrist, writing in the low-life Whiz-Bang, a Monthly, describes the death of Ephraim Tutt in a short story imitating Train's style. Tutt, Train, the Saturday Evening Post, and illustrator Arthur William Brown bring suit. The issue: can one author kill off another's fictional character? Otherwise, this is a Tutt collection of average interest, with the old lawyer's fishing enthusiasm more prominent than ever. Squire Mason is vanquished by clever ploys in "Tit, Tat, Tutt," "Just at That

Age," and "Mr. Tutt Goes Fishing." In "Jefferson was Right," villainous D.A. O'Brion prosecutes a broad-daylight murder case and has the help of a blatantly biassed judge. Others with trial action: "Black Salmon" and "Mr. Tutt Takes the Count."

345. Mr. Tutt Comes Home. New York: Scribner's, 1941. (C)

The later Tutt stories are characterized by more variety of setting, more dependency on odd quirks of law, more emphasis on the central character of Mr. Tutt with fewer appearances by Tutt and other members of the firm, a sparer style involving less addressing of the reader or first-person interpolations, and a generally increased reliance on the slick-magazine formula.

Rich in SatEvePost Americana, the penultimate Tutt collection takes the elderly lawyer to New Mexico, Montana, Kentucky, Maine, Canada, and New York's Arab community. All but the last of the eleven stories, "The King's Whiskers" (one of the stronger in the book, with Tutt confronting a lynch mob), provide courtroom action, and all but the Kentucky tale ("Old Duke," involving sheep-killing accusations against a well-loved local dog) have intriguing legal points. The strongest tales are probably "A Salmon for the White House" and "Clean Hands," both involving the ins and outs of probate law. The latter tale has a villain with a name out of Victorian melodrama: Enoch Gooch! It goes well with the saving-the-farm plot.

346. Mr. Tutt Finds a Way. New York: Scribner's, 1945. (C)

The last original Mr. Tutt collection gathers some war-time stories with conventional sympathies, heroes, villains, and attitudes. Most of the young-hero types are in uniform. In later Tutts, the shades of gray are always in the law, never in the characters. Eight of the eleven stories have trial action. Best of the lot is "The Camels are Coming," in which Squire Mason, thwarted once again in his ambition to become a Sacred Camel, tears down his Brick Block building, expecting the adjacent Camel lodge hall to topple, leaving him legally in the clear. The satire on service club pageantry is wonderful. (The story also has some sequences that seem offensively racist by today's standards, albeit mild and gentle by standards of the time.) "With his Boots On," concerning a New Jersey will contest involving a college friend of Mr. Tutt, is a fair-play tale with a well-laid clue to the solution of the problem. "The Wanga" is a Harlem voodoo story. Can the old lawyer find a legal way to thwart a witch doctor for attempted murder by suggestion? Unfortunately, the solution is more histrionic than legal. Other stories with courtroom action: "Mr. Tutt Tries Live Bait" (a very brief probate hearing), "Exit Mr. Machiavelli," "Colonel Tutt of Savannah," "Mr. Tutt Corners a Fox," and "King Wagamoc's Revenge." The most interesting parts of this volume are Train's beginning and ending essays, concerning the controversy about Mr. Tutt's supposed volume of memoirs, Yankee Lawyer, and the astonishing number of people who took it for a real autobiography.

The Adventures of Ephraim Tutt (Scribner's, 1930) is an omnibus volume including 27 tales from the early collections and a preface by Train describing the genesis of his famous character. Mr. Tutt's Case Book (Scribner's, 1936) is a similar regathering, repeating about half the stories and Train's preface from the earlier volume with an introduction by John Henry Wigmore and scholarly legal annotations to each of the 26 tales by Ferdinand J. Wolf. There is even a subject index, giving the volume the appearance of a legal textbook. The honor thus accorded Train may be unique in the annals of legal fiction. Mr. Tutt at his Best (Scribner's, 1961) gathers sixteen stories from the earlier collections with a good introduction about Train and his creation by Judge Harold R. Medina.

TRAVER, Robert, pseudonym of John Donaldson Voelker (1903-)

347. Anatomy of a Murder. New York: St. Martin's; London: Faber, 1958. (¼)

This massive best seller, which contributed hugely to the trial fiction vogue of the late fifties and early sixties, is almost universally regarded as one of the classic courtroom novels.   Forty-year-old lawyer Paul Biegler, recently ousted by voters as District Attorney of Iron Cliffs County on Michigan's Upper Peninsula, opposes his ex-football-star replacement Mitch Lodwick in the murder trial of Army Lieutenant Frederick Manion. Laura, Manion's wife, who brings the case to Biegler, claims the shooting victim, Barney Quill, had raped her. The defense is based on an insanity plea.

Thanks to the expertise of the author, a former D.A. and a Michigan Supreme Court Justice, the trial of nearly two hundred pages is one of the most detailed and authentic in fiction. It goes from jury selection through to closing arguments, judge's charge, and verdict, giving a sense of completeness not provided by more abbreviated trial sequences. Judge Harlan Weaver, memorably played in the screen version by Joseph Welch, is one of the most nearly perfect jurists in fiction, and Claude Dancer, the hired gun from the State Attorney General's office who assists Mitch, is one of the most memorable prosecutors, vain and aggressive as Hamilton Burger but far more formidable.

In introducing the 1983 reissue, Traver writes, "For a long time I had seen too many movies and read too many books and plays about trials that were almost comically phony and overdone, mostly in their extravagant efforts to over-dramatize an already inherently dramatic human situation. I longed to try my hand at telling about a criminal trial the way it really was. . . I felt. . . that a great part of the tension and drama of any major felony trial lay in its very understatement, its pent and almost stifled quality..." This was his achievement, one that was duplicated remarkably closely in Otto Preminger's film version with James Stewart in the role of Biegler.

Traver's Laughing Whitefish (New York: McGraw-Hill, 1965; London: Allen, 1967) describes a nineteeth-century Michigan trial.

348. People Versus Kirk. New York: St. Martin's, 1981. (½)

Though this is a generally inept novel (and one that probably could not have found a major publisher had its author not written a classic twenty years before), it still has some enjoyable material for trial buffs. The novel exemplifies educational fiction, with much research apparent and even reference notes at the end. Randall Kirk claims to have no memory of killing his lover, heiress Constance Spurrier. Lawyer Frederic Ludlow defends, at times playing very dense Watson to the Holmes of Dr. Hugh Salter, an expert on hypnosis, the key subject of the tale. Unlike Anatomy of a Murder, this can accurately be called a detective story, though a painfully transparent one. Outside the courtroom, Traver is the dullest novelist imaginable, but in it he can still be fascinating.

TREE, Gregory, pseudonym of John Franklin Bardin (1916-1981)

349. The Case Against Myself.   New York: Scribner's, 1950. London: Gollancz, 1951. (¾)

Catherine Benedict, wife of Broadway gossip columnist Bernard Benedict, is accused of the poisoning murder of Melissa Chambers, her husband's mistress. Smitten young lawyer Bill Bradley defends and eventually finds the truth with the help of psychiatrist Noel Mayberry. Bardin's pseudonymous work is reputedly more conventional than the psychological mysteries published under his own name, but his approach is still innovative. The tale is told in shifting first-person accounts (or interior monologues) by jurors, lawyers, defendant, judge, witnesses and suspects, a private detective, psychiatrist-sleuth Mayberry, and finally the murderer. Though readable and inventive, the story is ultimately unconvincing. In the trial scenes, Bradley uses the three I's (singly and together) as loosely and inappropriately as any advocate in fiction, and the prosecuting attorney takes a useless exception when he loses a ruling. There is some humor in the testimony: an assistant Medical Examiner who says an event would occur "once in a blue moon" is admonished to "confine himself to familiar systems of chronology."

Bradley and Mayberry return in The Case Against Butterfly (Scribner's, 1951), which may also have courtroom action.

TWAIN, Mark, pseudonym of Samuel Langhorne Clemens (1835-1910)

350. The Tragedy of Pudd'nhead Wilson.   Hartford: American, 1894. As Pudd'nhead Wilson, London: Chatto and Windus, 1894. (B)

In the town of Dawson's Landing, Missouri, unsuccessful lawyer David (Pudd'nhead) Wilson pursues a hobby of collecting fingerprints, an unrecognized pursuit in 1830. Roxana, a 15/16 white slave owned by leading citizen Judge

Driscoll, is caring for two virtually identical babies, her
own son and the judge's Thomas. She switches them and
watches her natural son grow up unpleasantly as the young
master. A very complicated plot culminates years later in
the trial of a pair of Italian twins for the stabbing murder
of the judge. The trial is mostly summary apart from
Wilson's closing argument and demonstration. The windup
is beautifully ironic. Besides being an early inverted
detective story and a pioneering fictional use of fingerprints, Twain's novel presents a chilling and undoubtedly
quite accurate view of nineteenth-century racial attitudes.

UNDERWOOD, Michael, pseudonym of John Michael Evelyn (1916-   )

351. Murder on Trial. London: Hammond, 1954. New York: Ives Washburn, 1958. (B)

The first novel by one of the best of the British specialists in legal detective fiction opens with a fifty-year-old senior clerk named John Pinty excitedly preparing for jury duty in the Old Bailey. He is seated as foreman in the trial of con man William Edgar Tarrant for the shooting murder of Police Constable David Moss. When the defendant is shot to death on his way to the witness box, presumably to make the startling revelations he loudly promised the day before, juror Pinty promptly vanishes and becomes suspect number one. Leading the investigation is 36-year-old Simon Manton, the Yard's youngest Detective Chief Inspector, the central character here though he will become a virtual bit player in some later Underwood novels. The novel offers an intriguing variation on the murder-at-a-public-performance situation, where a large number of witnesses unaccountably saw nothing. While quite a bit of time is spent in the courtroom, for most of it court is not actually in session. Though Underwood would get even better with the years, his debut, finishing with a traditional gathering-of-the-suspects finale, is a neat job.

352. False Witness. London: Hammond, 1957. New York: Walker, 1961. (B)

Young barrister Jeremy Harper loves wealthy heiress Jennie Rawlins, who is the daughter of the local mill owner and High Sheriff in Seahaven, first Assize town on the Coastal Circuit. But Jennie's fiancé is Derek Yates, an employee of the paper mill who claims he was robbed in the park of the firm's payroll. Jeremy becomes a key witness at his robbery trial. The thirty-or-so pages of trial action come early. A murder in the Clerk of Assize's office follows Yates' conviction and sentencing, and Detective-Superintendent Simon Manton of the Yard is called in. The least-suspected-person plot is cleverly done.

353. <u>Lawful Pursuit</u>.   London: Hammond; Garden City, NY: <u>Doubleday</u>, 1958. (B)

As in <u>Murder on Trial</u>, the sparse courtroom action primarily serves as a jumping-off place for the plot. In West End Magistrate's Court, defendant Alexander Burfa, accused of pimping, fails to appear for his hearing. It is the sixth bail-jumping incident in the same court in six months, and the first five had apparently been spirited away to Algeria. Detective Constable Roy Cordari goes underground to try to solve the case. Under the name Rafaele Skourasi, he is arraigned for drug possession. Simon Manton finally wraps up the fairly intriguing plot.

354. <u>Adam's Case</u>.   London: Hammond; Garden City, NY: Doubleday, 1961. (B)

Adam Cape, another of the young barristers that populate the author's early novels, receives a brief to prosecute Frankie Young in the Old Bailey on a charge of "wounding with intent" his wife Carole. Opposing Adam is his more experienced office-mate Charles Imrey. Feeling responsible for her death when Mrs. Young's strangled body is fished out of the North London Canal, Adam turns amateur detective, even getting hit over the head at one point, private-eye style. Simon Manton enters the case after the murder, springing a police trap and a surprise solution. Courtroom action is effective but still (at under fifteen pages) fairly brief.

355. <u>The Crime of Colin Wise</u>.   London: Macdonald; Garden City, NY: Doubleday, 1964. (¼)

The titular character is a bent TV repairman who plans the "perfect" murder for gain of novelist Geoffrey Goodwin. Wise goes through the full course of the criminal justice system (arrest, remand hearings, full hearing in Magistrate's Court, Old Bailey trial, retrial, and Court of Criminal Appeal hearing), clued in to the way things work by an old hand, firestarter Inky Pooler. This is a sort of inverted detective story, with Wise playing cat and mouse early on with series cop Manton, a relatively minor character this time. With a sharp ironic ending, this is one of the author's better books.

356. The Anxious Conspirator.   London: Macdonald; Garden City, NY: Doubleday, 1965. (B)

Manton leads a successful police raid on a forged-traveller's-cheque ring. But informer Tony Dayne is mistakenly taken with the rest of the gang and refuses to be released after arrest, fearing their reprisals. Thus, the police are in the odd position of trying to help get him off without revealing his treachery to his former cohorts.   Solicitor Roger Elwin gets the task of representing Dayne.   The ring's European contact, Freda Fischer, is strangled in Vienna. This is one of the author's stronger novels, though trial action is again very light (about eight pages), including an action climax in Magistrate's Court.

357. The Silent Liars. London: Macmillan; Garden City, NY: Doubleday, 1970. (¼)

Chris Laker is charged in the Old Bailey with the shooting murder of Gheorge Dimitriu, a successful businessman with whom he had no known connection.   Laker, a fairly unsympathetic character, is contemptuous of the whole business, but Underwood carefully conceals the truth of his guilt or innocence.   The trial is a very well-balanced presentation of a case that really could go either way. Less diverting is the aftermath, involving much chasing about the victim's native Rumania, as Chief Inspector Adams tries to tie up the loose ends.

358. A Trout in the Milk. London: Macmillan, 1971. New York: Walker, 1972. (B)

Robin Appleman, an apprentice barrister assisting James Geddy in the defense of racketeer Frank Manion on charges of grievous bodily harm, blackmail, extortion, and related offenses, is found murdered in chambers. As Chief Superintendent Roffery investigates, the Old Bailey trial goes on, totaling about twenty pages, though the actual testimony is not extensively reported. It's a sound mystery but not among the author's best.

359. A Pinch of Snuff.   London: Macmillan; New York: St.
     Martin's, 1974. (B)

     Brian Tanner, assistant wine steward at the Blackstone
     Club, of which many leading judges and lawyers are mem-
     bers, becomes involved in a plan to steal the club's famous
     snuff-box collection. When his contact Harry Green is
     murdered, he finds himself mistakenly accused of a much
     more serious crime. Rosa Epton, the young female lawyer
     who stars in Underwood's most recent novels, here makes
     her debut in a slightly less prominent role as assistant to
     solicitor Robin Snaith.   The trial, with barrister Martin
     Ainsworth arguing Brian's case, features a fine cross-
     examination of the main prosecution witness. Going on
     concurrently and briefly viewed is the trial of some politi-
     cal dissidents.   The novel belongs in the upper third of
     Underwood's reliable work.

360. Menaces, Menaces.   London: Macmillan; New York: St.
     Martin's, 1976. (¾)

     It's hard to believe the incomparable Henry Cecil didn't
     write this meticulously plotted novel of courtroom comedy,
     devious chicanery, and careful police work. It includes
     some of Underwood's most extensive (and surely funniest)
     Old Bailey action. Henry Sipson is defending himself on
     charges of trying to extort ten thousand pounds from a
     bingo company.   While he's locked up, a second crime
     (involving threats of ground glass in the product if a sugar
     manufacturer doesn't pay up) has all the earmarks of his
     familiar m.o., providing a fortuitous boon to the defense.
     Most of the investigative chores fall to the cop-and-wife
     detecting team of Nick and Clare Attwell. (They earlier
     appeared unmarried in the promisingly titled 1975 novel
     The Juror, which spends almost no time in court).

361. Murder With Malice.   London: Macmillan; New York: St.
     Martin's, 1977. (B)

     Here suspended Nick Attwell tiresomely nurses his self-
     pity while plucky Clare goes to work to clear him of
     soliciting a bribe from 17-year-old Paul Frenshaw, murder
     suspect and son of a powerful TV personality. The trial
     action (about thirty pages) comes in Magistrate's Court.

It's a smooth enough job, though not one of his very best. A later Attwell novel, The Fatal Trip (1977) has only very brief courtroom action in the opening chapter.

362. Anything but the Truth. London: Macmillan, 1978. New York: St. Martin's, 1979. (B)

This one begins and ends in the Old Bailey with 19-year-old Ian Tanner on trial for killing his friend Mick Burleigh by running him down in a stolen car. Judge Matthew Chaytor, in his first Old Bailey case, has a possible conflict of interest, discovering after the case begins that his wayward son Peter is in the employ of the stolen car's shady owner. A likeable young policeman, Temporary Detective Constable Patrick Bramley, handles the detecting chores. In the 48 pages of scattered court action, prosecutor Bruce Ridge proves to be one of the most breathtakingly incompetent advocates in fictional annals. This is fair to good Underwood, though not without the boring patches that occur in nearly every novel about smalltime professional felons.

363. Crooked Wood. London: Macmillan; New York: St. Martin's, 1978. (¼)

Clive Donig, alleged professional hitman, is in the Old Bailey dock for the murder of solicitor Stanley Fulmer. Nick and Clare Attwell again investigate. This is decidedly lesser Underwood with courtroom action more plentiful but less exciting than usual.

364. Smooth Justice. London: Macmillan; New York: St. Martin's, 1979. (B)

The action begins in Bloomsbury Magistrate's Court, where Donald Ferney tries to live up to the newspaper tag of "the kindly magistrate," a sobriquet those who work most closely with him cannot endorse. The court's elderly usher is found clubbed to death outside the magistrate's private entrance, and it is generally assumed he died in the hated Ferney's place. The book is in and out of court throughout, the main case concerning corruption charges against Detective Sergeant Wilkley. Underwood is entertaining as always, though his least-suspected-person killer will surprise few readers.

365. Victim of Circumstance. London: Macmillan; New York:
     St. Martin's, 1980. (¼)

     In the first sentence we are told that schoolmaster John
     Farndon intends to kill his French wife Monique, and in the
     second part of the book we have the case of Queen vs.
     Farndon in Chelvey Crown Court, but...   Representing
     Underwood at his trickiest, this is the kind of novel where
     too much plot summary spoils the fun. The trial is one of
     his longest (some 74 pages) and best, and the tale is fast-
     moving, well-peopled, and soundly constructed.

366. Crime Upon Crime. London: Macmillan, 1980. New York:
     St. Martin's, 1981. (B)

     When Tony Ching, the homosexual prostitute whose ses-
     sions with Judge Gerald Wenning of West Middlesex Crown
     Court form the basis for blackmail, is found strangled,
     long-time successful villain Arthur Kedby is ironically
     accused of the one crime he didn't commit. His solicitor is
     Rosa Epton, previously met in A Pinch of Snuff, now a
     qualified solicitor and a partner in the firm of Snaith and
     Epton.   As in the past, Underwood's courtrooms can be
     violently dangerous places, and the Old Bailey trial is not
     carried to a verdict. But the author delivers a strong plot
     and a satisfactorily surprising (if not quite believable)
     solution.

367. Double Jeopardy.   London: Macmillan; New York: St.
     Martin's, 1981. (B)

     Rosa Epton defends Toby Nash, whom she had just met at a
     friend's New Year's Eve party, on a charge of raping Tricia
     Langley. While Toby is out on bail, Tricia is murdered by
     suffocation, and Rosa, who has an occasional tendency to
     fall for her clients, is his alibi. This is one of Underwood's
     most satisfying pure whodunits, with an interesting and
     varied group of suspects. Trial action is limited to about a
     dozen pages, describing a series of three hearings on the
     initial charge in Petersham Magistrate's Court, an example
     of the piecemeal preliminaries Underwood's characters
     frequently rail against.

368. Hand of Fate. London: Macmillan, 1981. New York: St.
     Martin's, 1982. (½)

The reader is made fairly certain from the start that self-made millionaire Frank Wimble is guilty of the murder of his vanished wife, but the question is how he did it and whether there is enough evidence to convict him. There is only a severed hand found in the woods by a dog-- despite a thorough police search, the rest of the body was never found. The jurors and the capable female judge are the real focal characters in the story of Wimble's trial, one of Underwood's longest and a typically interesting one. The truth, when it comes following the verdict, is a nice surprise. (For an earlier treatment of a similar no-corpse situation, see Roderic Jeffries' The Benefits of Death.)

Since Underwood is himself a lawyer, one has to assume his procedure hews reasonably close to actual practice. But the novel suggests a considerable difference in jury selection and handling in British vs. American courts. Though the judge charges them not to discuss the case "outside the walls of the jury room" (an admonition some follow and some do not), they are apparently expected to discuss it among themselves before evidence is finished. A woman previously convicted of murder (her conviction subsequently quashed on appeal) sits on the jury, albeit under a new identity.

369. Goddess of Death.   London: Macmillan; New York: St. Martin's, 1982. (B)

Philip Arne engages solicitor Rose Epton to represent his brother Francis, charged with "loitering with intent to commit an arrestable offense" in the vicinity of a classic Rolls-Royce. Before Francis' trial in Shepherd's Bush Magistrate's Court, Philip is murdered by a blow from a bronze statuette of an Indian goddess, and it appears Francis may be charged with this as well. Also in the picture is an Indian villain named Shiv Kapur. The 20-page trial on the seemingly minor charge has a hint of Henry Cecil-style comedy, as the magistrate quite clearly has a crush on Rosa. Brisk and diverting, this is about average for Underwood.

370. A Party to Murder. London: Macmillan, 1983. New York: St. Martin's, 1984. (B)

At the annual Christmas party of the Grainfield Prosecuting Solicitor's office, staff member Tom Hunsey, known

for his indecisiveness and love of gossip, is found clubbed
to death. Is his murder connected to the controversy over
newly-appointed Chief Prosecuting Solicitor Murray Riston? Caroline Allard, another staff member and a former
lover of Riston, is accused of the crime, and Rosa Epton,
an old law school friend, comes from London to represent
her. By the time of Caroline's trial in Grainfield Crown
Court, Rosa has already figured out who did it but, lacking
solid evidence, instructs barrister Martin Ainsworth to
"play the role of Perry Mason" and expose the real killer in
court. By evidence of this novel, Underwood is at least as
good and maybe better than ever, and Rosa is surely the
most interesting of his series detectives.

371. <u>Death in Camera.</u>   London: Macmillan; New York: St.
Martin's, 1984. (B)

At the opening ceremonies of the new Runnymede Crown
Court, Mr. Justice Ambrose falls to his death from a
balcony during a photo session. Which of the line of
photographers fired the poison pellet that did him in?
Chief suspect is ne'er-do-well nephew Nigel Ambrose, who
is Rosa Epton's client. There is lighter court action (about
fifteen pages on a narcotics case the dead judge was to
have heard) and heavier carnage than in most Underwoods.
This is the least impressive of the half-dozen Epton novels
to date.

Some Underwood novels, published only in Britain, were not
examined for the present work. The following were
published by Hammond: <u>Death on Remand</u> (1956), <u>Arm of
the Law</u> (1959), <u>Cause of Death</u> (1960), and <u>Death by
Misadventure</u> (1960). The following were published by
Macdonald: <u>The Case Against Philip Quest</u> (1962), <u>Girl
Found Dead</u> (1963), <u>A Crime Apart</u> (1966), <u>The Man Who
Died on Friday</u> (1967), <u>The Man Who Killed Too Soon</u>
(1968), <u>The Shadow Game</u> (1969), and <u>Shem's Demise</u>
(1970). Also unexamined was <u>Murder Made Absolute</u> (Hammond, 1955; Washburn, 1957). Presumably, most of these
include some courtroom activity.

URIS, Leon (1924-   )

372. <u>QB VII.</u> Garden City, NY: Doubleday, 1970. (¼)

Dr. Adam Kelno, a naturalized citizen of Britain who has
been knighted for his contributions to medicine, brings a
libel action against American novelist Abraham Cady,
whose book The Holocaust alleged Kelno committed war
crimes while working in a Nazi concentration camp. Uris'
contribution to the courtroom blockbuster school is com-
pellingly readable, obviously deeply felt, and astonishingly
gracelessly written for an author of his reputation. Most
of the last half of this 500-page book covers the trial, with
testimony quoted at considerable length. Uris offers much
travelogue-ish information about the British legal system.

V

VIDAL, Gore (1925-   )

373. <u>Burr</u>. New York: Random House, 1973. London: Heinemann, 1974. (B)

Vidal's learned and witty fictionalized biography of Aaron
Burr includes about ten pages on Burr's treason trial in the
U.S. Circuit Court, District of Virginia, and the Grand Jury
proceeding that led up to it, summarized from the defendant's first-person point of view. The material about the
court's ability to subpoena documents from the President
had special relevance at the time Vidal's novel appeared.
Other trials are visited glancingly, including that of Richard Robinson for the murder of Helen Jewett, attended by
Burr's biographer Charles Schuyler, one of the few fictional
characters in the novel.

VON ELSNER, Don (1909-   )

374. <u>Don't Just Stand There, Do Someone</u>. New York: Signet,
1962. (B)

Many readers will approach the trial sequence in this
outrageously fast-moving, over-populated, excessively
eventful, and rather messy novel hoping for a coherent
summary of what's been going on. Fortunately, the trial is
by far the best part of the book. The beautiful founder of
a cosmetics firm tells lawyer-detective David Danning
(accurately) that her husband will be murdered and she
accused. Danning winds up as a co-defendant with her, as
his son Bob aids him in the defense. (Somewhat confusing-
ly, Danning <u>pere</u> and <u>fils</u> call each other "Duke.") Gangsters
are heavily involved (there is a rather gratuitous machine-

gun attack at one point) and Von Elsner manages to bring in
his bridge specialty in explaining (at least to fellow players) the admirably tricky solution. It's somewhat reminiscent of the way S.S. Van Dine used poker in The "Canary"
Murder Case.

375. Pour a Swindle Through a Loophole. New York: Belmont,
1964. (¼)

In Von Elsner's second courtroom novel, the vehicular
homicide trial of truck driver Luigi Ramazetti begins
inauspiciously: the prosecuting attorney segues from his
opening statement into his first witness without passing go.
After that, however, the trial action improves. This is one
of those courtroom novels, somewhat in the manner of a
Perry Mason, that involves itself as much with the ins-and-
outs of the law, questions of admissibility and procedure,
as with the sheer drama of evidence-taking. Danning's
client, it is demonstrated, had his rights trampled on in
best pre-Miranda style in his interrogations by the police,
and the lawyer (later to turn spy as the winds of fashion in
the mystery changed) does a fine job of reaching the real
solution.

VULLIAMY, C(olwyn) E(dward) (1886-1971)

376. Don Among the Dead Men. London: Joseph, 1952. (B)

Prof. Kerris Bowles-Ottery, research chemist at the University of Ockham, practices what he calls "Social Service
through Selective Elimination," providing via a newly discovered poison called DGX very pleasant deaths for people
he believes the world better off without. In an inverted
tale perhaps too similar in structure to the author's earlier
The Vicar's Experiments (as by Anthony Rolls; see below),
the savant is gradually found out and is tried in Ockham
Assizes for the murder of his former student and mistress,
Delia Thriddle. The author's satirical social observations
and proclivity for whimsical character names can be very
funny, even when he seems to follow his special formula
rather too slavishly.

377. Cakes for your Birthday. London: Joseph; New York:
British Book Centre, 1959. (B)

Messrs. Berecastle, Ripsguard, and Lollesworth (a retired headmaster, a lawyer, and an engineer-poet respectively) comprise the Liquidation Committee. They have identified 27 methods of elimination, but their attempts at actual murder tend to misfire. In their second attempt on Raddlesgate town gossip Millicent Euphonia Peaswillow, they send her some liberally poisoned cakes. There is a brief trial at Waldringham Assizes, where Sir Patcham Claydaw and Robert Lumjaw-Puddleboy, K.C., battle it out before "that enthusiastic supporter of the hangman, Mr. Justice Ambledew." Who is tried for the murder of whom is best left unmentioned here. The author's inexhaustible supply of funny names also provides Sir Quintus Taploft, Mr. and Mrs. Meatring-Peelyard, Mrs. Farrier-Sludge, and Sir Bedwith Bathwedder. An entertaining novel even more broadly satirical than the author's usual.

378. Tea at the Abbey. London: Joseph, 1961. (B)

This time Vulliamy deserts his usual inverted form to produce an enjoyable and more-or-less straight whodunit. Violet Oskinlowe, fiancée of well-born University of Mansterbridge senior lecturer Hindley Bascombe, is stabbed to death while a house party guest at Stathering Abbey, home of Hindley's aunt Anna Belinda Mortinghouse. Bruce Westerman is charged with the murder at Mansterbridge Magistrate's Court in a hearing marked by more adversarial speechifying than is usual in a preliminary. The author includes the deliberations of the five sitting magistrates, one of whom (incredibly enough) is Anna Belinda. As often with Vulliamy, the plot involves a newly-discovered chemical compound, in this case one that reverses human character.

379. Floral Tribute. London: Joseph, 1963. (B)

The distinctive author's final novel begins with a very effectively described graveside scene. A hideous wreath with an embarrassing inscription turns up at the burial of an old man named Lobscot, who had lived his final days in Weatherblow House, a nursing home operated by Dr. Theophilus Phudd. Through Lobscot's letters and the anonymous narrator's accounts, the story flashes back to life at the home, culminating in the strangulation murder of a disliked patient, Mrs. Crawky, with which the equally disliked Lady Pounce is charged. The Magistrate's Court hearing deals mostly with the defendant's competence to stand trial.

Of the other Vulliamy titles under his own name, Body in the Boudoir (1956) was not examined and Justice for Judy (1960) includes only an inquest.

(as Anthony Rolls)

380. The Vicar's Experiments. London: Bles, 1932. As Clerical Error. Boston: Little, Brown, 1932. (B)

The Reverend Gregory Virgil Pardicott, well-respected local vicar in the village of Lower Pydal, takes up a career as a poisoner. When he finally attracts notice to at least one of his murders (that of the irritating Colonel Cargoy) through a combination of blunders, the author presents his hearing in Magistrate's Court and his trial at Belchester Assizes. The manner in which he reaches his final fate is rich in irony, and the author's satiric eye is at its sharpest. The other Rolls novels seem to lack trial action, though Family Matters (1933) does have an inquest, and Lobelia Grove (1932) was not examined.

W

WADE, Henry, pseudonym of Henry Lancelot Aubrey-Fletcher (1887-1969)

381. The Evidence of You All. London: Constable, 1926. New York: Payson and Clarke, 1927. (B)

Wade's first novel is a Golden-Age police tale in the Freeman Wills Crofts manner, concerning the death of a financier with the ever-present male secretary (engaged to the wealthy victim's daughter) a logical suspect and defendant in the Old Bailey trial. Though the courtroom action is not especially notable, this is an exceedingly clever detective novel with some very cute reader misdirection.

WAINWRIGHT, John (1921-   )

382. Acquittal. London: Macmillan; New York: St. Martin's, 1976. (B)

Building contractor Harvey Russell is surprised to be acquitted of his wife's murder. His search for what really happened occasionally flashes back to extracts from the trial transcript, mostly from his cross-examination by the prosecutor. Trial parts total less than twenty pages and include little notable give-and-take. At one point a police witness is asked by the prosecutor (apparently without challenge from the defense) to offer his non-expert opinion of where the fatal fire started. This is below average Wainwright-- his customary overwrought prose is at its least effective when used for padding. There's some compelling technical trickery nonetheless, including both telegraphed and untelegraphed surprises in the solution.

383. The Jury People.   London: Macmillan; New York: St.
     Martin's, 1978. (A)

     A production schedule of four books a year is not neces-
     sarily fatal to quality, but it rarely makes for a good deal
     of variety. Wainwright, a retired Yorkshire policeman with
     much to say about the British police and legal systems, is
     remarkably uncommitted to a set formula, however. His
     books are all different, all adventurously constructed and
     forcefully (sometimes too forcefully) written. Here he
     presents the murder trial of a Pakistani youth through the
     eyes of the twelve jurors, culminating in their delibera-
     tions. The general attitude to racial minorities is well-
     intentioned but patronizing, and there is some over-simpli-
     fication in the presentation of the various jurors' attitudes.
     At the end, there is some doubt as to what Wainwright is
     saying about the British system of justice. His answers are
     almost always ambiguous, which underscores their reality.

384. Man of Law.   London: Macmillan, 1980; New York: St.
     Martin's, 1981. (¼)

     Simon Whitehouse, Q.C., and Dr. Martin Webb, a psychiat-
     ric expert witness, are former college friends now court-
     room adversaries.   The dramatic trial of Whitehouse's
     client on a charge of wife murder covers some eighty pages
     and, given a measure of artistic license, is very effectively
     done, especially the cross-examination of Webb by his old
     friend. The plot has all the twists and turns that typify a
     Wainwright product.

385. An Urge for Justice. London: Macmillan, 1981; New York:
     St. Martin's, 1982. (B)

     Elderly village recluse Annie Miller is found dead in her
     home, hanged with piano wire, and the crime is soon
     revealed to have its roots in the horrors of Nazi Germany.
     Barrister Simon Whitehouse defends Samuel Gold, the hun-
     ter of war criminals charged with the crime, telling his
     junior, "In law, we'll be fighting for what we know to be a
     wrong verdict." Trial action is relatively brief, but there
     are some interesting observations about the relationships
     between barristers and solicitors, and Wainwright delivers
     his usual knockout punch at the end.

WALLACE, Irving (1916-)

386. <u>The Seven Minutes</u>.   New York: Simon and Schuster;
London: New English Library, 1969. (B)

Most of the perpetual best sellers turn to the Big Trial
Novel eventually, and this is Wallace's contribution. The
defendant is a bookstore owner charged with selling an
obscene novel, <u>The Seven Minutes</u> by the pseudonymous J J
Jadway. Defense lawyer Michael Barrett is the hero. The
identity of the mysterious Jadway is one of the central
questions of the novel. While this is hardly a distinguished
work of fiction, it is a highly involving one for anyone
interested in problems of censorship and First Amendment
rights. It is distinguished by Wallace's usual heavy research, all of which he seems determined to get into the
story one way or another.

The trial covers slightly less than a quarter of the 600-page
novel. The questioning is less abbreviated than in many
courtroom novels, giving it more of a feel of reality.
Whatever charges can be laid on this book as a work of
fiction, the trial scenes ring true.

WARD, Edmund (1928-   )

387. <u>The Main Chance</u>. London: Weidenfeld and Nicolson, 1976.
New York: Coward, McCann, Geoghegan, 1977. (B)

This account of ambitious, aggressive solicitor David Main,
a character who will produce mixed feelings in most
readers, is basically a law office procedural. An enthralling legal melodrama, it reads like a British TV serial,
which indeed it was, produced by Yorkshire Television.
The novel flits in and out of court but never lights for long
aside from a six-page sequence involving Main's action to
recover custody of his two children.

WAUGH, Hillary (1920-   )

388. <u>Parrish for the Defense</u>.   Garden City, NY: Doubleday,
1974. London: Gollancz, 1975. (B)

With all the dedicated and heroic defense attorneys that

populate fiction, it seems only fair that at least one should be a thoroughly despicable opportunist. The legendary Cleveland Parrish, who fills even judges with awe, comes to Connecticut to defend Dr. Gerald Whittaker, accused of the murder of his wife. Among the noble advocate's first actions: 1) offering his client a paperback book contract for the ghost-written story of his married life and 2) going to bed with the client's mistress. Waugh, best known for some classic police procedural novels, is a writer well-suited to formalized situations. His trial scenes, occupying 60+ pages in the latter part of the novel, are superb.

389. A Madman at my Door.   Garden City, NY: Doubleday, 1978. London: Gollancz, 1979. (B)

This effective pure suspense novel begins with a 30-page sanity hearing in the Superior Court of New Haven County, Connecticut.   Orville Elliot, found to be insane when he raped and murdered three women several years before, is now deemed cured by his doctors and ready to reenter society.   The two sides are even-handedly presented, though the author's ultimate sympathies are little in doubt. Elliot, whose sex organs were shot off by the husband of one his victims, swore vengeance, and high school teacher Herbert Murdoch (now with a new life and a new family) is convinced Elliot will come after him.   An ambitious and insensitive young reporter helps stir things up, giving the novel a full complement of conservative villains: courts, psychiatrists, press.

WELCOME, John, pseudonym of John Needham Huggard Brennan (1914-   )

390. Go For Broke.   London: Faber; New York: Walker, 1972. (B)

One of this author's non-fiction volumes was Cheating at Cards: The Cases in Court (1963), and he uses such a situation here.   Series spy Richard Graham (who would have been a great part for the late David Niven) consults a solicitor to file a slander suit in response to a charge of cheating at poker.   Most of this novel, a rare combination of legal and espionage fiction, gives the impression of a good writer on an off day, but the climactic trial (of only twelve pages) has a couple of interesting twists to it.

WHEAT, Carolyn

391. <u>Dead Man's Thoughts</u>. New York: St. Martin's, 1983. (B)

This fine detective novel is steeped in the law and enters many courtrooms briefly. But it never stays long after a vivid and effective opening sequence in a Brooklyn night court. Protagonist and sleuth is Legal Aid attorney Cass Jameson, who tries to solve the murder of her lover, a fellow defender. The title is from a telling quote by Carl Sandburg: "The lawyers know a dead man's thoughts too well."

WILLIAMS, Brad (1918-   ), and J(acob) W(ilburn) EHRLICH (1900-1971)

392. <u>A Conflict of Interest</u>.   New York: Holt, Rinehart, and Winston, 1971. (B)

This is the second hardcover novel about Sam Benedict, following Howard Oleck's feeble <u>A Singular Fury</u> (q.v.). (For a novelization from the time the Benedict program was on television, see LEE, Elsie.)   The character of Benedict was, of course, based on San Francisco lawyer Ehrlich, and the reader of this book pictures him in the role rather than actor Edmond O'Brien.

Eccentric millionaire Cyrus Thurman, bearded and resembling a hippie, returns to San Francisco from Mexico and tells his three children (a varied group) that he must see Benedict. Then he is murdered in the evening fog while driving a decorated VW bus borrowed from the less Establishmentarian of his sons. He may or may not be a victim of the Astro killer, a serial slayer patterned after the real-life Zodiac killer. Trial action occurs in probate court, where Sam is ill-matched against an error-prone corporation lawyer. An interesting legal question is addressed: does a testator's reference to the "heirs of my body" exclude an offspring conceived by artificial insemination? This is a slick, competent, and professional job, but it lacks the excitement of a prime Perry Mason novel.

In a collaboration like this, it is natural to wonder how much was the work of the fiction pro (Williams) and how much of the subject matter expert (Ehrlich). In his 1965

autobiography, A Life in My Hands, Ehrlich states that he
wrote many of the Benedict TV scripts himself and that he
(not NBC) cancelled the show. He states he wanted to deal
with more adult material than an early evening timeslot
allowed. "For instance," he writes, "I had a tremendous
script idea involving artificial insemination." Presumably
the origin of this novel.

393. A Matter of Confidence. New York: Holt, Rinehart, and
Winston, 1973. (B)

Benedict becomes involved with two seemingly unrelated
killings that occur on the same night: of a stewardess who
has delivered two pieces of a possibly-stolen jade chess set
to a wealthy San Francisco collector, and of a Chinese
gangster discovered in bed with another man's wife. Again
the thirty-or-so pages of trial action (in a preliminary
hearing on the murder of the gangster) are knowledgeably
and capably done, and the Chinatown background and chess
lore are interesting, but this is the lesser of the two
Benedict cases by these authors. It was published after the
death of Ehrlich, and no further novels in the series
appeared.

WOLFE, Carson

394. Murder at La Marimba. New York: St. Martin's, 1984. (B)

When violence erupts between Puerto Rican and Dominican
teen-agers at a South Bronx disco, Ricky Betancourt is
accused of the shooting murder of Pablo Alvarado. Attorney Carlito Rivera, called in by Ricky's girlfriend's mother,
investigates and wraps things up in 35 pages of trial action.
Carlito seems to have it too easy in court, and the ending
of the rather thin plot is all too neatly dovetailed. The
background and characters are effectively done, however.

WOLFF, William Almon (1885-1933)

395. The Trial of Mary Dugan. Garden City, NY: Doubleday,
Doran; London: Heinemann, 1928. (¼)

The novelization of Bayard Veiller's famous play is a bit of
a museum piece but still entertaining. There are some nice

narrative touches in reporter Steve Barrow's breezy account, and the many topical references (especially to celebrated criminal cases of the time) give a strong sense of the period. Former Ziegfeld girl Mary Dugan is accused of the stabbing murder of her wealthy lover, Edgar Rice. Though trial procedure seems mainly accurate, there is quite a bit of dramatic license taken. On an unlikely but highly theatrical note, the judge interrupts proceedings just as the Dugan trial begins to sentence a young Italian woman, convicted of killing her lover, to be executed. Prosecutor Galwey, who has the usual gubernatorial aspirations, is allowed an appallingly prejudicial opening. It's easy to imagine the melodramatic stunt solution knocking them dead in the stage and early-talkie versions.

WOODS, Sara, pseudonym of Sara Hutton Bowen-Judd (1922-   )

396. Bloody Instructions.   London: Collins; New York: Harper, 1962. (B)

This is the first book in the longest British series of legal detective novels. To date there are about half as many Antony Maitland books as Erle Stanley Gardner wrote about Perry Mason, and the majority of them include courtroom action. Beyond these similarities, it would be hard to imagine two crime writers as dissimilar as Gardner and Woods, who is among the coziest of the cozy British school of tea-and-sherry mystery writers. The Maitland series is one of the most uneven in the field, with the gap between best and worst a wide one indeed. And the earliest are not necessarily the best, as this entry shows. It is exactly the kind of book some readers are thinking of when they wrongheadedly pronounce all British detective stories dull.

The series traditions are all in place in this first volume. Antony and wife Jenny share a large house in Kempenfeldt Square with Antony's uncle, the celebrated and irascible barrister Sir Nicholas Harding. It is a "temporary" arrangement begun after World War II, in which Antony acquired a continually painful shoulder wound, and continuing into the mid-seventies of the more recent novels. A large group of other recurring characters also debut here: Sir Nicholas' disagreeable butler, Gibbs; Detective-Inspector Sykes (friendly cop) and Superintendent Briggs (hostile cop) of Scotland Yard; actress Meg Hamilton; perpetual junior counsel Derek Stringer; and frequent prosecuting nemesis Bruce Halloran.

In the first chapter, the body of elderly solicitor James Winter is found in his office, knife in back. Actor Joseph Dowling, a current stage Macbeth whose souvenir dagger appears to have been used in the crime, is accused, and Sir Nicholas accepts the brief. Antony, on the scene at the time of the crime, will be a witness at the trial. It is a role in which he gets away with murder, as he later would as an advocate. The 25-page Old Bailey sequence is the liveliest part of the novel. Only the prospect of a trial will get some readers through the slow middle area of the book. But the following quote, coming during Halloran's questioning of Antony, illustrates just how loose procedure can get in a Woods trial: "Halloran had been making a jury speech, but nobody seemed to notice it except Sir Nicholas, and he held his peace." Later, Sir Nicholas would also be allowed to argue his case during examination of a witness.

At the end of the novel, Woods uses the early Gardner technique of plugging (though not by name) the next novel in the series, the non-courtroom Malice Domestic (Collins, 1962), published only in Great Britain. Another early Woods novel never published in the U.S., Error of the Moon (Collins, 1963), may have courtroom action.

397. The Taste of Fears. London: Collins, 1963. (As The Third Encounter, New York: Harper, 1963.) (B)

The strangulation murder of Dr. Henry Martin is linked to World War II espionage and the search for faceless British traitor Teddy Morris. When Sir Nicholas Harding is briefed to defend the victim's ne'er-do-well cousin Gerry Martin, Antony Maitland once more becomes involved with a wartime nemesis, German master spy Ernst Ohlendorff. The novel is considerably livelier than Bloody Instructions, providing some detail about Antony's secrecy-shrouded war service, a nice cat-and-mouse scene with Sykes and Briggs where Antony claims amnesia following a second murder, and some invigorating if not precisely believable cloak-and-daggering. The Magistrate's Court hearing, though a full-dress battle between Halloran and the Harding-Maitland team, runs scarcely over a dozen pages.

398. Trusted Like the Fox. London: Collins, 1964. New York: Harper, 1965. (½)

Photographer Michael Godson is tried in 1962 for alleged treason committed twenty years before while working under the name Guy Harland as a famous biologist's assistant. The result of his supposed treachery is a deadly biological experiment carried out by the SS on a Polish city's water supply. In his first big case since taking silk, Antony Maitland defends, initially on grounds of mistaken identification but later from a different angle. This is one of the most extensive trials in Woods' novels, with much detailed testimony and shifting points of view, and one of her very best. The witness stand give-and-take crackles.

399. This Little Measure. London: Collins, 1964. (B)

Roddy Gaskell brings Antony Maitland an intriguing situation: in a codicil to his will, shipping magnate Roderick Gaskell bequeathed to his son Andrew (Roddy's father) "the problem of the Velasquez." No one in the family knew he had a Velasquez, and when found it proved to be stolen property. Then Andrew is poisoned and Roddy (who had visited Nepal, whence came the poison) accused. Bruce Halloran (Woods' nearest equivalent of Gardner's Hamilton Burger) leads for the prosecution and Sir Nicholas Harding carries the defense, finally confronting the killer on the witness stand in dramatic fashion. Though the trial action is okay, this is substandard Woods for the period, its failure to find an American publisher understandable.

400. Though I Know She Lies. London: Collins, 1965. New York: Holt, Rinehart, and Winston, 1972. (B)

Sir Nicholas is defending the beautiful Barbara Wentworth, accused of poisoning her sister. Junior counsel Derek Stringer is smitten. Maitland enters as a consulting detective rather than a barrister. This is average Woods with good trial action (a little over forty pages) and an effectively drawn child character but a somewhat disappointing solution. As she frequently does, Woods resorts to attacks on Antony (tiresome whether they're needed or not) in an attempt to liven up things.

401. Let's Choose Executors. London: Collins, 1966. New York: Harper, 1967. (B)

This splendid novel shows Woods at the top of her game. Vera Langhorne, a barrister practicing in the West Midland town of Chedcombe whose telegraphic speaking style will become a regular feature of the later Maitland novels, here makes her series debut, bringing Antony into the defense of solicitor's clerk Fran Gifford (distractingly named for American football fans). Fran is accused of poisoning her elderly benefactor Alice Randall, who had just changed her will in Fran's favor. The courtroom climax is a fine one, and the least-suspected-person murderer is both surprising and fairly clued.

402. And Shame the Devil. London: Collins, 1967. New York: Holt, Rinehart, and Winston, 1972. (B)

Maitland makes the first of several visits to the grim Yorkshire industrial town of Arkenshaw. He is briefed to defend Sgt. Fred Duckett and Constable James Ryder, police officers accused of wrongful arrest by Pakistani immigrants Ghulam Beas and Chakwal Mohamad. A journalist and a medical student respectively, they have been acquitted of burglary. A setting in her native Yorkshire often brings out the best in Woods, and this is another above average entry.

Another Yorkshire-based case, They Love Not Poison (1972), an eery tale of supposed witchcraft set in 1947, is one of Woods' best novels, though it eschews courtroom action.

403. Past Praying For. London: Collins; New York: Harper, 1968. (¼)

The story begins in the Old Bailey in 1957. Maitland is acting as Bruce Halloran's junior in the murder prosecution of Camilla Barnard, accused of the shotgun killing of husband Richard. Action jumps to 1965, with the same woman accused of killing by arsenic poisoning her second husband, Oliver Barnard, the cousin of her first. Sir Nicholas Harding defends at Northdean Assize Court with Vera Langhorne (later to be Lady Harding) as his junior. The climax involves one of those evil master criminals that often turn up, rather incongruously, in Woods' novels. This is a strong entry, with a good plot and a dramatic in-court finale.

404. Tarry and be Hanged. London: Collins, 1969. New York: Holt, Rinehart, and Winston, 1971. (B)

Dr. Henry Langton is accused of murder when the body of a strangled and mutilated woman is dug up in his garden. His wife had been killed fifteen months before in the same way and by the same kind of weapon: a venetian blind cord. Antony's investigation uncovers an elaborate and unusual serial murder scheme. Highlights are his troubled relationship with prickly Inspector Conway and a nice suspenseful finish. Trial action is good but minor, covering only about twenty pages.

405. An Improbable Fiction. London: Collins, 1970. New York: Holt, Rinehart, and Winston, 1971. (B)

TV commentator Lynn Edison, the sister of a deceased actress (supposedly a sleeping-pill suicide) accuses entertainer Paul Granville of murder on a national telecast. He sues for libel and Antony defends her. The brief trial (about seventeen pages) is capable but not Woods at her best. There is some heavy-handed humor with a long-haired witness who speaks in sixties slang. (Witness: "Like the chick was out of sight." Judge: "I thought it was a television broadcast...") When the trial is interrupted by the shooting of Granville, the charge becomes murder, but this is wrapped up out of court. Solid, average Woods.

406. Serpent's Tooth. London: Collins, 1971. New York: Holt, Rinehart, Winston, 1973. (B)

Antony returns to Arkenshaw to defend seventeen-year-old Joe Hartley, one of thirteen foster children of Alfred and Agnes Baker. Joe, an office boy employed by solicitor Chris Conway's firm, does not deny clubbing his foster father to death with a poker, nor does anyone seriously doubt he did it. This is an interesting, off-trail Maitland novel, representing that rarest of detective story variants, the whydunit.

It is an honored literary tradition that English judges must have slang, jargon, and other current references explained to them by counsel. But would a judge of the late 1960's actually be unfamiliar with the word "flabbergasted"?

407. Yet She Must Die. London: Macmillan, 1973. New York:

Holt, Rinehart, and Winston, 1974. (B)

Mystery writer Jeremy Skelton is accused of the nylon-scarf strangling of his wife Lydia in circumstances that seem to parallel the Julia Wallace case, which Jeremy was researching for a book. Antony Maitland, called to the West Midlands town of Chedcombe by barrister Vera Langhorne, detects outside court while Uncle Nicholas leads for the defense. Again, this is a good average Woods with solid trial action of more than forty pages. The witness-stand confession of the real killer seems to come a little too easily, however.

408. A Show of Violence.   London: Macmillan; New York: McKay-Washburn, 1975. (B)

In another visit to the Yorkshire city of Arkenshaw (which could be called Maitland's Wrightsville), Antony is briefed by solicitor Chris Conway to defend a 13-year-old runaway youth. Tommy Smith is accused of stealing three Holbein miniatures in a burglary and of beating to death Alfred Neale, with whom he had been living, when the old man discovered the stolen art works hidden under the boy's mattress. Trial action is typically expert, and the Northern setting is again a plus.

409. The Law's Delay.   London: Macmillan; New York: St. Martin's, 1977. (B)

Ellen Gray, whose father was convicted of murder twenty years before, is accused of shooting to death stockbroker John Wilcox, one of the key prosecution witnesses in her father's trial. Antony, though believing Ellen guilty, manages to get her acquitted in the first half of the novel. Then he is asked to prove the verdict right by finding the real killer. The telephoned and written threats to get off the case are as tiresome a cliché of the series as the attacks on Antony. Still, this is better than average for Woods, with a fairly-clued if foreseeable murderer.

410. A Thief or Two.   London: Macmillan; New York: St. Martin's, 1977. (½)

Antony defends Malcolm Harte, a young jeweler's assistant accused of stealing some jewels and murdering his employer, George DeLisle, in a weekend-house-party crime complete with wealthy guests and butler. More time is spent in court than usual, the trial running its full course to a jury verdict, and much of the combat there is adroitly done. On the whole, however, this is not one of Woods' better efforts. The thumbnail sketches of individual jurors, a welcome plus in some books, prove an annoying distraction in this one.

411. <u>Proceed to Judgement</u>. London: Macmillan; New York: St. Martin's, 1979. (B)

Kate Johnstone is jointly charged with her alleged lover, Dr. James Collingwood, with the murder of her husband, Douglas, a diabetic whose insulin injection was replaced with a fatal dose of morphine. Her barrister, Kevin O'Brien, QC, who induces Antony to join the defense representing the doctor, may want him more for his detective skill than his courtroom ability. The Old Bailey trial of 40+ pages is expert as ever, and the whole cozy enterprise reminds one of a Perry Mason novel as written by C. P. Snow.

412. <u>Cry Guilty</u>. London: Macmillan; New York: St. Martin's, 1981. (¼)

In a sequel to the non-courtroom (and <u>very</u> weak) <u>Weep for Her</u> (1980), Antony continues the search for the mysterious leader of a ring of art thieves. He untypically appears for the prosecution, assisting old opponent Bruce Halloran and opposing usual allies Kevin O'Brien and Derek Stringer, in the case of Louise Chorley, who has admitted to shooting her husband but is claimed by her advocates to be insane. Antony enters the case for the purpose of cross-examining three defense witnesses, one of whom may have killed Alan Kirby, whom Antony had been slated to represent on a charge of stealing a Rubens painting. The gimmick for making a prosecutor the hero aside, this is a distinctly substandard Woods both in and out of the courtroom. The witness-stand chats lack the driving force of good Q-and-A, rendering even the trial scenes dreary. In his 1982 reference volume <u>Whodunit?</u>, H. R. F. Keating says this is the only Maitland novel in which he "allow(s) himself a touch of the Perry Masons." I'm not sure what Keating means, but this sluggish enterprise would disappoint any Erle Stanley Gardner fan.

413. <u>Dearest Enemy</u>.   London: Macmillan; New York: St. Martin's, 1981. (B)

Leonard Buckley, male half of the London stage's elderly "Perfect Couple," believes the female half, Victoria, is trying to poison him. In a play appropriately called <u>Done in by Daggers</u>, Victoria becomes the victim of an on-stage opening-night murder. In the course of defending Leonard, Antony subpoenas Superintendent Briggs as a witness. Though the central situation is intriguing, the execution is below par. One of the most unconvincing aspects of the plot is the prosecution claim that the defendant was taking Vitamin A to improve his night vision in preparation for a murder in the dark.

414. <u>Enter a Gentlewoman</u>.   London: Macmillan; New York: St. Martin's, 1982. (B)

Sir Nicholas is briefed to represent Elizabeth Coke in a divorce action, while Antony is representing her solicitor husband Edward in a libel action against her. She alleges he forced her into a kinky triangle along the lines of the Adelaide Bartlett case. The courtroom battle of uncle and nephew in the libel suit is less interesting than one might hope. Much of Woods' latter-day court action loses impact because witness-stand encounters are too much like conversations and too little like examinations. Two murders occur on the eve of closing arguments, and Antony is briefed to represent a different client on those charges. The matter only gets to Magistrate's Court, however, with action summarized in a couple of pages. The plot is all right, but the whole novel is less enthralling than it should have been.

415. <u>Villains by Necessity</u>.   London: Macmillan; New York: St. Martin's, 1982. (B)

Antony defends Jim Arnold, a shopkeeper and supposedly-reformed felon accused of burglary. The client claims he returned to his old ways to foil a protection racket. Arnold's climactic trial follows the murder of a tenant of the house which apparently has among its residents the racket's coordinator.   The central situation has some originality, but execution is routine. The witness-stand exposure of the murderer seems much too easy.

416. The Lie Direct. London: Macmillan; New York: St. Martin's, 1983. (¼)

Out of friendship, Maitland accepts on no notice the defense of a client who seems to be clearly guilty: John Ryder, accused of treason (and, almost incidentally, bigamy). Ryder, charged with arranging the passage of state secrets to a Soviet agent on the evidence of the defecting Russian and his supposed "town wife," claims to be the victim of an extremely elaborate frameup. In mid-trial, one of his wives is arrested for the murder of the other. Maitland's climactic confrontation with one witness is more like a speculative conversation about the evidence in the case than a cross-examination. The extreme (and not really explained) tolerance of both judge and prosecutor is rightly remarked on in the family post mortem. On the whole, though, this is above average latter-day Woods.

Another 1983 Maitland case, Call Back Yesterday, takes on the fascinating subject of reincarnation but (alas) includes no courtroom scenes.

417. The Bloody Book of Law. London: Macmillan; New York: St. Martin's, 1984. (B)

Young journalist Vincent Gilchrist is accused of burgling the jewels of family friend Denise Thurlow. After successfully defending the case in the first half of the book, Antony is suspected by Superintendent Briggs of suborning perjury and murdering his own client. Though the plot is neat enough, the novel is marked by the increased padding evident in later Maitland novels, expecially in the family council scenes at Kempenfeldt Square.

WOOLRICH, Cornell

See IRISH, William

WOUK, Herman (1915-   )

418. The Caine Mutiny. Garden City, NY: Doubleday; London: Cape, 1951. (B)

Steve Maryk, executive officer of the Destroyer Mine-

sweeper U.S.S. Caine, relieves his captain, Lt. Cmdr. Philip
Queeg, of command during a typhoon, believing him to be
mentally ill and applying the little-known Article 184 of
Naval Regulations. Maryk's court-martial, not for mutiny
but for "conduct to the prejudice of good order and
discipline," is one of the most famous trials in American
fiction, but it actually takes up less than sixty pages of the
novel, a fuller account appearing in Wouk's play, The Caine
Mutiny Court-Martial. Barney Greenwald, an injured Navy
pilot assigned to defend on the basis of his civilian career
as a self-described "red-hot lawyer," is good example of
the advocate who goes to the limit for a client with whom
he has limited sympathy. The courtroom scenes are
excellently done, but the shipboard scenes that make up
most of the book are the key to this Pulitzer Prize winner's
massive appeal. Wouk obviously loves the Navy, and it is
interesting that the villain of the piece is not Queeg but a
novelist, Tom Keefer, the third-in-command officer whose
facile amateur psychiatric diagnosis spurs Maryk to his act.

While the novel is deserving of its stature as one of the
fine books about World War II, it demonstrates that some
fiction of the early fifties no longer seems contemporary.
Wouk, though not denying the relentless obscenity of
servicemen's conversation, goes through great pains (including repeated references to Shinola) to avoid duplicating
it, an effort that reviewers of the time thanked him for
and so might some readers today. The only black characters, the faceless messboys, are something no one will
thank him for, "yassuh, nossuh" caricatures that belong to
another time.

Readers who come to the novel for the first time, as I did,
after repeated viewings of the film version, will note how
well most of the parts were cast. Wouk's descriptions of
his characters are so vivid and fully-realized, though, that
most readers will see them rather than their screen coun-
terparts. Maryk is far less handsome than Van Johnson;
Ensign Willie Keith, the book's protagonist, is a more
complex and interesting character than Robert Francis was
able to project on the screen; and Barney Greenwald looks
nothing like Jose Ferrer (and even less like his stage
portrayer, Henry Fonda). Humphrey Bogart's Queeg and
Fred MacMurray's Keefer are the hardest images to erase.

YAFFE, James (1927-   )

419. Nothing but the Night. Boston: Atlantic/Little, Brown, 1957. London: Cape, 1958. (B)

Yaffe had the bad luck to come up with a fictionalization of the Leopold and Loeb case too close on the heels of the publication of Meyer Levin's classic Compulsion (q.v.) Although Barry Morris (the somewhat sympathetic Leopold character) and Paul King (the sociopathic Loeb equivalent) are fifties New Yorkers rather than twenties Chicagoans, the parallels are clear and unconcealed. Trial action covers about thirty pages, with more summary and speechifying than detailed give and take. Defender Brennan's closing argument, though eloquent, is not as impressive as the speech it is patterned after: Clarence Darrow's defense of Leopold and Loeb, quoted verbatim in the Levin novel. Yaffe is a wonderful writer, and this is a readable, affecting story, though not especially distinguished as a courtroom novel.

YGLESIAS, Helen

420. Sweetsir. New York: Simon and Schuster; London: Hodder and Stoughton, 1981. (B)

In the New England town of Eatonville, 32-year-old Sally Sweetsir stabs her abusive husband Morgan (Sweets) Sweetsir with a kitchenknife. Is it accident? self-defense? manslaughter? premeditated murder? an outpouring of rage accumulated over years of ill use by men? This is an immensely powerful novel, offering a hard and uncompromising depiction of male-female relationships at their worst. It is a feminist book but not a black-and-white one-- feminist do-gooders are not spared a jaundiced look, and few of the men are pure villains. The relationship between Sally and Ellen Mahoney, the one female member of her Public Defender team, is interestingly done, and the book gives more attention than usual to pre-trial rehearsals. The trial itself, told from Sally's point of view in some 38 pages, is very effective, though State's Attorney Lyman Bannister seems too much in the grand tradition of obnoxious prosecutors. The jury's slowness to agree on whether or not a husband has the right to strike his wife is a telling (and haunting) incident.

Z

ZIRAN, Goland

421. The Counsellor. New York: Arbor House, 1982. (B)

The saga of New York trial lawyer Saul Belinsky, who goes from idealistic young attorney to mob mouthpiece, has its moments, but ultimately it is flat and disappointing, mostly because Saul never really comes to life as a character. The book also needed better editing: a 1946 reference to "Third World" countries is the kind of sore-thumb anachronism that can severely damage the reader's faith in a work of historical fiction. The two main trial sequences, totaling some 45 pages, concern Belinsky's representation of the heir of a senile 75-year-old woman, who was sold an annuity by an insurance company shortly before her death; and his defense of his senior partner, Hiram Lewis Sears, accused of the murder of a judge. The trial scenes are competent but nothing extraordinary.

SUPPLEMENTARY BIBLIOGRAPHY
OF COURTROOM FICTION

The following are additional novels and collections that may be of interest to trial buffs. Although not all of these titles have been examined, nearly all of them are assumed to have substantial courtroom scenes. Unexamined titles are from the following sources: Fiction Catalog, Book Review Digest, the Los Angeles Public Library fiction subject index, and suggestions by the individual authors, critics, and collectors noted in the acknowledgements. Additional titles by authors represented in the annotated section may be found in the annotations. Authors and titles listed below have not been included in the index.

ACHESON, Edward (1902-   )

Red Herring. New York: Morrow, 1932. As Murder by Suggestion, London: Hutchinson, 1933.

ADAMS, Frederick Upham (1859-1931)

The Bottom of the Well. New York: Dillingham; London: Upham, 1906.

ADAMS, Samuel Hopkins (1871-1958)

Sunrise to Sunset. New York: Random House, 1950. London: Long, 1951.

AINSWORTH, W(illiam) H(arrison) (1805-1882)

Guy Fawkes. London: Bentley; New York: Nafis, 1841.

Star Chamber. London: Routledge, 1854. American editions various.

AUCHINCLOSS, Louis (1917-   )

A Law for the Lion. Boston: Houghton-Mifflin; London: Gollancz, 1953.

AVALLONE, Michael (1924-   )

Stag Stripper. New York: Midwood, 1961.

BANNING, Margaret Culkin (1891-1982)

The Iron Will. New York: Harper, 1936.

BARRE, Michael.

The Case Against the Andersons. New York: Delacorte, 1983.

BENJOYA, Mitchell

Final Judgment. Chicago: Contemporary, 1978.

BENNETT, Arnold (1867-1931)

Buried Alive. London: Chapman and Hall; Garden City, NY: Doubleday, Page, 1908.

BENTLEY, Barbara

Mistress Nancy. New York: McGraw-Hill, 1980.

BENTLEY, Phyllis (1894-1977)

Inheritance. London: Gollancz; New York: Macmillan, 1932.

Modern Tragedy. London: Gollancz; New York: Macmillan, 1934.

BESANT, Sir Walter

The Orange Girl. London: Chatto and Windus; New York: Dodd, Mead, 1899.

BESSIE, Alvah (1904-   )

Bread and a Stone. New York: Modern Age, 1941. London:
Swan, 1948.

BICKEL, Mary

Brassbound. New York: Coward-McCann, 1934. As The
Trial of Linda Stuart, London: Hamilton, 1935.

BIER, Jesse (1925-   )

Trial at Bannock. New York: Harcourt, Brace, and World,
1963.

BINKLEY, Anne

What Shall I Cry? New York: Harcourt, Brace, and World;
London: Gollancz, 1968.

BLACK, William (1841-1898)

Highland Cousins.   London: Sampson Low; New York:
Harper, 1894.

BLOOMFIELD, Robert, pseudonym of Leslie Edgley (1912-   )

Vengeance Street. Garden City, NY: Doubleday, 1952.

BONNET, Theodore

Dutch. Garden City, NY: Doubleday, 1955. London: Allen,
1956.

BRAND, Max, pseudonym of Frederick Schiller Faust (1892-1944)

Destry Rides Again. New York: Dodd, Mead, 1930. London: Hodder and Stoughton, 1931.

Dr. Kildare's Trial. New York: Dodd, Mead, 1942. London:
Hodder and Stoughton, 1944.

BROWN, J(ohn) E(dward) (1920-   )

Incident at 125th Street.   Garden City, NY: Doubleday,
1970.

BROWN, Katharine Holland (?-1931)

   The Father. New York: Day, 1928. London: Heinemann, 1929.

BUCKMASTER, Henrietta, pseudonym of Henrietta Henkle Stephens (1909-   )

   Deep River. New York: Harcourt, Brace, 1944. London: Edwards, 1948.

BULWER-LYTTON, Edward (1803-1873)

   Eugene Aram. London: Colburn; New York: Harper, 1832.

BURKE, Alan Dennis (1949-   )

   Getting Away with Murder.   Boston: Atlantic/Little, Brown, 1981.

CANAVOR, Frederick

   Rape One. Seattle: Madrona, 1982.

CHANDLER, David

   The Ramsden Case. New York: Simon and Schuster, 1967.

CHATTERTON, Ruth

   The Betrayers.   Boston: Houghton Mifflin, 1953.   London: Harrap, 1954.

CHEVALIER, Haakon (1902-   )

   For Us the Living. New York: Knopf; London: Secker and Warburg, 1949.

COLUM, Kelly

   Hear That Train Blow. New York: Delacorte, 1970.

COLUM, Padraic (1881-1972)

   Castle Conquer. New York: Macmillan, 1923.

COLVER, Anne (1908-)

   Theodosia, Daughter of Aaron Burr. New York: Farrar and
   Rinehart, 1941.

COMSTOCK, Harriet T.

   Smothered Fires. London: Heinemann; New York: Doubleday, Page, 1924.

CONNERS, Bernard F. (1926-)

   Dancehall. Indianapolis: Bobbs-Merrill, 1983.

COOPER, I(rving) S(pencer) (1922-)

   It's Hard to Leave When the Music's Playing. New York:
   Norton, 1977.

COOPER, Kent (1880-1965)

   Anna Zenger Mother of Freedom. New York: Farrar,
   Straus, 1946.

COWAN, Sada

   Bitter Justice. Garden City, NY: Doubleday, Doran, 1943.
   London: Gifford, 1946.

CRONIN, A(rchibald) J(oseph) (1896-1981)

   Beyond This Place. London: Gollancz; Boston: Little,
   Brown, 1953.

DAVIDSON, David (1908-)

   The Quest of Juror 19. Garden City, NY: Doubleday, 1971.

DAVIDSON, Louis B., and DOHERTY, Eddie

   Captain Marooner. New York: Crowell, 1952.

DAVIES, Rhys (1903-1978)

   The Black Venus. London: Heinemann, 1944. New York:
   Howell, Soskin, 1946.

DAVIS, Robert P. (1929-)

The Divorce. New York: Morrow; London: Hale, 1980.

DEAL, Borden (1922-)

The Advocate. Garden City, NY: Doubleday, 1968.

DENTON, Kit

The Breaker: The Novel Behind Breaker Morant. Sydney and London: Angus and Robertson, 1973. New York: St. Martin's, 1981.

DIBNER, Martin (1911-)

The Trouble with Heroes. Garden City, NY: Doubleday, 1971.

DINNEEN, Joseph.

Anatomy of a Crime. New York: Scribner's, 1954. London: Cassell, 1955.

Underworld U.S.A.. New York: Farrar, Straus, 1956. London: Cassell, 1957.

DODGE, Constance W.

In Adam's Fall. Philadelphia: Macrae-Smith, 1946.

DOHRMAN, Richard

Vonda Rosegood. New York: Harper and Row, 1965. London: Transworld, 1966.

DOUGLAS, M(arjory) S(toneham)

Road to the Sun. New York: Rinehart, 1952.

DOWNING, J(ohn) Hyatt (1888-)

Sioux City. New York: Putnam, 1940. As They Built a City, London: Jarrolds, 1941.

DOYLE, Arthur Conan (1859-1930)

    Micah Clarke. London: Longman; New York: Harper, 1889.

DRATLER, Jay J. (1911-)

    The Pitfall. New York: Crown, 1947.

DRURY, Allen (1918-)

    Decision. Garden City, NY: Doubleday, 1983.

DUKE, Winifred (?-1962)

    Skin for Skin. London: Gollancz; Boston: Little, Brown, 1935.

DUMAURIER, Daphne (1907-)

    Mary Anne. London: Gollancz; Garden City, NY: Double-day, 1954.

DUNCAN, Thomas W. (1905-)

    Ring Horse. Garden City, NY: Doubleday, 1940.

DUNNE, John Gregory (1932-)

    Dutch Shea, Jr. New York: Linden Press/Simon and Schuster; London: Weidenfeld and Nicolson, 1982.

ECKERT, Allan W. (1931-)

    The Court Martial of Daniel Boone. Boston: Little, Brown, 1973.

EGAN, Lesley, pseudonym of Elizabeth Linington (1921-)

    A Case for Appeal. New York: Harper, 1961. London: Gollancz, 1962.

EGGLESTON, Edward (1837-1902)

    The Graysons. New York: Century, 1887. Edinburgh: Douglas, 1888.

EHRLICH, Jack (1930-)

Court Martial. New York: Pyramid, 1959.

The Chatham Killing. New York: Pocket Books, 1976.

ELLSBERG, Edward

Mid Watch. New York: Dodd, Mead; London: Heinemann, 1954.

ENDORE, Guy (1900-1970)

Methinks the Lady. New York: Duell, Sloan, and Pearce, 1945. London: Cresset, 1947.

FARJEON, J(oseph) Jefferson (1883-1955)

The Judge Sums Up. London: Collins; Indianapolis: Bobbs-Merrill, 1942.

FAST, Howard (1907-)

Conceived in Liberty. New York: Simon and Schuster; London: Joseph, 1939.

The Winston Affair. New York: Crown, 1959. London: Methuen, 1960.

FERBER, Edna (1887-1968)

Cimarron. Garden City, NY: Doubleday; London: Heinemann, 1930.

FOLLETT, James (1939-)

Crown Court. London: Barker, 1977. New York: St. Martin's, 1978.

FORBES, Esther (1891-1967)

Mirror for Witches. Boston: Houghton, Mifflin; London: Heinemann, 1928.

General's Lady. New York: Harcourt, Brace, 1938. London: Chatto and Windus, 1939.

FORD, Jeremy

    Murder Laughs Last. New York: Bouregy, 1956. London: Ward, Lock, 1959.

FORD, Leslie, pseudonym of Zenith Brown (1898-   )

    Reno Rendezvous. New York: Farrar and Rinehart, 1939. As Mr. Cromwell is Dead. London: Collins, 1939.

    The Girl from the Mimosa Club. New York: Scribners; London: Collins, 1957.

    Trial by Ambush. New York: Scribners, 1962. As Trial from Ambush, London: Collins, 1962.

FORREST, Williams

    Stigma. New York: Crown, 1957. London: Redman, 1959.

FORSTER, E(dward) M(organ) (1879-1970)

    A Passage to India. London: Arnold; New York: Harcourt, Brace, 1924.

FOWLER, Sydney, pseudonym of Sydney Fowler Wright (1874-1965)

    The King Against Anne Bickerton. London: Harrap, 1930. As The Case of Anne Bickerton, New York: Boni and Liveright, 1930, as by S. Fowler Wright.

GAINES, Ernest J. (1933-   )

    Of Love and Dust. New York: Dial, 1967.

GAITHER, Frances Ormond

    The Red Cock Crows. New York: Macmillan, 1944.

    Double Muscadine. New York: Macmillan; London: Joseph, 1949.

GANN, Ernest K. (1910-   )

    Of Good and Evil. New York: Simon and Schuster; London:

Hodder and Stoughton, 1963.

The Magistrate. New York: Arbor House, 1982.

GARVE, Andrew, pseudonym of Paul Winterton (1908-   )

Death and the Sky Above. London: Collins; New York: Harper, 1953.

GILBERT, Anthony, pseudonym of Lucy Beatrice Malleson (1899-1973)

The Night of the Fog. London: Gollancz; New York: Dodd, Mead, 1930.

GLOAG, Julian (1930-   )

A Sentence of Life. London: Secker and Warburg; New York: Simon and Schuster, 1966.

GODWIN, William (1756-1836)

Things as They Are; or the Adventures of Caleb Williams. London: Crosby, 1794. New York: Rice, 1795.

GORDON, Arthur (1912-   )

Reprisal. New York: Simon and Schuster; London: Hamilton, 1950.

GRAHAM, Winston (1909-   )

The Merciless Ladies. London: Ward, Lock, 1944.

Take My Life. London: Ward, Lock, 1947. Garden City, NY: Doubleday, 1967.

The Tumbled House. London: Hodder and Stoughton, 1959. Garden City, NY: Doubleday, 1960.

GRAVES, Robert (1895-   )

"Antigua, Penny, Puce". London: Constable, 1936. As The Antigua Stamp, New York: Random House, 1937.

GREENE, F(rances) N(immo)

The Devil to Pay. New York: Scribner's, 1918.

GREENE, Ward (1892-1956)

Death in the Deep South. New York: Stackpole, 1936.
London: Cassell, 1937.

GREGOR, Manfred (1929-   )

Town Without Pity. Translated from the German Das
Urteil by Robert Brain. New York: Random House; London: Heinemann, 1961.

GUTHRIE, A(lfred) B(ertram), Jr. (1901-   )

Murders at Moon Dance. New York: Dutton, 1943.

HAGGARD, H(enry) Rider (1856-1925)

Mr. Meeson's Will. London: Spencer Blackett; New York:
Harper, 1888.

HALE, Edward Everett (1822-1909)

Philip Nolan's Friends. New York: Scribner, Armstrong,
1877.

HARDWICK, Elizabeth

The Simple Truth. New York: Harcourt, Brace; London:
Weidenfeld and Nicolson, 1955.

HARRIS, John (1916-   )

Light Cavalry Action. London: Hutchinson; New York:
Morrow, 1967.

HARTE, Bret (1836-1902)

Gabriel Conroy. Hartford: American Publishing; London:
Warne, 1876.

HENRIQUES, Robert

> No Arms, No Armor. New York: Farrar and Rinehart; London: Nicholson and Watson, 1939.

HERBERT, A(lan) P(atrick) (1890-1971)

> Holy Deadlock. London: Methuen; Garden City, NY: Doubleday, 1934.

> Uncommon Law. London: Methuen, 1935. Garden City, NY: Doubleday, 1936.

HESKY, Olga (?-1974)

> Life Sentence. Garden City, NY: Doubleday, 1972.

HIGGINS, George V. (1939-   )

> The Judgment of Deke Hunter. Boston: Little, Brown; London: Secker and Warburg, 1976.

HILLIARD, A(lec) R(owley) (1908-   )

> Justice Be Damned. New York: Farrar and Rinehart, 1941. London: Cassell, 1944.

HOSTER, Grace (1893-   )

> Trial by Murder. New York: Farrar and Rinehart, 1944. London: Hammond, 1952.

HOWELLS, William Dean (1837-1920)

> A Modern Instance. Boston: Osgood; Edinburgh: Douglas, 1882.

HUGHES, Rupert (1872-1956)

> Stately Timber. New York: Scribner's; London: Jarrolds, 1939.

HUIE, William Bradford (1910-   )

> Mud on the Stars. New York: Fischer, 1942. London: Hutchinson, 1944.

HUNT, Harrison, pseudonym of W. T. Ballard (1903-1980) and
Norbert Davis

Murder Picks the Jury. New York: Mystery House, 1947.

HUTCHINS, A(rthur) S(tuart) M(enteth)

If Winter Comes. Boston: Little, Brown, 1921.

JENNINGS, John

Next to Valor. New York: Macmillan; London: Hamilton,
1939.

Call the New World. New York: Macmillan; London:
Hamilton, 1941.

JESSE, F(ryniwyd) Tennyson (1889-1958)

A Pin to See the Peepshow. London: Heinemann; Garden
City, NY: Doubleday, Doran, 1934.

JOHNSTON, Mary (1870-1936)

Lewis Rand. Boston: Houghton Mifflin; London: Constable, 1908.

JOHNSTON, Myrtle (1909-)

A Robin Redbreast in a Cage. London: Heinemann, 1950.
Boston: Houghton Mifflin, 1951.

KAMPF, Harold

My Brother, O My Brother. London: Chapman and Hall,
1953. As When He Shall Appear, Boston: Little, Brown,
1954.

KANE, Harnett T. (1910-)

New Orleans Woman. Garden City, NY: Doubleday, 1946.
London: Davies, 1947.

KANE, Henry (1918-)

Decision. New York: Dial, 1973.

KAYE-SMITH, Sheila (1888-)

Rose Deeprose. London: Cassell; New York: Harper, 1936.

KAZAN, Elia (1909-)

Assassins. New York: Stein and Day; London: Collins, 1972.

KEENE, Day (?-1969)

Seed of Doubt. New York: Simon and Schuster, 1961. London: Allen, 1962.

KELTON, Elmer (1926-)

Medicine Hill. Garden City, NY: Doubleday, 1984.

KERR, James

The Clinic. New York: Coward-McCann, 1968.

KINGSLEY, Henry (1830-1876)

Austin Elliott. London: Macmillan; Boston: Ticknor and Fields, 1863.

KLINGSBERG, Harry

Doowinkle, D.A. New York: Dial, 1940.

KLUGER, Richard (1934-)

Member of the Tribe. Garden City, NY: Doubleday, 1977.

KOMROFF, Manuel (1890-1974)

A New York Tempest. New York: Coward-McCann, 1932.

LAING, Alexander (1903-1976)

Jonathan Eagle. New York: Duell, Sloan, Pearce; Boston: Little, Brown, 1955.

LAMSON, David

   Whirlpool. New York: Scribners, 1937.

LANCASTER, Bruce (1896-1963)

   Bright to the Wanderer. Boston: Little, Brown, 1942.

LANE, Elinor (1864-1909)

   Nancy Stair. New York: Appleton-Century, 1904.

LANHAM, Edwin (1904-1979)

   The Wind Blew West. New York: Longmans, 1935. London:
   Heinemann, 1936.

   Thunder on the Earth. New York: Harcourt, Brace, 1941.
   London: Heinemann, 1942.

LEVY, Barbara (1921-   )

   Place of Judgment. Garden City, NY: Doubleday, 1965.

LEWIS, Hilda (1896-1974)

   Send Dr. Spendlove. London: Jarrolds, 1940. As The Case
   of the Little Doctor, New York: Random, 1949.

   Strange Story. London: Jarrolds, 1945. New York: Random, 1947.

LEWISOHN, Ludwig (1882-1955)

   Stephen Escott. New York: Harper, 1930. As The Memories of Stephen Escott, London: Butterworth, 1930.

LICHFIELD, Richard

   Diana K.C.. London: Harry Walker, 1930.

LIEBELER, Jean Mayer (1900?-   )

   You, the Jury. New York: Farrar and Rinehart, 1944. As
   by Virginia Mather, London: Skeffington, 1946.

LIEBER, Joel (1937-1971)

How the Fishes Live. New York: McKay, 1967. London: Allen, 1968.

LIEBMAN, Ron

Grand Jury. New York: Ballantine, 1983.

LINCOLN, Victoria (1904-1981)

A Dangerous Innocence. New York: Rinehart, 1958.

LINN, Edward (1922-)

The Adversaries. New York: Saturday Review/Dutton, 1973.

LOWNDES, Marie Belloc (1868-1947)

Letty Lynton. London: Heinemann; New York: Cape and Smith, 1931.

LOWREY, Walter B.

Watch Night. New York: Scribner's, 1953.

LUND, Roslyn

The Sharing. New York: Morrow, 1978.

LYNDE, Francis (1856-1930)

Young Blood. New York: Scribner's, 1929.

LYON, Winston

Criminal Court. New York: Pocket Books, 1966.

MCCABE, Cameron, pseudonym of Ernest Borneman (1915-)

The Face on the Cutting Room Floor. London: Gollancz, 1937. New York: Gregg, 1981.

MACDONALD, William Colt

> Wheels in the Dust. Garden City, NY: Doubleday, 1946. London: Hodder and Stoughton, 1949.

MCGIVERN, William P. (1927-1982)

> Summitt. New York: Arbor House, 1982.

MACKENZIE, Donald (1908-   )

> The Juryman. London: Elek, 1957. New York: Houghton-Mifflin, 1958.

MCMORROW, Thomas (1886-   )

> The Sinister History of Ambrose Hinkle. New York: Sears, 1929.

MANKIEWICZ, Don M. (1922-   )

> Trial. New York: Harper; London: Deutsch, 1955.

MARGOLIN, Phillip

> Heartstone. New York: Pocket Books, 1978.

MARSHALL, Archibald, pseudonym of Arthur Hammond Marshall (1866-1934)

> Claimants. Boston: Houghton, Mifflin, 1934.

> Nothing Hid. London: Collins, 1934. Boston: Houghton, Mifflin, 1935.

MARSHALL, Robert K.

> Little Squire Jim. New York: Duell, Sloan, and Pearce, 1949. London: Macdonald, 1950.

MASEFIELD, John (1878-1967)

> Dead Ned. London: Heinemann; New York: Macmillan, 1938.

MASTERMAN, Walter S. (1876-)

The Perjured Alibi. London: Methuen; New York: Dutton, 1935.

MASTERS, Edgar Lee (1869-1950)

Kit O'Brien. New York: Boni and Liveright, 1927.

MAVITY, Nancy Barr (1890-)

The State Versus Elna Jepson. Garden City, NY: Doubleday, 1937.

MENEN, Aubrey

Prevalence of Witches. London: Chatto and Windus, 1947. New York: Scribners, 1948.

MERGENDAHL, Charles

The Bramble Bush. New York: Putnam; London: Muller, 1958.

MERRITT, Miriam (1925-)

By Lions Eaten Gladly. New York: Harcourt, Brace, and World, 1965. London: Gollancz, 1966.

MILLER, Alice Duer (1874-1942)

Manslaughter. New York: Dodd, Mead, 1921. London: Parsons, 1922.

MILLS, Osmington, pseudonym of Vivian Collin Brooks (1922-)

Trial by Ordeal. London: Bles; New York: Roy, 1961.

MITCHELL, Paige, pseudonym of Judith S. Ginnes

Love is not a Safe Country. New York: Dutton; London: Barker, 1967.

MOLLOY, Robert (1906-1977)

Afternoon in March. Garden City, NY: Doubleday, 1958.

MORRIS, Jean (1924-   )

    Man and Two Gods. London: Cassell, 1953. New York: Viking, 1954.

MORROW, Honoré Willsie

    The Devonshires. London: Hodder and Stoughton; New York: Stokes, 1924.

MOTLEY, Willard (1912-1965)

    Knock on Any Door. New York: Appleton-Century, 1947. London: Collins, 1948.

NELSON, Truman (1911-   )

    The Sins of the Prophet. Boston: Little, Brown, 1952.

NILES, Blair

    East by Day. New York: Farrar and Rinehart, 1941.

NORDHOFF, Charles (1887-1947), and HALL, James Robert (1887-1951)

    Mutiny on the Bounty. Boston: Little Brown, 1932. As Mutiny!, London: Chapman and Hall, 1933.

OATES, Joyce Carol (1938-   )

    Do With Me What You Will. New York: Vanguard, 1973. London: Gollancz, 1974.

PAGE, Elizabeth

    Tree of Liberty. New York: Farrar and Rinehart; London: Collins, 1939.

PANGBORN, Edgar (1909-1976)

    The Trial of Callista Blake. New York: St. Martin's; London: Davies, 1961.

PARKER, James Reid

Attorneys at Law--Forbes, Hathaway, Bryan, and Devore. New York: Doubleday, 1941.

PARSONS, Helen Beal

The Trial of Helen McLeod. New York: Funk and Wagnalls, 1938.

PAUL, Raymond (1940-   )

The Thomas Street Horror. New York: Viking, 1982.

PEARCE, Dick (1909-   )

The Darby Trial. Philadelphia: Lippincott, 1954. London: Hodder and Stoughton, 1955.

PEARL, Jack (1923-   )

Stockade. New York: Simon and Schuster, 1965.

A Jury of his Peers. Englewood Cliffs, NJ: Prentice-Hall, 1975.

PEARSON, William (1922-   )

A Fever in the Blood. New York: St. Martin's, 1959.

PONICSAN, Darryl (1938-   )

The Accomplice. New York: Harper and Row; London: Joseph, 1975.

POPE, Dudley (1925-   )

Ramage. London: Weidenfeld and Nicolson; Philadelphia: Lippincott, 1965.

POPKIN, Zelda (1898-1983)

A Death of Innocence. Philadelphia: Lippincott, 1971. London: Allen, 1972.

PORTER, Monica

    The Mercy of the Court. New York: Norton, 1955.

PORTER, Rebecca N. (1883-)

    The Rest Hollow Mystery. New York: Century, 1922.
    London: Long, 1924.

POWELL, Richard (1908-)

    The Philadelphian. New York: Scribners, 1956.

QUICK, Herbert (1861-1925)

    Invisible Woman. Indianapolis: Bobbs-Merrill, 1924. Lon-
    don: Brentano's, 1925.

RAYMOND, Ernest (1888-1974)

    We, the Accused. London: Cassell; New York: Stokes,
    1935.

REACH, James (1909?-1970)

    Late Last Night. New York: Morrow, 1949. London:
    Heinemann, 1950.

RECHY, John (1934-)

    This Day's Death. New York: Grove, 1969.

REYWALL, John

    The Trial of Alvin Boaker. New York: Random, 1948.

RHODE, John, pseudonym of Cecil John Charles Street (1884-
1964)

    The Davidson Case. London: Bles, 1929. As Murder at
    Bratton Grange, New York: Dodd, Mead, 1929.

RHODES, Eugene Manlove (1869-1934)

    Stepsons of Light. Boston: Houghton, Mifflin, 1921. Lon-
    don: Hodder and Stoughton, 1922.

RHODES, James A. and JAUCHIUS, Dean

Trial of Mary Todd Lincoln. Indianapolis: Bobbs-Merrill, 1959.

RICE, Elmer L. (1892-1967)

Imperial City. New York: Coward-McCann; London: Gollancz, 1937.

ROBINSON, Lewis (1886-   )

The General Goes Too Far. London: Nicholson, 1935. New York: Putnam, 1936.

ROLLINS, William, Jr.

The Shadow Before. New York: McBride, 1934.

ROSEN, Norma Stahl (1925-   )

Touching Evil. New York: Harcourt, Brace, and World, 1969.

ROSSITER, John (1916-   )

The Villains. London: Cassell, 1974. New York: Walker, 1976.

ROTH, Holly (1916-1964)

Shadow of a Lady. New York: Simon and Schuster; London: Hamish Hamilton, 1957.

ROYDE-SMITH, Naomi Gwladys

For Us in the Dark. London and New York: Macmillan, 1937.

RYAN, James H. (1928-   )

Suffer the Little Ones. Nashville: Aurora, 1972.

RYLEE, Robert

Deep Dark River. New York: Farrar and Rinehart; London:

Heinemann, 1935.

SABATINI, Rafael (1875-   )

Sea-Hawk. London: Secker; Boston: Houghton, Mifflin, 1915.

Captain Blood. London: Hutchinson; Boston: Houghton, Mifflin, 1922.

The Minion. London: Hutchinson, 1930. As King's Minion, Boston: Houghton, Mifflin, 1930.

SCHWEITZER, Gertrude (1909-   )

Born. Garden City, NY: Doubleday, 1960.

SEAMAN, Donald (1922-   )

The Defector. London: Hamish Hamilton, 1975. As The Chameleon Course, New York: Coward-McCann, 1976.

SETON, Anya

My Theodosia. Boston: Houghton, Mifflin 1941.

SHAPIRO, Lionel (1908-   )

The Sealed Verdict. Garden City, NY: Doubleday, 1947. London: Jarrolds, 1950.

SHEARING, Joseph, pseudonym of Gabrielle Margaret Vere Campbell Long (1886-1952)

Airing in a Closed Carriage. London: Hutchinson; New York: Harper, 1943.

SHELDON, Richard

Poor Prisoner's Defense. London: Hutchinson; New York: Simon and Schuster, 1949.

Harsh Evidence. London: Hutchinson, 1950.

SHELDON, Sidney (1917-   )

   Rage of Angels. New York: Morrow; London: Collins, 1980.

SHEPARD, Martin (1934-   )

   A Question of Values. New York: Saturday Review/Dutton, 1976.

SIEGEL, Benjamin (1914-   )

   The Jurors. New York: Delacorte; London: Hale, 1973.

SILBERSTANG, Edwin (1930-   )

   Rapt in Glory. New York: Pocket Books, 1964.

SINCLAIR, Upton (1878-1968)

   Boston. Long Beach, CA: Sinclair, 1928. London: T. Werner Laurie, 1929.

SLAUGHTER, Frank G. (1908-   )

   Sword and Scalpel. Garden City, NY: Doubleday, 1957.

SPARKS, Dorothy

   Nothing as Before. New York: Harper, 1944.

SPICER, Bart (1918-   )

   Act of Anger. New York: Atheneum, 1962. London: Barker, 1963.

   The Adversary. New York: Putnam; London: Hart-Davis, 1974.

STEEN, Marguerite (1894-1975)

   The Sun is my Undoing. London: Collins; New York: Viking, 1941.

STEGNER, Wallace (1909-   )

   The Preacher and the Slave. Boston: Houghton, Mifflin,

1950. London: Hammond, 1951.

STEIN, Sol (1926-   )

   The Magician.   New York: Delacorte; London: Joseph,
   1971.

STILLWELL, Hart

   Border City. Garden City, NY: Doubleday, Doran, 1945.
   London: Hurst and Blackett, 1948.

STONE, Irving (1903-   )

   False Witness. Garden City, NY: Doubleday, 1940.

   Immortal Wife. Garden City, NY: Doubleday, 1944. London: Falcon, 1950.

   Adversary in the House.   Garden City, NY: Doubleday,
   1947. London: Falcon, 1949.

STUART, Francis

   Julie. London: Collins; New York: Knopf, 1938.

STUART, Jesse (1907-   )

   Trees of Heaven. New York: Dutton, 1940.

STUBBS, Jean (1926-   )

   My Grand Enemy. London: Macmillan, 1967. New York:
   Stein and Day, 1968.

SWINNERTON, Frank (1884-1982)

   The Two Wives. London: Hutchinson, 1939. Garden City,
   NY: Doubleday, 1940.

   A Woman in Sunshine. London: Hutchinson, 1944. Garden
   City, NY: Doubleday, 1945.

TARKINGTON, Booth (1869-1946)

   Conquest of Canaan. London and New York: Harper, 1905.

TAYLOR, Joan

   Asking for It. New York: Congdon and Lattes, 1980.

TERROT, Charles

   Miss Nightingale's Ladies. London Collins, 1948. As
   Passionate Pilgrim, New York: Harper, 1949.

THOMPSON, Estelle

   The Lawyer and the Carpenter. London: Hodder and
   Stoughton, 1963. New York: Washburn, 1964.

TREAT, Lawrence (1903-   )

   Trial and Terror. New York: Morrow, 1949. London:
   Boardman, 1958.

TROLLOPE, Anthony (1815-1882)

   Phineas Redux. London: Chapman and Hall; New York:
   Harper, 1874.

TRUMBO, Dalton (1905-1976)

   The Remarkable Andrew. Philadelphia: Lippincott; London: Lane, 1941.

TURNBULL, Agnes Sligh (1888-1982)

   The Wedding Bargain. Boston: Houghton, Mifflin, 1966.
   London: Collins, 1967.

UPWARD, Allen (1863-1926)

   The Queen Against Owen. London: Chatto, 1894.

WAKEFIELD, H(erbert) Russell (1888-1965)

   Hearken to the Evidence. London: Bles, 1933. Garden
   City, NY: Doubleday, Doran, 1934.

WALLIS, James Harold (1885-1958)

   The Neice of Abraham Pein. New York: Dutton, 1943.

London: Jarrolds, 1944.

WALSH, William Thomas (1891-1949)

Out of the Whirlwind. New York: McBride, 1935. As A
Murder Makes a Man, London: Longmans, 1935.

WALZ, Jay (1907-   ) and Audrey

The Bizarre Sisters. New York: Duell, Sloan, and Pearce,
1950. London: Gollancz, 1951.

WAMBAUGH, Joseph (1937-   )

The Blue Knight. Boston: Little, Brown, 1972. London:
Joseph, 1973.

WARREN, J(ohn) Russell (1886-   )

Gas-Mask Murder. London: Heinemann, 1939. As Murder
in the Blackout, New York: Sheridan, 1940.

This Mortal Coil. London: Melrose, 1947. As This Inward
Horror, New York: Dutton, 1948.

WARREN, Robert Penn (1905-   )

Night Rider. Boston: Houghton, Mifflin, 1939.

World Enough and Time. New York: Random House, 1950.
London: Eyre and Spottiswoode, 1951.

Meet Me in the Green Glen. New York: Random House,
1971. London: Secker and Warburg, 1972.

WARREN, Samuel (1807-1877)

Experiences of a Barrister and Confessions of an Attorney.
Boston: Wentworth, Hewes, 1859. 2 volumes.

WEBSTER, Bill

One by One. Garden City, NY: Doubleday, 1972.

WELLMAN, Manly Wade (1903-   )

    Not at These Hands. New York: Putnam, 1962.

WELLMAN, Paul I. (1898-1966)

    Walls of Jericho. Philadelphia: Lippincott, 1947.

WENTWORTH, Patricia, pseudonym of Dora Amy Dillon Turnbull (1878-1961)

    Silence in Court. Philadelphia: Lippincott, 1945. London: Hodder and Stoughton, 1947.

WEST, Anthony (1914-   )

    The Vintage. Boston: Houghton, Mifflin, 1949.

WEST, Jessamyn (1907-1984)

    The Massacre at Fall Creek. New York: Harcourt, Brace, Jovanovich; London: Macmillan, 1975.

WEST, Pamela Elizabeth

    Madeleine. New York: St. Martin's, 1983.

WHITNEY, Janet (1894-   )

    Jennifer. New York: Morrow, 1940. London: Harrap, 1941.

WICKWARE, Francis Sill (1911-   )

    Dangerous Ground. Garden City, NY: Doubleday, 1946.

WILLIAMS, Ben Ames (1889-1953)

    Death on Scurvy Street. New York: Dutton, 1929.

    Crucible. New York: Dutton, 1937.

    Leave Her to Heaven. Boston: Houghton, Mifflin, 1944. London: Hale, 1946.

WILSON, C(harles) M(orrow)

  A Man's Reach. New York: Holt, 1944.

WINSLOW, Walker

  Man in Paradise. New York: Smith and Durrell, 1941.

WINWAR, Frances (1900-)

  Gallows Hill. New York: Holt, 1937.

WOOD, Mrs. Henry (1814-1887)

  East Lynne. London: Bentley; New York: Dick, 1961.

WOODRUFF, Philip, pseudonym of Philip Mason (1906-)

  Call the Next Witness. London: Cape, 1945. New York:
  Harcourt, Brace, 1946.

WOOLFOLK, William

  Opinion of the Court. Garden City, NY: Doubleday, 1966.

WORSENCROFT, Mona Esly

  An Echo From Salem. S. Thomaston, ME: American
  History, 1981.

WRIGHT, Richard (1909-1960)

  Native Son. New York: Harper; London: Gollancz, 1940.

YOUNG, Francis Brett (1884-)

  Mr. and Mrs. Pennington. London: Heinemann; New York:
  Harper, 1931.

YOUNG, Phyllis Brett

  A Question of Judgment. New York: Putnam, 1969.
  London: Allen, 1970.

GENERAL INDEX

Index references are to entry number. The index includes authors and titles included as entries, as well as authors, titles, and names of real people or real cases mentioned within the annotations. <u>References to titles and authors of entries have been underlined and appear first.</u> No references have been made for fictional characters. Book titles appear in all capitals, short story titles in quotation marks. This index has been compiled by Rita A. Breen. Omissions, errors, and dubious policy decisions should be blamed on the author, however.

A

D

Hanshew, Mary E. 207
Hanshew, Thomas W. 207
"Happy Couple, The" 270
HARD CAIN 29
Hare, Cyril 208, 209
Harness, Charles L. 210, 211
Harrington, William 212-215
Harris, John Norman 216
Hart, Frances Noyes 217
Harte, Bret 2, 270
Hastings, Sir Patrick, K.C. 17
Hayes, Ralph 218
HE SHOULD HAVE DIED HEREAFTER 209
Hecht, Ben 270
HELL IS A CITY 4
HELTER-SKLELTER 24
Henderson, Donald 255
Henry, O. 2
Hensley, Joe L. 219-221
"Hepplewhite Tramp, The" 336
Herbert, A. P. 18
HERMIT OF TURKEY HOLLOW, THE 337
Hichens, Robert 222
Hinkemeyer, Michael T. 223
HIS LORDSHIP THE JUDGE 255
Hitchcock, Alfred 13, 222
Hitler, Adolf 249
"Hocus-Pocus" 339
"Hopeless Defense of Mrs. Dellford, The" 232
HOUSE OF THE WHISPERING PINES, THE 199
Hubin, Allen J. 251
HUBSCHMANN EFFECT, THE 272
Hughston, Dana 224
"Human Element, The" 336
Hume, Fergus 225
Hunt, Kyle 64, 65
HUNT THE SLIPPER 56
Hunter, Evan 226-228
Hurwitz, Ken 24

I

"I Killed Gordon McNaghten" 49
"I Thought I'd Die" 304
I, TOO, NICODEMUS 19

N

"Naboth's Vineyard" 2, 291
"Name, The" 35
NATURAL CAUSES 38
Nevins, Francis M., Jr. 4, 31, 180, 232, 251, 297
NEW MADE GRAVE, THE 91
Newman, Paul 303
Nichols, Mike 286
"Night of Charity, The" 2
"Nine Points of the Law" 340
Niven, David 390
Niven, Larry 284
Nixon, Richard M. 18
NO BAIL FOR THE JUDGE 37, 39
NO FEAR OR FAVOUR 52, 35
NORTH STAR 231
NOT I, SAID THE VIXEN 8
Notable British Trials 34
NOTHING BUT THE NIGHT 419, 250

O

O (Theo Mathew) 18
O'Brien, Edmond 392
O'Connor, Frank 270
Olander, Joseph D. 285, 18
"Old Duke" 345
OLD MAN TUTT 344
Oleck, Howard 286, 257, 392
Oliansky, Joel 9
"On Appeal" 35
"Once in Jeopardy" 292
ONE MORE RIVER 100
ONE MORE UNFORTUNATE 271
ON INIQUITY 317
ONLY IN NEW ENGLAND 308
Ostlere, Gordon 195
Oursler, Will 287
OUTRAGE 74, 24
OVERDRIVE 189
OVER THE RIVER 100

P

CAUSE OF ACTION INDEX

Listed are offenses and types of legal proceedings that are the subject of works listed in the book. Since the vast majority of fictional trials covered here concern charges of homicide, indexing has been limited to causes of action <u>other</u> than homicide. Other offenses combined with homicide have <u>not</u> been indexed. (For example, entries listed under rape below concern pure rape prosecutions, not combined prosecutions for rape-murder.)

JURISDICTION INDEX

The following index includes individual states of the United States, countries outside the United States, and territories and possessions of English-speaking countries.